MALICIOUS INTENT:
A Writer's Guide
to How Murderers, Robbers, Rapists
and Other Criminals Think

MALICIOUS INTENT:
A Writer's Guide
to How Murderers, Robbers, Rapists
and Other Criminals Think

by
Sean P. Mactire

WRITER'S DIGEST BOOKS

Cincinnati, Ohio

Malicious Intent: A Writer's Guide to How Murderers, Robbers, Rapists and Other Criminals Think. Copyright © 1995 by Sean Mactire. Printed and bound in the United States of America. All rights reserved. No part of this book may be reproduced in any form or by any electronic or mechanical means including information storage and retrieval systems without permission in writing from the publisher, except by a reviewer, who may quote brief passages in a review. Published by Writer's Digest Books, an imprint of F&W Publications, Inc., 1507 Dana Avenue, Cincinnati, Ohio 45207. 1-800-289-0963. First edition.

99 98 97 96 95   5 4 3 2 1

Library of Congress Cataloging-in-Publication Data

Mactire, Sean P.
    Malicious intent: a writer's guide to how murderers, robbers, rapists, and other criminals
think / by Sean Mactire. — 1st ed.
      p. cm. — (The Howdunit series)
    Includes bibliographical references and index.
    ISBN 0-89879-648-2
    1. Detective and mystery stories — Authorship. 2. Crime. 3. Criminals. 4. Criminal psy-
chology. I. Title. II. Series
    PN3377.5.D4M33 1995
    364.1'02483 — dc20   94-44387
                                                              CIP

Edited by Jack Heffron
Designed by Angela Lennert

Dedication

To my darling, beloved Jan,
An outstanding lady, who has enriched my life and is
my inspiration.

About the Author

Sean Mactire is a research analyst and technical writer specializing in criminal justice issues, international and strategic studies, and health and medical care issues. In addition to his book *Lyme Disease*, Sean has written articles, monographs and handbooks on the prevention of child abuse and domestic violence, the relationship of psychological stress and violence, and crimes against women and children. He designed and developed a public awareness program promoting child safety, crime prevention and family wellness. This project was adopted by the U.S. Public Health Service and was implemented as a community service program by RKO Radio and their affiliate stations. Sean also wrote the booklet "Safe Traveling With Your Child." He lives in Denver, Colorado.

Table of Contents

Introduction: The Face of Evil   *1*

1 The History and Hallmarks of Violent Crimes   *8*

A review of criminal history to eliminate misconceptions.
> In the Beginning
> Violence Escalates
> The Invention of Police
> Jack the Ripper
> Other Serial Killers

2 Understanding Human Behavior   *23*

Some basic principles of how the human mind works.
> The Rules of Human Behavior
> Psychology and Criminal Justice
> Labels
> The Anatomy of Behavior
> Crime, Violence and Criminal Behavior
> Outlining the Criminal Mind

3 Profiling the Criminal   *39*

Developing a criminal portrait by evaluating behavioral characteristics.
> The Development of Profiling
> The Murder Types
> Computer Profiling

4 Crime Fact, Crime Fiction   *53*

Examining the relationships between crime and the entertainment of popular culture.
> Crime Fact
> Crime Fiction

5 **Serial Murder** *66*

The new source of gothic horror.

  The Fantasy
  The Facts
  Hunting Humans
  Definition of a Serial Murder
  Types of Murderers
  Types of Sexual Behavior Involved in Serial Killings
  Social Structure
  The Predatory Types
  Theater of Blood
  The Disease Cycle
  Crime Scene Characteristics

6 **Cult-Related Murder** *81*

Exploring the crimes attributed to the spiritual and paranormal realms.

  Satanism
  Witchcraft
  The Occult
  Christian Cults

7 **Sexual Predators** *93*

Dealing with the complex and sensitive issues of sex crimes.

  Rape Defined
  Forms of Rape
  Patterns of Sex Crimes

8 **Child Molesters and Child Murderers** *105*

Dispelling the myth that these offenders are "nonviolent" criminals.

  The Child Molester
  The Pedophile
  The Types of Offenders
  Sex Rings
  Incest
  Female Offenders

Teenage Offenders
The Pedophile Profile
Pornography and the Pedophile
Child Murderers

9 **Victims** *127*

Portraying victims of violent crimes objectively.

To Know the Victim Is to Know the Criminal
How Victims Think
General Reaction to Traumatic Crisis

10 **The Career Criminal** *141*

Examining the different types of criminal vocations.

The Quiet Criminals
The Grand Showmen
The Robbers
The Deadly Outlaws

11 **Wise Guys and Hitmen** *158*

The multifaceted world of organized crime.

"Wise Guy" Behavior
Historical Background of Organized Crime
What Is Organized Crime?
Hitmen
The Modern Mobster

12 **Drug Abuse** *171*

Understanding the most pervasive influence on criminal behavior.

Alcohol Abuse
Polydrug Abuse
Prescription Drug Abuse
Nonprescription Drug Abuse
Motivation for Drug Abuse

13 **Terrorists** *180*

The ultimate predator, the great white shark of criminals.

What Is Terrorism?
The Elements of Terrorism

The Mind of the Terrorist
Strategy, Tactics and Victims

14 **Women Who Kill** *194*

Profiling a recently increasing group of killers.
Characteristics
Victims and Hunting Techniques
Methods and Motives
The Assassins

15 **Psychology in the Courtroom** *206*

Dealing with the relationship of mental health and crime.
The Defendant's Mental Health
The Insanity Defense
Battered Wife Syndrome
Civil Commitment
The Issue of Dangerousness
Suicide
Attempts to Fool the Courts

Bibliography   *221*
Index   *223*

Introduction: The Face of Evil

May 1993 — Cult leader David Koresh leads his followers to a fiery death. Terrorists strike the World Trade Center with a massive car bomb. June 1993 — Joel Rifkin, a Long Island gardener, is arrested and confesses to the murders of seventeen prostitutes in and around New York City. October 1993 — A young girl is kidnapped from her own home, in the middle of a slumber party, and is later murdered. The suspect is linked to other child murders. November 1993 — A serial killer is stalking St. Louis, abducting and killing small children. January 1994 — A suspect, Lewis Lent, Jr., is arrested who may be linked to the abduction/murders of almost a half-dozen children in the New England/New York area. The horrors are growing faster than the media can keep pace but not faster than the public's fascination with and consumption of real-life horror. In the cases of the Waco Massacre and the World Trade Center bombing, the dead are not even buried before the book contracts are signed and the made-for-TV movies go into production.

Today's serial killer, mass murderer, terrorist and stalker are tomorrow's media celebrities.

Two questions come to mind concerning the public's craving for the nightmare world of true crime: (1) Why is the public fascinated with the criminal subculture? (2) What causes criminal behavior, and how do the monsters of our fascination behave? The answer to the former may be found in the answer to the latter.

There are no simple answers to these questions, but this book will try to give you a look into the mind of evil and show you what makes criminals tick.

The twentieth century has justifiably become known as the Century of Violence. While two world wars have been fought in this period, this label is not concerned with wars between nations but with the interpersonal violence that has turned our streets into combat zones. Today, more than any other time in the course of human history, criminal behavior exists at every level of society. If you look at the police blotters in the newspapers and the FBI crime reports, you can't help but feel that criminals are everywhere.

Ironically, this is not far from the truth, because until they are apprehended, those monsters, whose debauched crime sprees are plastered all over the front page, may be the Mr. or Ms. "Nice Guy" you always thought so highly of. No one can really tell who the murderers, rapists, mobsters or pedophiles are. They can be anybody, from the casual acquaintances you meet while shopping to those good neighbors just down the street to the people you work with. This is the frame of mind you have to have when you try to define who is a criminal.

Since the dawn of time, human beings have wondered why other humans commit crimes. Except for some of the higher apes, humans are the only creatures that intentionally — with malice aforethought — kill, maim, torture, rape and rob their own species. Other species may fight over mates and territory, but this behavior is motivated by primal needs and holds no comparison to the destructive behavior patterns that human beings are capable of. We are also the only creatures on the planet that hunt for pleasure and kill for pleasure and sport.

Humans also are the only creatures that can turn anything into a weapon. Unlike our Stone Age and Bronze Age ancestors, people do not own and use weapons of any kind as tools of survival. Everyone may blame guns, especially handguns, for violence and criminal behavior, but the reality is that all destructive or nonproductive behavior is motivated by *power*.

Beginning with the Iron Age, when weapons became objects of power, we see the foundations of criminal behavior being built in human society. In a nutshell, crime is about power. However, this is not the only key factor. Today's crime statistics reflect that many crimes, especially a high number of murders, are motivated by *sex* and *power*.

Definition

What makes a criminal think and act in such a destructive manner? In the simplest of terms, criminals are parasites. While criminals fall into various categories within their own social structure and the definitions set by the justice system, they all need to feed a particular, and sometimes insatiable, appetite. The majority are sociopathic, and in this context, another appropriate term is *vampire*. While this term may sound exaggerated and sensationalistic, it fits the very nature of the evil behind all criminal behavior. While many criminals do have an insatiable "blood lust," the majority simply crave fear and danger. Like a junkie who can't live without drugs, the average criminal comes to crave the psychic energy expended by the victims or the high derived from the danger involved in committing criminal acts. As a result of this hunger/addiction, many criminals are driven to seek increased or more frequent levels of danger or to commit increasingly horrific crimes.

Webster's and other standard dictionaries define *vampire* as:

1. A reanimated corpse that is believed to rise from the grave at night to suck the blood of sleeping people.
2. A bloodsucking ghost.
3. The soul of a ghoul who takes over a body in order to hunt for blood.

This is the vampire myth.

However, the *Oxford English Dictionary*, *Webster's*, and others offer another definition that is closer to reality and the purposes of this book. This definition of *vampire* is:

1. A person of a malignant and loathsome character; a vile and cruel exactor; a parasite.
2. A person, such as an extortionist, who ruthlessly preys upon others.
   Noun: A perversely bad, cruel or wicked person; beast, monster, fiend, ghoul, arch fiend, ogre.

Generally we apply the term *malevolent* to criminals. *Malevolent* is defined as:

1. Having or exhibiting ill will; wishing harm to others; malicious.
2. Having an evil or harmful influence.
   Adjective: Characterized by intense ill will or spite; black, evil, mean, vicious, wicked, nasty, poisonous, malicious, venomous, malign, malignant, spiteful.

While both definitions are similar, the *vampire* description seems to fit the parasitic nature of criminal behavior in general. Since most criminals are sociopathic parasites who feed on the fear of ordinary people, these definitions illustrate why the vampire legend has a lot of basis in fact.

In our society it is difficult for the majority of people to imagine that such a dangerous evil really exists. In the Dark Ages and the Inquisition, the illiterate public and the unenlightened lawgivers wanted to believe that only devils, demons, monsters, and other such imaginary minions of Satan could be responsible for any vicious, unexplained crimes that might strike their communities. However, many times they discovered, to their shock and horror, that the evil monsters that terrorized them were their neighbors.

In the twentieth century, we do not have superstition to comfort us from our fears. But this evil does exist. According to the FBI, one hundred to two hundred fiends are "hunting humans" all over the United States and Canada. This number may be higher as some experts feel that the serial killer population could be five hundred or more, with some estimates going as high as two thousand. Therefore it is safe to estimate the serial killer population to be anywhere from one hundred to twenty-five hundred. While any number in this range is feasible, it would still be reasonable to conclude that the higher numbers are closer to the truth. Considering that a 1990 Justice Department report estimated that these modern, real-life vampires account for over 75 percent of all non-family/acquaintance homicides and 100 percent of all abduction disappearances, it is hard to believe that a small number of killers is responsible for such a huge body count. The FBI noted that many of these killers are also pedophiles and the reported serial killer population numbers were very conservative. The FBI concluded that the numbers could be much higher. Thus, as the twentieth century draws to a close, the dawn of the twenty-first century will be darkened by a whole new folklore of terror.

To really understand criminal behavior and the criminal's lifestyle, you have to reassess your own perceptions of people. Federal crime statistics show that one out of four households is experiencing some form of domestic violence. This statistic alone illustrates that any type of criminal can be your acquaintance and you may never know it. Because most people have tunnel vision when it comes to evil, these perpetrators are able to hide while in plain sight. Serial killers, rapists, child molesters, mobsters, terrorists, robbers and other fiends have been found in the best communities, wearing masks of respectability.

Because appearances can be deceiving, you may be looking at the face of evil without realizing it. Everyone lets their preconceptions and personal biases prejudice their opinions about people. So when Mr. or Ms. "Nice Guy" next-door neighbor turns up with two or three dozen bodies in his or her backyard or is arrested for some insidious crime or crimes, many people say, "I never knew." A lot of people simply don't want to acknowledge that creatures of pure evil may live in their midst. Look at the public view of mobster John Gotti. "A real nice guy!" said many, even after he was convicted of murder. This is the psychological environment that allows these vampires to exist and provides them with the darkness and secrecy they need to hunt and acquire new targets almost every day.

What Evil Looks Like

In the 1800s, the public's perception of evil was manipulated and distorted by the media, which was becoming a powerful social influence. Prior to the Jack the Ripper case, the middle and upper classes lived sheltered lives, shielded from any such outrage, unless they were the victims or perpetrators. The only knowledge they had was shrouded in Gothic mystery that filled volumes of books. When Jack the Ripper appeared, these more fortunate classes were still shielded. The public of Victorian London devoured the newspaper accounts, which contained more fiction than truth and scoffed at the idea that this monster could be one of their own. The image that the press of the day was selling, that of a lower-class "Leather Apron" or heinous immigrant or impoverished Jewish butcher, fit more of the middle and upper classes' idea of what a murderer should look like.

In the 1990s, little has changed, except for the variety of media that is available to the public. Crime, criminals and monstrous evil have become the major subject of mountains of books, plays and films. Since the advent of film, there have been over three hundred vampire films made to feed the public's curious hunger for terror and horror. Television, the electronic educator, has made its own unique contribution to public perceptions with countless recreations of true-life horrors and creations of its own that mimic reality.

It is unlikely that you will ever meet someone like a character envisioned by Bram Stoker or Anne Rice, though you may live next door to someone like Dr. Hannibal Lecter, of *Silence of the Lambs* infamy. As the current cases of Joel Rifkin and a handful of other recent multiple or mass murder arrestees demonstrate, a vicious criminal can be someone you know and the last person you would ever suspect. Dracula's or Lestat's real-life counterpart will be either a pallid-faced little man with a greasy tie and carpet slippers, like John Christie; a pillar of the community, like John Wayne Gacy;

or a handsome, friendly stranger with chameleon traits and deadly charm who does volunteer community service, like Ted Bundy. These killers and other violent criminals benefit from the public's distorted perceptions and the camouflage that biased social attitudes provide. They are chameleons, and they can be very charming, seductive liars. There is little difference between Kenneth Bianchi, one of the hillside stranglers, and John Gotti, the convicted Mob boss and fashion plate, except Gotti was a little more high profile in his crimes. Deception is the cloak of darkness that the sadistic hunters of the criminal subculture use to hide the pursuit of their chosen prey.

For you, regardless of whether you are a writer or a curious layperson, this book is a road map to the shadow world of the criminal mind. It is also a tool—a torch to light the darkness, a key to open up the doors to a world that everyone wants to view, like a voyeur—but one that few really want to take a long, hard look at in order to understand how it works. As you read this book, maintain an objective attitude and never underestimate or take for granted the potential for human destructiveness that lives within us all. This book is about the anybodies who are nobodies. These are the monsters of the real-life nightmares who haunt the streets of your community, who have chosen a life of evil to try to be a somebody. So, before you, as a writer, set out to paint your own portrait of the criminal mind and the face of evil that goes with it, look around your neighborhood, your community, and even your town or city. Take a good, hard look at the people you see. Don't be surprised if one day you see them plastered across the front page of your daily newspaper or headlining the evening news because they have been arrested for some horrible crime. Anybody's neighbor, co-worker, college classmate or even a spouse, lover, family member or in-law can be concealing the face of evil behind a mask of civility.

Always keep in mind that a criminal subculture exists within the norms of the law-abiding sectors of our society. Like Whitley Strieber's *The Hunger* and Anne Rice's vampire classics, the 1990 cult-classic film *Near Dark* suggests that among the human race lives a race of vampires, hunting to feed its hunger, feeding simply to survive, and generating more of its own kind, not through procreation, but by infecting others with the disease of its lust and teaching its neophytes in the ways of the hunter/killer. This is a perfect example of fiction reflecting the images of reality. The truths of *Near Dark* have dawned: Crime is part of a disease cycle that is infectious; the face of evil can be anywhere; and with their sheer numbers alone, violent criminals, career criminals, and killers of all types are a society and race unto themselves.

O N E

The History and Hallmarks of Violent Crime

For writers, it is imperative to know the history behind a subject so they can avoid misconceptions. With the subject of human behavior, the history of certain aspects of behavior, such as criminality, is just as important as the pathology. All human behavior is governed by the course of events in the history of human civilization. And since all human behavior is learned behavior, it is important to know about the events that spawned the innovation of such behavior.

In the Beginning

Cannibalism and human sacrifice by our cave-dwelling ancestors are the foundation of all human crime. We know from archaeological evidence that humans were massacred in droves for the purpose of sacrifice and consumption of their brains, over 1.5 million years ago. This activity was still a part of human culture as recently as the Cro-Magnon era, over forty thousand years ago. Back when Homo erectus walked the lands of Europe, the motive was blood.

It is strange though, for as Homo sapiens were settling down into an agricultural society, human beings only seem to have fought wars over territorial disputes. Cruelty was a much later invention when the hordes of Assyrians brought their reign of terror down upon the Middle East about 2000 B.C. But it did not come about with the building of cities or with the invention of writing. A bright spot in the history of humanity that lasted for thirty thousand years came about between the last time Cro-Magnon man had brains for lunch and the "dark ages" brought by the Assyrians. The Sumerians invented writing about 3500 B.C., but the first "recorded" crime was not documented until one thousand five hundred years later, which was about the same time that humans were developing their penchant for cruelty and destruction.

So what went right before things went wrong in the evolution of human behavior? Some anthropologists have proposed that because most of our Stone Age (40,000 B.C. and later) ancestors were such devout servants of nature and of the gods, their high spiritual values made them hold all life as sacred. During this "enlightened" period of time, humanity seemed to be able to keep its ego in check. However, the advent of and growth of city-states changed all this around 2500 B.C. Now that there were kings exercising real power, humans felt the need to exercise a high degree of ruthlessness. And here is where the human ego seems to have deviated into corruption, and the epidemic of violence spread throughout the known world. Around 1100 B.C., King Tiglath-pileser I of Assyria, instituted a "policy of frightfulness," as he and his people built an empire on the blood and bones of thousands of innocents. Then in 1077 B.C., this butcher-king was murdered. With his death, Assyrian power declined, but in 911 B.C., it rose again with even greater viciousness. In 689 B.C., the Assyrians conquered Babylon, killing all of its inhabitants until the streets were piled high with bodies. Then the Assyrians destroyed the entire city. Finally, the people who were oppressed by the Assyrians revolted, bringing down the Assyrian Empire.

Greece and Rome

Even though the fall of Assyria brought to an end a long reign of terror, it was, unfortunately, only the beginning. The civilizations that followed only refined the cruelty of their predecessors. The Golden Age of Greece may have contributed much to the growth of human civilization, but this legacy was the product of blood, barbarity and tyranny. Almost from the beginning of its civilization, Greece was plagued by wars. These consisted mostly of Greeks killing Greeks for very petty reasons, like the wars between Athens and Sparta, which generally started over offenses to personal honor, or Greek egos attacking their neighbors for other petty reasons, as in the Trojan War. Between wars, the Greek populace had to put up with out-of-work soldiers who supplemented their income by robbing, raping and killing their own people. But the Greeks regarded crime as an extension of war and commerce.

Still, while Greece was bad, Rome was worse. When Rome was founded in 473 B.C., civilization seriously digressed. From the aspect of criminality, the Glory of Rome and the so-called Pax Romana, the Roman Peace, were built on the blood and bones of slaves and the corpses of massacred innocents. From the time of Julius Caesar (44 B.C.) to the Fall of Rome (A.D. 500), Rome exercised its own policy of frightfulness and terror, that has only been rivaled by the Nazi occupation of Europe and the Communist domination of Eastern Europe. It was Rome that invented "ethnic cleansing." However, they regarded this campaign of cleansing as a way to pacify and civilize the known world. Cities were razed and the millions who resisted were put to death. The millions who survived were deported into slavery and their land was settled by Roman citizens. When the conquered occasionally protested some policy of Rome, such as increases in taxes or the confiscation of food stocks, they were subjected to some of the cruelest punishments that humankind has ever devised. Among these were:

- *Crucifixion* — the hanging of victims from trees, walls or crosses so that the person would slowly asphyxiate over the course of days from the weight of their own bodies crushing the lungs
- *Decimation* — the indiscriminate execution of every tenth person by slow impalement or other means
- *Flogging* — the beating to death of a victim with a whip or rod
- *The death of a thousand cuts* — victim slowly bleeds to death from one thousand small incisions made all over the victim's body.

Once a promising republic, Rome degenerated into an empire of injustice dominated by a selfish, cruel people who had egomaniacs for emperors until around A.D. 350. After 350, the empire was bi-

sected and each half was governed by a succession of juvenile delin-
quents. Rome grew as a matter of survival and security in the face
of aggression from its neighbors, but it was like a snowball rolling
downhill. Its own accretion gave it strength, size and power, but it
fell because, like the snowball, it could only grow so big before,
sooner or later, it had to crash. When it did crash, the fall of the
Roman Empire left behind a tragic wake of chaos.

For Assyria, Greece and Rome, there is no singular crime or
criminal that stands out as significant in the history of crime. It
is simply that the acts of criminal aggression committed by these
civilizations in the name of imperial expansion were to lay the foundations for future evils.

The Middle Ages

Except for the stupidity of feudalism and the childishness of
the Crusades, the Middle Ages was mostly a mirror image of the
barbarity of Rome. The birth of the "Hashishims," the Assassins
Cult, was the only major innovation in criminal behavior. This was
the forerunner of modern political terrorism and ironically, this
movement, even though it was stamped out twice, is the root of the
problems now posed by Iran as it tries to impose its own agenda on
the entire Middle East. Founded in 1090 by Hasan ibn-al-Sabah in
what is now modern day Iran, the Assassins Cult was very much like
the PLO or Islamic Jihad. It was a small army of devoted fanatics
bent on overthrowing the society of its time. To their enemies, the
cult members were criminals; to their supporters, they were highly
trained revolutionaries, overthrowing oppression by the only means
at their disposal. Hasan and his Assassins were Shiite Muslims and
were determined to establish their own religious empire.

To add to the power of their terror, Hasan established the
cult's base of operations in an impregnable fortress appropriately
called the Alamut or Eagle's Nest. This fortress sat high on a single
peak in the Elburz Mountains of what is now Iran. The Turks, who
were the main enemies and targets of the cult, laid siege to the
Alamut twice but failed to take it. For years, no one felt safe and
no one spoke out against Hasan's agenda, lest that person be permanently silenced. No people in authority—princes, governors, generals and religious leaders—dared go out in public without armor
under their clothes.

The power of fear soon made the majority of Hasan's opponents yield and become his unwilling allies. One victim was stabbed to death in a mosque as he knelt in prayer surrounded by his guards. Another arose one morning to find a dagger driven into the ground close to his head with a note attached, telling him how easily he could have been killed.

With this kind of influence, it should have been a certainty that Hasan's political and military agenda would succeed. However, Hasan and the cult made the mistake of trying to take on the entire Arab world. He suffered numerous defeats in the years prior to his death, even though the cult's influence had infiltrated the Turkish army and reached as far as Egypt and Syria. Hasan died a bitter failure in 1124, and within a few years, the leaderless cult was annihilated. Had Hasan and his followers taken the position of honorable men who fought like lions, they might have achieved their goals politically, even though they held a weak military position. However, even though they were widely feared, Hasan's cult was loathed and mostly regarded with extreme contempt. Though Hasan had the military capability to take over the existing government, he felt that his self-righteous tactics would win the day. Without a position of respect, the cult was doomed to defeat.

Hasan's ego was also a major factor in his undoing. He felt his cause was so just, he allowed his overconfidence to warp his judgment, and he refused to set limits on his ambitions. This is a classic example of an ego out of control, and Hasan stands as a model of the nature of criminality. Hasan was a righteous man, and there is nothing more dangerous than a person obsessed with his own beliefs. He was inflexible and felt that all those who opposed him or did not believe as he did were wrong and deserved to die.

Ego, of course, is an essential tool of constructive behavior, but when the human becomes a slave to his ego, the human ultimately degenerates into destructive behavior.

The Right Man

Hasan, the founder of the Assassins Cult, and the autocratic criminals who ruled Assyria and Rome were self-righteous tyrants whose own irrational sense of being right led them to slaughter countless people. History has repeated itself with the careers of many tyrants and serial killers such as Tiberius, Caligula, Vlad the Impaler, Gilles de Rais, H.H. Holmes, Al Capone, John Wayne Gacy, John Gotti and the Green River Killer. Their brutality and contempt for human life stems from what appears to be a belief that they are outside or above society and the law.

In his 1954 novel, *The Violent Man*, A.E. van Vogt identifies a phenomenon that has come to be known as "The Right Man" type. In all human beings, as Maslow noted, there is a need for self-esteem and self-confidence. However, with the Right Man, there is a need for dominance. This is a child in an adult body who thinks of himself as the center of the universe and demands to be respected as such. Unlike psychotics, the Right Man's delusions are voluntary. He wants to be destructive. He also fully recognizes the consequences of such conduct, but he chooses to satisfy his starving ego.

From the Crusades on, humanity stumbled along through the mayhem of bickering, warring, murderous popes; the stupidity and sadism of the Mongols, whose hyperactive egos put hundreds of thousands of innocents to the sword for the fun of it; and the devastation of the Black Death. After all this, the people of Western civilization somehow managed to reach the enlightenment of the Renaissance. However, things were not all that bright. Shortly after the Renaissance began, Europe was plunged into darkness again by the start of the Hundred Years War.

All wars produce crimes, but this one had a singular significant atrocity that made its mark on history—the murder of Joan of Arc. However, her murder was of a political nature, of the kind that would be classified as a "war crime."

Gilles de Rais and Vlad Dracula

The era of the fourteenth and fifteenth centuries was a period when sick egos were flying out of control everywhere, but two in particular could be termed "cancerous" and are hallmarks of absolute evil. The first was Gilles de Rais. Technically, he was one of the first recorded "sex murderers." While many of the mass murderers who came before him enjoyed killing, their crimes were mostly political. Gilles de Rais killed for fun, and his crimes were definitely nonpolitical. He was a French nobleman and one of the richest men in France. He had fought with Joan of Arc, and his bravery was unquestioned. However, after the English were driven out of France, he went back to his estates and indulged in spending money and killing children to satisfy his sexual desires. Before he was executed in 1440, he raped, tortured and killed hundreds of children. His other perversions included drinking their blood, eating their flesh, and having sex with the corpses of his victims. He was the prototype of Jeffrey Dahmer, except that instead of luring or kidnapping his victims, he would simply order his servants to fetch a child for slaughter.

The second was Prince Vlad Tepes Dracula, the son of Vlad Dracul and a contemporary of de Rais and the historical source for the Dracula legend. He was also the first to gain celebrity status as a vicious murderer during his lifetime. Even though he was a minor prince in what is now modern Rumania, the stories of his atrocities were the talk of every royal court in Europe, earning him the moniker Vlad the Impaler. Like Gilles de Rais, Vlad was an extraordinary soldier. He spent much of his life fighting the Turks, and he was a brave and resourceful leader, who found terror to be one of his best weapons. After he forced the Turks out of his country, he kept them from invading again with warnings of the fate that awaited them. He delighted in having hundreds, sometimes thousands, of Turkish prisoners of war impaled on sharp stakes and left to die slowly. Since Vlad was typical of absolute rulers of the period, one might regard these murders as political; however, his use of terror was not limited to his military and political enemies. As one of the original "blood monsters," which is the literal translation of the word vampire, Vlad displayed a sexual hunger for the tremendous pleasure he derived from killing. In 1460, on one of many murderous occasions, he had a number of Saxon merchants impaled and four hundred apprentices burned alive as dinner entertainment. Later, he invited all the beggars and sick people in his domain to a feast, and once they were all inside the banquet building he built for the occasion, he ordered the doors locked and he burned the building. Vlad Dracula, "the Dragon," was killed in battle in 1476, but the power of his blood lust has lived on for centuries, resulting in his romantic immortalization by Bram Stoker in the 1800s.

Witch-Hunts

During the sixteenth century, the people of Western civilization became obsessed with religion and with exploration and conquest. Furthermore, thousands of political and nonpolitical crimes were committed in the name of the Christian faith. The worst of these was the "witchcraft craze." This was the first organized holocaust and it lasted 150 years.

In a forty-year period in France alone, over one thousand people were burned alive, after being tortured into confessing to crimes they did not commit. During the same period, another thousand perished in the same manner. Ironically, the whole concept of Satan and Devil worship was a lie the Church invented to help consolidate its power. So, during the explosion of witch-hunting that occurred from 1600 to the beginning of the Thirty Years War in 1618, thousands of innocents were killed to save their souls from a Lucifer who didn't exist and no one really believed in enough to worship. Only the Church and the witch-hunters ardently believed in the Devil, and it was they who invented the rituals they accused the victims of practicing. Many of these victims were children, whose ages ranged from three to fifteen. Technically, these witch-hunters were serial killers who had government and church approval to kill. They can be appropriately labeled serial killers because they loved their murderous work, they derived sexual pleasure from the torture and executions they performed, and they felt justified, calling it "the Lord's work," in persecuting and murdering their fellow human beings.

England and its colonies suffered from the storm as well, but they quickly regained control of their senses. Only a handful of innocent men, women and children were murdered in England, and until the Governor's wife was accused of witchcraft in Massachusetts, the Salem witch hysteria claimed a few dozen lives.

The witchcraft craze demonstrated that no one was safe from persecution. The concept of "justice" was not to gain any real meaning until the American and French Revolutions. Besides witchcraft, it was easy for anyone to accuse another of a crime and the accused to be convicted with little or no evidence. Consequentially, it was the poor who suffered, and many became criminals either to survive or because of persecution.

Violence Escalates

The level of violence and mayhem that commonly existed from 1500 to 1800 makes today's violence on the streets look like a pillow fight. The streets of towns and cities were the hunting grounds of gangs of thieves, and the country roads were prowled by hordes of bandits. It was not uncommon for homes to be besieged and looted regularly, and grave robbing was a daily occurrence. Only the very rich nobles, who could afford small armies of personal guards, large walled estates and stone tombs, had the luxury of traveling, living and dieing in peace. The less fortunate risked their lives just by getting out of bed. There was no police force, and government troops and local civilian militias were impotent in controlling crime.

One example of the insanity of this period was the crimes of the Beane family. For twenty-five years (circa 1430), this ever growing clan of what can only be called monsters launched a reign of terror that claimed over one thousand unwary travelers. It took the intervention of King James I to put the Beane's crime spree to an end and discover the horrible secret behind the attacks and disappearances that had plagued the area east of Edinburgh: the Beanes were not only incestuous, inbred robbers and murderers, they were cannibals. The king took a force of four hundred troops to this area, and they discovered a huge cave where the Beanes had lived and hidden for over two decades. With little resistance, the entire family of forty-eight men and women was taken to Edinburgh. Without benefit of trial, the arms, legs and genitals of the men were cut off, and the men were left to bleed to death. The women were burned alive after they were forced to watch the men die. If King James had not stepped in, the Beanes could have gotten away with their inhuman crimes indefinitely because the local magistrate held the same view about who or what had committed the crimes as the local populace and nobles — they believed that werewolves did it.

The Invention of the Police

Law enforcement, as we know it today, is a recent innovation, only a little over two hundred years old. Prior to this, nothing, except in rare cases like the Beane family, from regular army troops to bands of vigilante militia, ever had any effect on crime. Criminals acted with absolute impunity, with gangs often conducting their criminal activities openly as if they were trade guilds. In 1753, the novelist Henry Fielding founded the first organized attempt at anything resembling a police force. Called the Bow Street Runners, they used good intelligence work to round up criminals. Detection was not used because Fielding felt that the crime gangs could be stopped simply by taking the trouble to become acquainted with the criminals and their habits. By knowing who did what and how, Fielding's Bow Street Runners captured criminals by the dozens. Day by day, the crime rate dropped as fast as the gallows trap fell under the feet of the criminals who were hung as a result of Fielding's attack on crime. Highway robberies and house breakings were just as easily halted by the institution of heavily armed horse patrols that roamed the countryside around London. Later, these patrols were increased to protect homes around other major English cities. Unfortunately, this innovation and the dramatic drop in crime it produced in the cities and countryside were short lived.

Before Fielding introduced the Runners, criminals acted and were treated as if they were an integral component of society, a separate class within the social fabric, just like merchants and tradesmen. Since they were out in the open, stealth and skill were unnecessary. The introduction of organized law enforcement not only forced the criminals to prey on the remoter parts of the country, it also alienated them from society.

Now criminals had to employ new methods of secrecy and cunning. The once public gangs were forced to operate as secret societies. In short, they had to think. Those who were clever enough to operate in this new clandestine environment carried on and ventured into new and riskier criminal endeavors, such as cat burglar-type raids. These were the foxes and they survived. This need for stealth did not change the way criminals behaved, but it forced them to use their brains, which was a major revolution for this new subculture. However, with alienation came an increase in the development of a variety of psychological traits. Chief among these was paranoia. Criminals had always been able to deal directly with the public and their fellow criminal. With the advent of the Runners, they couldn't tell friend from foe, especially since the Runners also used paid informants. Those whose wits were too slow to allow them to adapt did not survive this social transition. They stuck to the old ways of smash and grab, rampaging as if nothing had changed, and were slaughtered like cattle.

This social transition of the criminal class into a covert subculture forced the Runners and the horse patrols to work harder. Their earlier successes declined and soon the crime rate rose to a point where it stabilized in the face of the new law enforcement efforts. When Fielding died, the crime rate rose like a flood because there was no one with the energy or desire to hound the criminals to the gallows.

With the coming of the Industrial Revolution, circumstances changed, and in 1805, the horse patrols were revived. Still, there was no organized police force because the public viewed the idea with great suspicion. People were afraid of criminals, but they were more afraid that the police would rob them of their rights. So, the public chose crime as the lesser of two evils until 1811, when a new dimension of horror became a basic part of the criminal behavior pattern. These were the mass murders that occurred on the Ratcliffe Highway. These crimes were significant because instead of being committed by gangs bent on robbery, the victims were believed to have been killed by a "lone" fiend who stalked the streets lusting for blood. In addition, the victims were slaughtered in their homes. These crimes and a series of other brutal murders were to finally galvanize the country with fear and fill the public with horrified fascination.

The Age of the Individual Ego-Assertive Criminal was now born. At the same time, the public was undergoing changes. First, the public was becoming addicted to a steady diet of gore and cruelty that the media of the time was feeding them. Second, society was becoming increasingly aware of the need for a full-time professional police force. However, it was not until the case of Burke and Hare in 1826-1829 that the public outgrew its distrust of a police force and allowed the concept to become a reality.

It is a strange irony that the notorious body snatcher of Edinburgh should be the catalyst that helped give birth to the police force the public dreaded. Burke and Hare started out as simple grave robbers who stole corpses for medical schools for dissection classes. They were paid about the equivalent in today's money of $50, but the supply of already dead corpses was growing short, so they began "making corpses." In the next year, Burke and Hare murdered over a dozen people to further the advancement of medical science and line their own pockets. In 1829, Hare turned evidence against Burke and Burke was hung, but their doctor client was not prosecuted even though the dissection of bodies was also a crime. In the same year, Sir Robert Peel and his newly organized police force undertook the guardianship of the public. In years to come, the public's distrust would disappear, and these new guardians would be affectionately known as "bobbies."

While the British and American public distrusted police forces at first because they thought the police were spies, the French public, and later other Europeans, had good reason for distrust — the police *were* spies. In fact, the original Surete, the French National Police Force, was founded by Eugène-Francois Vidocq, a former criminal and police spy. When he started his police force, he employed other ex-criminals and police spies. Still, the institution of organized law enforcement did not prevent the advent of the next new horror to plague society—the sex crime. Now that the police occupied the place that criminals once held as a class within society, this social displacement forced the criminals to be further alienated into the darkness. They were now totally isolated as a subculture, and they were fast developing a social structure of their own. From this subculture was born the alienated lone monster who would prey on the society that had ostracized him. He would be the prototype of today's modern serial killer.

Jack the Ripper

In 1888, history's most notorious blood monster burst on the scene to inaugurate the Age of the Sex Crime. This, of course, was Jack the Ripper, and whoever Jack was, he or she set several precedents. Up to this point, almost no one killed for sexual motives and/or sexually mutilated the victims, so when Jack committed his or her first murder/mutilation, it set the stage for the vicious crimes we are so familiar with today. Jack was the first murderer to become a media celebrity and the first to manipulate the public and government with terror.

While it has usually been believed that Jack killed only five prostitutes, there is evidence that indicates the killer began his or her career with a series of slash-and-run killings in the spring of 1888 and then dispatched and horribly mutilated six women from August 1888 to November 1888 before signing off with one last killing in July 1889. In most modern serial killer cases, there is generally a pattern of experimentation that precedes the main series of killings. Since sex killings were extremely rare in the 1800s, the possibility of such experimentation is difficult to ignore. Whoever did the killings also possessed masterful skill with a knife, similar to that of a surgeon. This is why there has been so much speculation that the killer was a mad doctor.

Now, for a little bit of academic fun, let us, as Hercule Poirot would say, "exercise the little gray cells" and see if we can paint a portrait of Jack based on history and the information contained in this book. First, let's consider the theory that Jack committed suicide after the final murder. Ask yourself this one key question: If you lived in the era when criminal detection was in its infancy and you were a serial killer who knew absolutely that you would never be caught, would you commit suicide after advertising how much you enjoyed killing and how this "fun" would continue?

Since Jack asserted that he or she was on a mission and exhibited little evidence of remorse, it is highly unlikely that he or she committed suicide. The suicide theory is more of a Victorian moral judgment, and there are no facts to support this conclusion. The diary that has popped up claiming that a middle-class merchant did the crimes should not be given credence until its authenticity can be fully documented. The all-important factor is that Jack was the prototype for his or her twentieth-century counterparts: The killer was a nobody who wanted to be a somebody. Jack could have been a member of the middle- or upper-class but more likely was on or near the same social plane as the victims and was a product of the same unfortunate social environment. It is also highly possible that Jack was a woman, possibly a fellow prostitute.

By today's standards of serial killers and mass murderers, Jack's known body count was a minor crime spree. Yet, to the Victorian public, this rampage had an overwhelming impact on all levels of society and almost toppled the government. Still, while Jack's crimes were significant in the history of crime, these crimes were not the first of their kind. Others came before Jack and many, many more would follow in the bloody footsteps of this fiend.

Other Serial Killers

In 1886, the career of H.H. Holmes began with the murder of a friend for life insurance money. Over the next eight years, Holmes, who was once a doctor, killed twenty-seven people. His motive was partly money, but mostly he did it, by his own admission, because he enjoyed killing. Holmes's criminal career started out in fraud, then graduated to murder, for which he was hanged in 1896. He had an insatiable sexual appetite, which lead him to commit several acts of bigamy, along with maintaining a long succession of mistresses. After killing his friend to collect the insurance, Holmes became partners with a Mrs. Holten in a pharmacy in 1886. Shortly afterward, Mrs. Holten disappeared. With the proceeds from his pharmacy, Holmes built an extravagant home, which he called "the Castle." It soon became a castle of horrors. Many people came in as guests, but few ever left, disappearing without a trace. Over a period of four years, Holmes used the rooms of the house as murder chambers. During the World's Fair of 1893, he rented rooms to tourists, killed them, and sold their bodies and skeletons to medical schools. To make his handiwork easier, he had set up a torture chamber in the basement that also had a work area with a furnace and acid bath for disposing of bodies.

The record of murders by Holmes made him America's first major serial killer. He was dubbed America's criminal of the century, and though he confessed to twenty-seven murders, it is realistically believed that his actual body count is over fifty. His record of twenty-seven or more was incredible for the period. It was not broken until 1979, when thirty-two young boys were discovered under the house of John Wayne Gacy. At any rate, Dean Corll may have broken both records, but we will never know. In 1973, twenty-seven of his victims were dug up from the Houston Boat Basin, and even though the authorities had indications that there were dozens more bodies, they simply refused to dig up any more.

In 1895, the prototype of Ted Bundy burst on the scene. His name was Theo Durrant and he only killed two women, but the savagery of his crimes made international news. Had he not been caught, he could easily have broken Holmes record for two reasons. First, law enforcement in America at the end of the nineteenth century, was, as in England, in its infancy. Second, he was one of those decent, respectable types who, like Bundy over eighty years later, fooled everyone with his deadly charm. He worked for Emanual Baptist Church in San Francisco, and he was studying to be a doctor. Dubbed the "Demon of the Belfry," Durrant lured his two victims to the church library, one on April 3, 1895, and the other on April 12, 1895, and murdered them as he tried to rape them. On both occasions, after he murdered his victims, he took the bodies to the belfry, mutilated the corpses, and had sex with them. The day after the bodies were found, he was arrested, and in 1898, he was hanged.

Across the Atlantic, Joseph Vacher was earning his reputation as the "French Ripper." Unlike other serial killers, whose monstrous minds can be concealed by either a charming, attractive exterior or an ordinary, everyman exterior, Vacher looked like the ogre he was. In 1893, Vacher was a soldier, and after almost killing his lover in a shooting accident, he tried to shoot himself in the head.

The bullet caused extensive facial and brain damage, leaving him horribly disfigured. Vacher was treated for mental instability, and after a year in an asylum, he was pronounced cured and released. He started killing within months of his release. As a disfigured, seedy tramp, he roamed the countryside begging for food and racking up a body count of eleven people. He was compared to Jack the Ripper because all his victims were raped, murdered and horribly mutilated. In 1897, he was arrested for assault, and after being sentenced to three months in jail, he confessed to the murders. After being subjected to five months of extensive study by a team of doctors, he was tried in October 1898. Though Vacher tried to plead insanity, he was found guilty and executed in December 1898. Interestingly, if Vacher had been tried in the 1990s instead of the 1890s, his plea of insanity would have been accepted on the grounds that brain damage made him unable to control his actions.

So, from the history of human destructiveness, we shall now proceed to explore the mystery of human behavior.

UNDERSTANDING HUMAN BEHAVIOR

Whenever you go on a trip to an unfamiliar place, you usually study a map to familiarize yourself with the landmarks and roads. Now you are about to travel to a very unfamiliar area — the human mind — to study a very dark corner — criminal behavior. Before you can follow this path, you need to become familiar with some basic principles of how the human mind works.

The Rules of Human Behavior

The world renowned psychologist Abraham Maslow defined some wonderful rules about what governs basic human behavior, and these rules are the foundation to understanding criminal behavior. In his book *Motivation and Personality*, Maslow proposed that all human motivation can be described in terms of a "hierarchy of needs," which he said fit into five categories:

1. *Physical* — those needs concerning such things as food

2. *Security* — those needs concerning such things as shelter

3. *Belongingness and love* — those needs concerning the desire for roots and the desire to be wanted

4. *Esteem* — those needs concerning the desire to be liked and respected.

5. *Self-actualization* — the need to know and understand the world around us, to invent and create, and to discover the joy of solving problems.

Every hour of every day, your every action, as the average citizen, is governed by this hierarchy of needs as it relates to your life. When you are hungry, you think of nothing else but food, and your primary motivation for working is directed at feeding yourself, buying clothes, and keeping a roof over your head. To a homeless person, life is a preoccupation with food, shelter and maybe liquor or drugs to ease the pain of suffering. After your physical and security needs are satisfied, you are faced with satisfying your sexual needs. This is not just the need for simple physical gratification. This also concerns the need for affection, emotional security and "belonging." Finally, after you have achieved this level, your life becomes directed toward the need to be liked, the need for self-esteem, and the need for the admiration of the people around you. After all four basic need levels are met, your need to be self-actualizing is free to develop; however, most people are never fortunate enough to reach this level. Writers do — *after* they get published often enough.

Criminals have the same needs as most people. This is why when you study criminal behavior, you will discover a number of things that are uncomfortably familiar. It is like staring into a dark distorted mirror, only to discover that the face peering back at you bears a taunting, hideous resemblance to yours.

But you're not a criminal, or are you?

You are an average person. The regular man or woman. You work from nine to five. You pay your bills on time (or at least you try to). You pay your taxes. You cross the street at crosswalks. You dot your *i*'s and cross your *t*'s. So, it's not possible for you to be a criminal, or is it?

What about those times you lied to your boss and defrauded him or her out of wages by calling in sick when all you really wanted was a day or two off? And how about those thefts you committed when you took home those pens, pencils and pads from the office?

Everyone is capable of committing a crime, but other than the petty stuff, the lives of crime of most people are limited to their dreams and daytime fantasies. So, what makes the average person so different from criminals? Trick question! There is no difference. The criminals you read about in your newspapers and who make headlines on the evening news are just a reflection of the darkness that dwells within every human being. The question that needs reflection is, Why did this darkness, the shadow side, come to dominate these people, turning them toward a life of crime and a chosen path of evil, and not you or any of the genuinely decent people of our society? The answer is simple. You and the decent people grew up into mature human beings, and the criminals stagnated in a perpetual childhood. This degeneration in behavior is accentuated by three basic traits that signify the "criminal personality":

1. *Weakness* — emotional and/or physical, lacking in discipline
2. *Immaturity* — childish egocentrism
3. *Self-deception* — distorted sense of personal reality, severely narcissistic.

Psychology and Criminal Justice

Criminal justice and psychology have one major element in common: They both involve understanding human behavior. To be more precise, both fields attempt to comprehend and control evil. As you follow our road map, you need to ask the following questions:

1. What is crime?
2. What is violence?
3. What is criminal behavior?

Other factors to keep in mind:

1. There is no such thing as "normal." The terms *normal* and *abnormal* are societal labels that change like the weather, such as the myth that all homosexuals are child molesters. As you will discover later on in this book, it is more likely that a child will be molested by a heterosexual relative than a homosexual stranger.
2. Mental illness, such as severe depression, can turn even the staunchest pillars of the community into murderers or other types of criminals.

Labels

Before you can gain a clear understanding of how criminals think, you'll need to have a clear understanding of terms used by the criminal justice officials and by psychologists. Unfortunately, these terms are often misused by the media, which can lead to errors in thinking about the makeup of the criminal mind.

There is no one single way to describe criminals, especially violent criminals, nor is there any one psychiatric label that would fit their behavior. Earlier, I referred to two terms, *parasite* and *vampire*. These terms are appropriate to criminal and violent criminal behavior, respectively. With respect to violent criminals, there are two main categories that psychology, but mostly society, has deemed to fit them into. These categories are psychotic and psychopath. Again, these are labels, and unfortunately, these terms are chronically misused by the public. Frequently, these terms are used interchangeably, and too often, the word *crazy* or *insane* is used to apply to both. Both types are mentally ill.

Psychotic fits the definition of being legally insane, which is why true psychotics are a minority among violent criminals. Psychotics are out of touch with reality, and they often hear voices or see visions or both. Ed Gein, the real-life model for the main character of Hitchcock's *Psycho*, is a classic example of a psychotic. There are also a number of mass murderers who fit this category. For these demented creatures, their madness has led them to kill.

Psychopaths, or as they are often called, sociopaths, are quite different. Psychopaths are also mentally ill, but they are in touch with reality and therefore are not legally insane. Psychopaths know right from wrong, and they are aware that their criminal behavior is wrong, yet they consciously choose to follow a path of evil. This is not the behavior of a crazy person. Psychopaths also lack any conscience and could care less about the harm they do. To them, their crimes are many times regarded as a sport, and they rampage through society without guilt or remorse.

For now, forget the labels and social misconceptions that almost everyone is guilty of allowing to prejudice his or her understanding of criminal behavior.

There are many types of criminals, and their personality traits are different, as well. However, there is one thing that the majority of violent criminals and career criminals have in common and it relates back to the term *vampire*. This is an addiction that can almost be described as a "hunger." In the past twenty years, numerous federal and university research projects have been conducted on the subject of violent criminal behavior. These investigations included the hundreds of interviews with convicted serial killers, serial rapists, child molesters and other violent criminals. From these investigations, we can conclude that these criminals seem to feed on the fear of their victims, feed on the power they derive from their acts, and feed on the pleasure, often sexual, that their acts provide. Even money-oriented mobsters have talked about the "kick" or "high" they get from a bloody perversion called "buckwheats," which is assassination by torture and mutilation. Many mobsters have been known to gloat and laugh over snapshots of such victims, while they proudly show them to fellow mobsters.

While the majority of the criminal population is generally motivated by greed (even though there is a "kick" involved in illegal economic activity), many criminals are bent toward more aggressive, antisocial, destructive desires that embody this hunger, a bloodlust that varies in degrees and a thirst for power and danger. In many serial killers, this insatiable hunger manifests itself in a disorder called "haematodipsia." This is a sexual compulsion to see, taste and touch human blood, and this problem, which is a form of necrophilia, is what can literally define the killers as vampires. However, unlike their mythical counterparts, these real-life vampires *desire* to inflict pain. The only thing this type of criminal shares with the mythical vampire is the *need* for blood. Many of these killers derive sexual gratification from strangling and/or torturing their victims, and many also derive further pleasure from mutilation of the corpse. Most female killers are generally motivated by greed, but a fair number of those caught have confessed that they found killing to be the ultimate sexual high.

Sometimes, these killers kill just for the thrill of the sight of blood, as in the cases of Peter Kürten, the Düsseldorf Ripper, who killed twenty-nine people, and Peter Sutcliffe, the Yorkshire Ripper. Some, like Jeffrey Dahmer, have been known to desire to drink the blood of their victims. The majority of these modern vampires are psychotic, and except for the aforementioned desire for blood, they are nothing like their occult forebears. They can be model citizens by day and monsters by night.

Another term that is appropriate is *necrophile*. These are criminals who derive sexual stimulation from seeing or touching corpses. As in the case of Theo Durrant, he derived greater sexual gratification from having intercourse with the dead bodies of his victims than from having sex with them while they were alive. This is not uncommon, as many serial killers have been known to have sex with the corpses. Necrophilia is divided into three types:

1. *Lust murder* — the sexual compulsion to kill
2. *Necrostuprum* — the theft of corpses for sexual pleasure
3. *Necrophagy* — a desire to eat the flesh of the dead.

The Anatomy of Behavior

To understand the true nature of criminal behavior, you must ingrain into your thinking and use as the foundation of your understanding: *Violence, and for the most part, all crime, is a disease.* Criminal behavior is part of a whole class of destructive human behavior disorders, which, contrary to the protestations of the social scientists, makes crime and violence a *medical problem.* Former surgeon general of the United States Dr. C. Everett Koop set the ground rules for a more realistic way of understanding and dealing with human destructiveness when he said, "Violence is every bit a public health issue for me and my successors in this century as smallpox, TB and syphilis were for my predecessors in the last two centuries." The dictionaries define *disease* as

1. A pathological condition of mind or body, a part, an organ, or a system of an organism resulting from various causes, such as infection, genetic defect, or environmental stress, and characterized by an identifiable group of signs or symptoms.
2. A condition or tendency, as of society, regarded as abnormal and harmful.

Since criminal behavior and violence are pathological conditions of the mind, they are truly diseases. In addition, there are other criteria that further define these problems as diseases. As Thomas Szaz, the world renowned psychiatrist, has pointed out, something is a disease if it meets any one of the following criteria:

1. *Proven and demonstrated lesion* — This includes those things that are proven to the naked eye. This is the core concept of what constitutes a disease. Since there is a proven pathology

to criminal behavior, this criterion fits our definition.

2. *Commonly accepted or suspected lesion* — This refers to an assumed rather than a proven condition. To a small degree, this criterion also fits.

3. *Suffering or things that cause suffering* — This is self-explanatory. Since criminal behavior and violence definitely cause suffering to those who inflict them and all those whom crimes and violence are inflicted upon, this criterion certainly fits.

4. *Bad habits or actions that are dangerous to self* — This concerns things like drug abuse, drunk driving and other similar complications. Since it is also proven that criminal behavior is dangerous to self, this criterion works here as well.

5. *Criminality or actions that are dangerous to others* — This is another self-explanatory item, and this final criterion puts the icing on the cake.

Having met all five medical criteria of what defines a problem as a disease, we can say with certainty that criminal behavior is an illness, that violence is a disease, and that most, if not all, criminals are mentally ill to varying degrees. This does not mean that such a definition is an excuse for criminal behavior, nor is this to be interpreted as mitigating circumstances because a person can be both mentally ill *and* legally sane. (A good example of this is Jeffrey Dahmer.) This is just a more realistic way of defining and understanding criminal behavior. Other components to consider are the ego and sex.

The Ego

When the Greeks were teaching the philosophy that said, "Above all else, know thy Self," they possibly knew long before the invention of psychoanalysis that humans do not like to acknowledge their Egos. While the Self is the center of the total human psyche, the Ego is the center of the conscious personality. It is what makes us individuals, separate from the "tribe," and is the source of creativity. Still, people don't really care for it, mostly because they don't understand it.

Carl Jung, the famous Swiss psychoanalyst, defined the Ego by its functions, which he put into two categories. First are those functions that relate the Ego to the surrounding environment. This group involves the four functions of sensation, intuition, thinking and feeling. Sensation tells the person that something *is*. Thinking tells us *what* a thing is and gives it a name. Feeling informs us of its *value*, and intuition tells us about the *possibilities* of things or situations. All these functions, combined with what Jung called the "energy of willpower," help the individual interact with society and the environment in which the person lives.

The second category of Ego functions are those that relate the Ego to the dark unconscious.

The second group is what links all humans to the "shadow world." People do not like this group and usually, and mistakenly, associate it with the Ego as a whole. Humans make this mistake because this group is out of their control. And generally, people detest all things in their lives that they cannot control. The primary component of this group is *memory*, which, more often than they like, reminds people of things they have repressed or just plain prefer to forget. Memory is pain.

The secondary component is that which controls our subjective reactions, those unmentionable misperceptions of things or people or situations that most people find painful to acknowledge and are creations of the shadow side of ourselves. Prejudice is a good example of a subjective reaction. These subjective reactions are another thing that are generally uncontrollable. Thus, the subjective reaction is pain.

The third component is emotion. As we all know, emotions are hard to control. As Jung said, when the emotions cut loose, "The decent Ego is shoved aside and something else takes its place." An example of this is when a person becomes angry and both looks and feels as if he or she is "possessed." This creation of the shadow side is where crimes of passion and irresistible impulses are born. Emotion is pain.

Finally, there is what Jung called "invasion." This is the shadow side at its worst, and it is when the darkness within us is in full control. These invasions do not necessarily represent deviant or criminal behavior unless they become habitual. It is from these invasions that temporary insanity emanates, as in the case of Lorena Bobbitt. Invasions are those moments of strange behavior that overwhelm a person with emotion or drain a person of energy or fill a person with a sense of strangeness. At these times, a person is capable of anything, including mutilating a spouse's sexual organs. These invasions are real pain, the kind of intense pain that can be lethal.

The Ego is good, and when the conscious mind is in control,

there is no pain. However, when the shadows invade and allow the Ego to go out of control, there is a lot of pain, along with its attendant alienation, fear, suffering, conflict and uncertainty.

Also companion to the dark side is the "death instinct" that dwells within all of us. Freud called the death instinct "Thanatos," and he expressed that when "Thanatos" is dominant, a person is compelled toward destructive behavior.

The Sex Factor

Pick up any newspaper today or turn on CNN or your local news and you may notice that the crime reports seem to be dominated by sex crimes or allegations of sex crimes. Don't worry, you're not imagining things. From Hollywood madams to celebrities to the Bobbitt trials to Joel Rifkin, who killed over a dozen prostitutes in New York City, sex crimes are the hottest items in the news. Even the clergy and teachers are the latest to be accused and/or convicted.

In our society, sex is the most pervasive influence that affects every aspect of our lives. Modern Western society has become one that demands instant gratification and instant relief from boredom. The result is what Freud says is the major drawback of civilization: frustration. And the stresses of modern society cause an overwhelming amount of frustration, with boredom as the main by-product of frustration. Boredom, in turn, creates an oppressive sense of nonreality. Unfortunately, most people have been duped by the media myths and think sex is one of the many ways to alleviate the pain that boredom causes.

In both men and women, the pain of boredom and its accompanying sense of nonreality can lead to addictions as people seek a cure for their suffering. In women, the predominant addictions are food, drugs and alcohol. However, in men, the addictions take a far more destructive bent with drugs, sex and violence being the male ideas of cures to their ills. Both Erich Fromm and Sigmund Freud developed their views of human destructiveness and self-destructiveness around sex. Fromm, an eminent psychoanalyst and researcher into human behavior, used the terms *sadism* and *necrophilia*, which are both psychiatric disorders of a sexual nature, to define the human desire to commit violence. Freud explained the human propensity for violence as stemming from the death instinct, which he said is related to human sexual desires.

As history and today's crime statistics bear out, sex and crime go hand in hand. This does not mean that all criminals are sexual deviants, but the desire for either conscious or unconscious sexual gratification is a common element in many crimes. It is the death instinct at work.

Crime, Violence and Criminal Behavior

With these reference points in hand, we can now examine the questions posed earlier in this chapter.

What Is Crime?

When H. Rap Brown said that violence "is as American as cherry pie," he wasn't far from the truth. This is the mentality that pervades society, and it is essential that, as you study how criminals think, you understand the social and environmental factors that create and contribute to such behavior. There are a lot of Band-Aid, quick-fix theories that blame almost anything as the cause of crime and violence and give society an excuse not to take responsibility for the real cause of crime. Currently, there is a move to blame television and movies as the cause of these problems. However, there is absolutely no conclusive evidence to support this claim, just as there was no evidence to support Hitler's justification for burning books, which he claimed were corrupting the minds of people. These baseless theories are all part of a new "witchcraft craze" that even claims there is a genetic cause for crime and violence. Again, these boats sink fast when you try to sail them without proof. Before these excuses became popular in the media and political arena, junk food was blamed and was even used as ground for an insanity defense. Well, the "Twinkie defense," which attempted to show that the defendant in this case only killed because he was addicted to junk food, specifically citing Twinkie snack cakes, failed just like the "extra chromosome defense," the defense that attempted to excuse a defendant's acts of murder because of a genetic mutation. There is no conclusive proof of the existence of a "criminal gene," just as there is no conclusive proof of a genetic cause for homosexuality or alcoholism or addictive/compulsive behavior.

What Is Violence?

Violence, as a disease, is referred to in medical terms as "intentional trauma," which includes, according to the Center for Disease Control, but is not limited to:

1. Murder
2. Assault
3. Sexual assault
4. Manslaughter
5. Spouse/partner abuse
6. Child maltreatment (abuse and neglect)
7. Physical and mental exploitation
8. Suicide
9. Drug/alcohol abuse
10. Deliberate negligence
11. Deliberate hazards
12. Criminal manipulation and duress
13. Peer confrontations
14. Parasuicide
15. Abduction
16. Robbery.

While this is a very complex issue, it can be simply stated that crime and violence are problems of *medical ecology*. This is a simple equation that defines the relationship between one or more individuals in conflict with one or more other individuals, their surrounding environment, and these factors as they relate to time. Unlike an accident, where you have a VICTIM + ENVIRONMENT (such as a rainy night) + AGENT (such as a car) + MECHANISM (such as a blown-out tire) = ACCIDENT INCIDENT, the equation for all acts of intentional trauma is:

[VICTIM(S) + VICTIMIZER(S) + TIME] + AGENT/
VECTOR FACTORS + MECHANISM + ENVIRONMENT
FACTORS = CRIME.

This is the mixture of the victim and the predator combined in the crucible of fate (TIME) with the criminal's motive, intent, opportunity and method (AGENT/VECTOR FACTORS), along with the environment, and the result is a crime. MECHANISM is the weapon or tool used. ENVIRONMENT FACTORS are not just the physical influences but also the social, political, legal and economic factors that give the criminal the latitude to commit his or her foul deeds.

Violence is not a social or a legal problem. It is a complication of mental illness. And herein lies the key to why the public is so fascinated with the "romance of violence." Crime and violence are the "dark" side of human nature and people are naturally drawn to it to fill their void of understanding about why criminals do what they do. The best-selling books and the most popular movies on TV, in the theater and on video are usually about violent crime. The popularity of *Silence of the Lambs* is a perfect example of the public's love affair with trying to understand the criminal mind.

What Is Criminal Behavior?

Even though we have discussed criminals as evil, it is important to understand that criminal behavior is not a deviancy bent on evil as a way of life because there are other factors involved. It is a constant desire to be childishly self-indulgent. A criminal wishes to do whatever he/she pleases with nothing but contempt and total disregard for the rights and feelings of others. The criminal always, like a child, wants something for nothing. Freud once said that a child would destroy the world if it had the power. Simply, a child is totally subjective. The child has no desire to consider nor accept the viewpoint of others because a child is incapable of acknowledging anything other than the desire to satisfy his or her own feelings. In short, a criminal is nothing more than a ruthless adult who never stops behaving like a child—the victim of a chronic disease that makes a person obsessed with taking shortcuts.

What is perplexing and terrifying at the same time, is that, tragically, many of the worst crimes are not committed by evil, simpleminded degenerates but by people of high intelligence. Research has indicated that a high proportion of the criminal population possesses a medium to high degree of intelligence. It is ironic that that as a person's intelligence potential develops, his or her intelligence can lead toward either creative, productive consequences or destructive, futile consequences. However, even as destructive as most criminal behavior is, some types of criminals, such as forgers and con artists and sometimes burglars and mobsters, display a unique ability to be highly creative, except that this talent is wasted on useless self-indulgence that benefits no one.

In essence, the basic components of criminal behavior are:

1. *A dominant Ego*—Self-interest is all important (weakness and self-deception interacting).

2. *A chronic lack of maturity* — Dominant childish mental and emotional qualities are present (the childish egocentrism running amok).

3. *An obsession with sex* — Sex is viewed as a form of crime and crime as a form of sex (weakness, the general lack of discipline, interacting with the need for power to compensate for weakness, along with self-deception working to compensate for immaturity).

Outlining the Criminal Mind

When psychologists and law enforcement officials want to gain a clear understanding of a criminal, they create an outline by asking six questions:

1. WHO are the victimizers? That is, what is their psychiatric type? WHO are the victims? That is, what is the victim profile?
2. WHERE did the crime occur? That is, what physical and social environment facilitated the crime?
3. WHEN, as in the parameters of the "window of vulnerability," was the crime committed? That is, what is the relationship of time?
4. WHAT occurred, as in the types of acts defined as intentional trauma?
5. HOW did it happen? That is, what was the mechanism of injury, the weapons and tools of the criminal trade, and the method of operation?
6. WHY was it done? What was the motive?

Once the answers to these questions are outlined, you will have a comprehensive understanding of the pathology of the sickness and disease that dominate the criminal mind. In addition, this outline will define the trauma suffered by the victim. Let's take a closer look at these questions to provide a clearer understanding of how they outline the criminal.

WHO? The pathology of criminal behavior and intentional trauma shows that victimizers are usually people suffering major behavioral/personality disorders. These disorders tend to be sadistic and narcissistic predilections. This group of criminals accounts for the majority of incidents of intentional trauma. The remainder are related to:

1. Emotionally disturbed children
2. Incidents of drug and/or alcohol abuse
3. Persons suffering extreme social and economic stress
4. Acts of intentional negligence
5. Criminal gang exploitation
6. Financial gain
7. Emotional disorders such as anxiety and stress disorders
8. Persons who have been subjected to prolonged abuse and exploitation and lash out as a result of Post-Traumatic Stress Syndrome and other relevant causes of temporary insanity.

Destructive (sadistic, narcissistic or sociopathic) personality disorders are the primary foundation of criminal behavior, especially violent criminal behavior. Unfortunately, these perpetrators don't wear signs that say "criminal," and they have an uncanny talent for hiding. As I mentioned before, this type of criminal has a very chameleon-like, average-person exterior that masks a wide range of problems that encompass any type of criminality or social deviancy.

Regardless of the label, the monsters we shall discuss in this book are people who delight in hunting down and preying upon the helpless and/or the vulnerable of our society. This not only results in death or injury to individuals; the community as a whole pays a high price in terms of the extreme emotional trauma that is suffered.

To these criminals, all the world is a stage, and they derive great satisfaction and gratification in deceiving everyone around them. Crime allows these monsters to play the role of master and satisfies their consuming need for power. Since they are inadequate in a number of ways, including impotence and a lack of emotional maturity, these perpetrators have to have that ultimate control, which includes control over life and death.

If you think this sounds like a description that would fit your common, garden-variety political terrorist, you are right. There is little difference between a terrorist and a serial killer or serial rapist or chronic violent offender or mobster/violent career criminal.

Finally there is the question concerning *victims*. Simply stated, *everyone* has an equal potential of becoming a crime victim at any time in life. So, forget those theories that blame the victim. Victims are neither responsible for the harm they suffer nor are they as culpable as the criminal, even if there is interplay between the victim and the criminal that creates escalation of the incident of trauma, as in the case of spouse/partner abuse or date rape. Until the first blow is struck, the victim of domestic violence, spouse abuse or partner abuse has no idea that the person she married or is living with is a vicious monster. The same situation exists in date rape. It is the deception factor that is so prevalent in the personality of violent perpetrators that is at play in trapping the victims.

So, how do people become victims? The only sane explanation to this insane issue can be found in the factor known as "victim vulnerability." Since it is the criminal who hunts the victim, lying in wait for the prey to come along, or snares the victim in the web of a deceptive relationship, it is impossible to blame the victim. The attacks only occur when the opportunity to exploit both the vulnerability of the victim and the victim's circumstance is available. This opportunity is called "the window of vulnerability."

WHERE? We all know that given any opportunity, crime can be inflicted anywhere. However, it is important to pay attention to the goals and desires of the criminal types in order to determine the patterns of locales used to commit crimes, such as serial killers who choose venues frequented by prostitutes. Given any unguarded moment in any vulnerable opportunity, no one is really safe. This is the case in most incidents of nighttime ATM robbery, many cases of rape, and all cases of child molestation. Since most rapes and murders are committed by people who are acquainted with the victim, no one ever knows he or she is being hunted or stalked until the predator makes his or her presence known. It is also important to pay attention to the social characteristics of the community in which the locales of crimes are situated to understand if the cause is a local or an outside factor. There is the interesting case of a small northern California town that had a reputation for being quiet, until someone decided to rid the area of prostitutes à la Jack the Ripper. The hookers thought they were safe hustling the tourists in this cozy burg, but either a tourist or a resident showed the prostitutes they were dead wrong.

WHEN? This is the time factor, which can be either random, uncontrolled or controlled, solely at the discretion of the criminal. If drugs are involved, this factor can be totally random or random only to the extent that the timing is based on the criminal's desires. If frequency of emotional intensity is the sole control factor of time, this can explain the unstable time factor that is common in many serial killer cases. While some serial killers murder by a timetable, others kill only when the mood is upon them. Some just wait until a victim *and* a window of vulnerability are available. This is why, in many crimes, time is a key factor relating to this window of vulnerability. With mass murderers, when the incident occurs, it usually involves time in relationship to some highly stressful or traumatic event that drives them over the edge. This is generally the case when postal employees turn their jobs into killing grounds.

WHAT? These are the acts of intentional trauma that have become a public health epidemic. These are the same elements listed earlier.

HOW? This concerns the mechanism of injury and the agent/vector factor of method involved in the criminal act. These factors involve the weapons or tools the criminals use, including their own limbs, and the techniques they use to harm people, as in their method of operation. These factors always vary according to the criminals' desires and motives in relationship to the circumstances surrounding the crimes or pattern of crimes. For example, in the case of Peter Kürten, he kept changing his weapons and attack/killing methods in an effort to achieve greater sexual gratification with each kill.

WHY? This is the great unknown. Deviant desires for and obsessions with pain or killing or death, a distorted concept of justice, or righting some nonexistent personal wrong. You name it — anything — and there is little chance that you will be wrong. All in all, *why* is wrapped up in the motives of the criminal, and this is an uncontrollable factor. However, there may be an answer to determining why certain crimes occur, and it could be found in the issue of self-esteem. In recent years, there has been an increase in crimes of self-esteem, crimes in which the criminals feel that society is to blame for their lack of dignity, justice and recognition of individuality. The criminal may also be seeking acceptance. Thus a crime can be an expression of protest or desire for status, a narcissistic statement of contempt or simply part of a ritual.

T H R E E

PROFILING THE CRIMINAL

From 1940, with a patriotic pause for World War II, to 1957, New York City was terrorized by an unknown subject who came to be known as the "Mad Bomber." The police were baffled and up against a stone wall until they consulted Dr. James A. Brussel. Dubbed by the press as the "Sherlock Holmes of the Couch," Brussel is the founder of the art of psychological profiling of criminals. After one interview with the police, Brussel, with almost psychic ability, provided a detailed portrait of the Bomber. But it was not magic nor was it pure science that led Dr. Brussel to his conclusions. He simply zeroed in on a single subject by combining identifiable behavioral characteristics with statistical probability, the skills of modern psychiatric examination and good intuition.

While this new "art" of criminal investigation was successful and pioneered the field of modern forensic psychology, the technique used by Dr. Brussel was limited and prone to error because it focused on individuals. For the next seventeen years, this technique rested in the shadows until, in 1974, the FBI's Behavioral Science

Unit based at Quantico, Virginia, debuted its new system of "profiling" based on the pioneering work of Dr. Brussel. To the ever expanding world of law enforcement and criminal detection entered the "psychological profiling team."

The Development of Profiling

Prior to 1974, profiling, the development of a psychological mug shot of an unknown suspect, was a very haphazard effort. Even though Dr. Brussel had earlier successes with his technique, it was not highly accurate, and when used as part of a team effort, the technique was totally off target. When Dr. Brussel was asked to join a team of experts to assist with the Boston Strangler case, the team concluded that there were two murderers: one a loner, who worked as a schoolteacher, and the other a homosexual with an intense hatred of women. In fact, this profile never led to the Strangler's arrest. He was apprehended by good old-fashioned police work. Once in custody, the profile proved to be dead wrong. Albert DeSalvo was a married man with children and a former soldier. He did not hate women and he did not hate his mother, as the Freudian theories put forth by the team suggested. He was a rapist who killed only when he became enraged over his own impotence. When he discovered that his impotence was "cured" after the last murder, he stopped murdering and returned to committing only rapes. But this failure to correctly profile the Boston Strangler did not cause law enforcement to throw the baby out with the bath water. Profiling was a good idea that only needed work to improve the technique's accuracy.

With a grant from the National Institute of Justice, the FBI set up its special project for profiling at the FBI Academy in Quantico, Virginia. The bureau began by compiling a library of known cases and defined psychological studies and interviews of murderers. (Coincidentally, such a project had been suggested by crime writer Colin Wilson in 1960.) This was the beginning of a new weapon in the war on crime.

This new system of psychological profiling focused in on reading *the crime scene* for behavioral clues in order to identify the *type* of criminal responsible for the crime. This was an advance over the method used by Dr. Brussel and his peers, which focused on the individual and greatly depended on the guidance and reputation of the psychologist or psychiatrist offering the professional assessment. Since most of Dr. Brussel's contemporaries had their own theories on criminal behavior, the old "profile" method was flawed by personal bias and the whims of chance. The new FBI method was highly systematic, allowing law enforcement professionals the flexibility of combining their years of investigative experience and intuitive judgment with the behavior clues deduced from the crime scene evidence, coroners reports and statistical probability. The central component of the system was the classification of unknown subjects into two types: the organized or the disorganized offender. However, this relied too much on experience and intuition, so a further component was added: the Criminal Personality Research Project. This began as criminal behavior surveys based on interviews with a series of imprisoned murderers and rapists that provided an ongoing database of behavioral characteristics. This component is now an encyclopedic data bank that is continually reviewed and updated.

In 1984, the system was enhanced by the establishment of the National Center for the Analysis of Violent Crime, also based at Quantico and run by the FBI's Behavioral Sciences Unit (BSU). NCAVC is a law enforcement clearinghouse and resource center for the collection and sharing of violent crime data. Together with the BSU, also known as the "think tank" of law enforcement, NCAVC uses the latest in cutting-edge computer technology to combat violent crime nationwide, especially serial crime. This includes specialized projects such as VICAP (the Violent Criminal Apprehension Program) and PROFILER (a computerized system that profiles serial murderers).

In 1973, the early system of the BSU was put into practice when seven-year-old Susan Jaeger was abducted and murdered while camping with her parents in Montana. When the FBI entered the case employing its new technique, it profiled the unknown subject as:

- A homicidal voyeur, who lived near the victim's campsite
- A young, white male, as statistics suggested
- An organized type, made evident by the use of a knife brought by the offender and taken away
- A loner of average or higher intelligence, also as statistical probability suggested.

These behavioral jigsaw puzzle pieces were put together with the investigators' experience, which also said that since no ransom note or word had come forth, the girl was dead and the killer most probably mutilated the victim for souvenirs.

In January 1974, the murder of a local teenager was linked to a suspect who was identified by an FBI informant. However, no evidence could connect him to the crimes. The suspect was David Meirhofer, a twenty-three-year-old single Vietnam veteran who lived near the campgrounds. Despite the fact that Meirhofer had passed two tests, a lie detector and a truth serum interrogation, the experts from Quantico were sure he was their man. Aided by Susan Jaeger's parents, the FBI induced the killer to tip his hand, enabling them to obtain a warrant for the search of Meirhofer's apartment. As they had predicted, body parts — the grisly souvenirs of Meirhofer's crimes, which proved his guilt — were found, and while in custody, he confessed to the killings of the two girls and also two local boys whose disappearances and deaths were then unsolved. Shortly thereafter, Meirhofer hanged himself in his jail cell. This was a breakthrough case, and David Meirhofer became the first serial killer to be caught by the new technique of criminal profiling. Within a decade, the system would be refined and would be known as the accurate, systematic profiling technique called CIAP (the Criminal Investigative Analysis Program).

While Dr. Brussel is credited with the founding of the art of profiling, the refiners of the technique to be known as CIAP were Howard Teten, Patrick Mullany, Robert Ressler and John Douglas. These pioneers of profiling put their careers on the line to advance the new technique, which included unofficial interviews with convicted murderers that could have wrecked their careers if there had been any problems stemming from the interviews. However, there were no complaints, and the risk paid off with invaluable answers to numerous questions about why these killers did such brutal acts.

The Elveson Murder

In 1979, their research, added to the infant technique, was put to the test to aid in the search for the killer of New York City schoolteacher Francine Elveson. Miss Elveson, 26, was the victim of a brutal sexual assault and mutilation murder. Her naked, maimed body was found on the roof of the apartment house where she lived with her parents. In this case, the FBI got an opportunity to examine a crime scene as that canvas of mayhem we discussed earlier. The killer literally arranged the body to create a portrait of murder and rage, and to use as a challenge to police that he would never be caught. He had even written his challenge on the victim's thigh. All her personal effects were carefully placed to accent the portrait, and the mutilation was also carefully done to dehumanize the dead woman, with the removed body parts placed back on the body with artistic intent. A pendant in the shape of the Jewish symbol for good luck, the Chai, was taken as a souvenir, and the woman's body was bent and twisted into the shape of the Chai, an almost mocking replica of the pendant.

The case was extremely bizarre, and there was a lot of publicity. Over two thousand suspects were interviewed, but by the time the FBI was called in, the police were no closer to catching the killer than the day the body was found. The police felt they had no clues.

However, John Douglas, one of the pioneers of profiling, found a number of clues in this ritual killing that the police could not see. Agent Douglas was looking for clues to the *type* of murderer, while the police were searching for the individual murderer.

The canvas the killer had created with crime science produced this portrait of the unknown subject:

1. The killer was both "organized" and "disorganized." The FBI called this a "mixed" crime scene; however, the killer was classified as a "disorganized" type because it was felt that the killer had acted out a fantasy ritual with a victim that he simply killed on the spur of the moment. There was no planning; the victim was not chosen and hunted. The victim was just unlucky enough to meet her killer by chance, and the killer took advantage of this meeting to act on his fantasy.

2. The portrait also indicated a white male, between twenty-five and thirty-five, of average appearance and who was familiar with the layout of the building and the habits of the tenants. The killer was confident that he would be uninterrupted during the ritual mutilation that he carried out.

3. Statistics pointed out that the killer was a school dropout and was unemployed, lived alone, and did not use drugs or alcohol.

4. The ritual and the sadistic rage involved in the killing indicated that the killer was sexually inadequate and could not relate to women normally, which was borne out by the fact that the victim was not raped but was object raped with a pen and umbrella

thrust into her vagina. The semen found on the body showed that the orgy of mutilation gave the killer the sexual gratification he desired. These factors also indicated that the killer had a history of mental illness and possibly had been in a psychiatric hospital. The killer's implied desire to shock and offend, along with his challenge to the police, also indicated the presence of mental illness.

5. The way in which the crime appeared to have happened seemed to indicate that the victim knew her killer, that the killer was a regular visitor to the building, and that given another similar window of opportunity, he would kill again.

Armed with this profile, the police closed in on Carmine Calabro, a thirty-year-old, unmarried, unemployed actor, who was a high school dropout and who regularly visited his father, a neighbor of the victim. However, Calabro had an alibi that almost cleared him. He had severe mental problems, and he was undergoing treatment in a psychiatric hospital at the time of the murder. But it was discovered that the hospital's security was very lax, and Calabro was absent without permission on the day of the murder.

Calabro pleaded "not guilty," but dental evidence matched the bite marks on Francine Elveson's body, and he was convicted, sentenced to life in prison. This was another impressive demonstration of the art of profiling, and the profile was so accurate that the police jokingly asked why the FBI hadn't given them the killer's phone number too. The jokes stopped and soon the new investigative tool was warmly embraced by the country's law enforcement community.

The Murder Types

As a result of its research, the FBI lists five categories of murder:

1. *Felony murder* — a homicide committed during the commission of a serious crime, such as armed robbery, hijacking or arson

2. *Suspected felony murder*

3. *Argument-motivated murder* — a homicide that occurs during a domestic dispute and is distinct from criminal-motivated murder, the proverbial "crime of passion"

4. *Other motives* — homicides with identifiable motives that are separate from the first three types of murder

5. *"Unknown" motives* — homicides with no clear motive present.

There are two categories of mass murder:

1. *Family mass murder* — This is the killing of four or more members of the same family by another family member, as in the case of John List. List was a New Jersey insurance salesman and Sunday school teacher who killed his mother, wife and three children in November 1971, then disappeared. He left behind a detailed confession that gave an exact account of how he carried out the murders, and the press implied that the motive was money. List was not arrested until June 1989 after an aged likeness and a bust were broadcast on *America's Most Wanted*.

2. *Classic mass murder* — This is the killing of four or more non-family victims in a single location at one time. This is a type of seemingly motiveless crime that is becoming more and more prevalent worldwide. The motive, if there is any, usually is only discovered well after the killings, but the pattern indicates that classic mass murderers are mentally ill men and women who vent their hostility against society in an orgy of stabbings and/or shootings of victims chosen at random. Such was the case of Charles Whitman, the Texas Tower killer, who shot up the University of Texas in Austin, killing sixteen men and women and wounding thirty in ninety minutes in 1966. In 1989, Marc Lepine declared war on women and killed fourteen at the University of Montreal. He wounded nine others plus four men. He complained that "feminists have always spoiled my life," and he blamed all women for a "life filled with disappointments." Police later found a "hit list" of fifteen prominent Quebec women. Lepine's rage ended with the one mass killing and then killing himself. Other notables are Richard Speck, who killed eight nurses in their apartment in 1966; James Huberty, who shot up a California McDonalds in 1984 killing twenty-one men, women and children and wounding nineteen — the worst mass murder in modern American history; and Richard Farley, who shot up his workplace in 1988 after being fired for sexually harassing a female coworker he was obsessively stalking and planning to kill for four years.

The FBI Behavioral Sciences Unit also lists two kinds of multiple murderers:

1. *Spree killer*—This is a person who commits murder in two or more locations, but the killings are linked by motive as a single event, as in the case of Michael Ryan, who killed sixteen people and wounded fourteen in 1987 in England. The Hungerford Massacre had two killing grounds nine miles apart, the second being the town of Hungerford itself, which is the reason that this is regarded as spree killing rather than a mass murder.

2. *Serial killer*—Sometimes, a serial killer will become a spree killer, as in the 1984 case of Christopher Wilder, a successful businessman who led the FBI and numerous state law enforcement agencies on a coast-to-coast manhunt. In seven weeks, Wilder kidnapped, raped, tortured and murdered as many as ten women in twelve states before being killed by a New Hampshire state trooper on Friday the 13th. It was this case that underscored the need for a national resource center that would help track and apprehend transient violent criminals. A little over a month after Wilder's death, NCAVC was established at Quantico.

Computer Profiling

With the enormous leaps in computer technology in the past six years, profiling is no longer being exclusively done by human minds. PROFILER is a computer based expert system that uses a very sophisticated "if-then" program to determine the type of criminal that human profilers do. So, now the computer is part of the profiling team, but the humans have the last word on what the final profile report will say.

However, it must always be remembered that profiling is an art, not a science, and it is far from perfect. Since 1982, Seattle's Green River Killer has not only defied detection after over fifty murders, the killer has also never been successfully profiled, thus remaining an absolute enigma. Ted Bundy was another that would have defied profiling because he did not really fit any specific type. He was not a genius, but he was an intelligent overachiever, who is far from the "loser factor" that somewhat flaws the profiling system. He had been a good student, dated women, interacted with people well, had a good work history, and been a modest success at the time he became a full-time serial killer. By the time Bundy was "profiled in a sense" and listed seventh on a list of ten suspects, he was already under arrest. By then he had killed as many as seventeen women, and after he escaped jail, he was suspect number one.

The Profile Matrix

In the same manner that crime-scene analysts outline a criminal, the practitioners of the art of profiling are governed by the same question outline utilized in journalism. So, to develop a portrait of evil, connect the dots by answering the following questions:

1. Who?
   - Who are the victims (women, children, gays, prostitutes, elderly or men)? Are they targeted specifically, or are the targets varied?
   - What type (organized or disorganized) of killer is involved? Is the killer:
     1. Visionary
     2. Mission oriented
     3. Comfort oriented
     4. Lust motivated
     5. Thrill motivated
     6. Power/control oriented?

2. What?
   - What was the cause of death?
   - What kind of deviant sexual behavior is evident?
   - What are the unusuals?

3. When?
   - When did the crime occur (time of day, time of month, time of year)?
   - Did the crime occur on or near a particularly significant event or date?
   - Did the crime occur on a religious-related date or occult-related date?
   - Is there anything special or unusual about when the crime was committed?

4. Where?
   - Where did the crime occur?

- Where was the body or victim (if still alive) found?
- Was the victim abducted from another place, and if so, where did the abduction occur?

5. How?

- How was the crime committed?
- Was the crime method specific, or does the method vary?
- Was there anything unusual about the methods?

6. Why?

- Does the crime appear to be sexual in nature?
- Does the crime appear to be profit motivated?
- Does the crime appear to be spontaneous?
- Does the crime appear to be planned?

Other Factors

As we have seen, the FBI has proven that there is more to the crime and crime scene than just the physical evidence, which emphasizes the importance of looking beyond these factors. In doing so, the BSU has specified two main types of violent criminals. These types are the *organized* and the *disorganized*. In addition, the personal characteristics of the criminal and the behavior of the criminal after the crime have been defined for each criminal.

The personal characteristics of the organized violent offender may include:

- High intelligence (IQ 135 +), may be college educated
- Social competence
- Sexual competence
- Living with a partner
- Being an only child or most favored child in family
- Having suffered abuse or harsh discipline in childhood
- Controlled moods
- Maintaining a stereotypical masculine image
- Being charming
- Having moods subject to situational cause
- Being geographically and occupationally mobile
- Following media coverage.

The behavior of this type after the crime may include:

- Returning to the crime scene
- Volunteering information
- Being a police groupie
- Anticipating being questioned
- Moving the body
- Disposing of the body to advertise the crime.

On the opposite side, the disorganized violent offender characteristics include:

- Having low to average intelligence (IQ 80-100)
- Being an unskilled worker (may be school dropout)
- Being socially immature
- Having had a rough childhood with a father whose work history was unstable
- Having suffered abuse in childhood
- Being anxious during the crime
- Using drugs or alcohol minimally
- Living alone
- Living and/or working near crimes
- Paying little or no attention to news media
- Being dominated by significant behavioral change
- Being a nocturnal person
- Having poor personal hygiene
- Having secret hiding places
- Not usually dating.

This type's behavior after the crime may include:

- Returning to the scene of the crime
- Attending funeral of victim
- Clipping obituary
- Turning to religion
- Keeping a diary and/or collecting news clippings
- Changing residence
- Undergoing a personality change.

How the crime scene is produced differs between the two types of offenders.

The organized criminal:

- Plans the offense
- Targets strangers
- Personalizes the victim
- Controls conversation with victim
- Controls crime scene
- Requires victim to be submissive
- Uses restraints
- Acts aggressively
- Moves body
- Removes weapon
- Leaves very little evidence.

The disorganized criminal:

- Acts spontaneously
- Targets people he or she knows
- Depersonalizes victim
- Keeps conversation with victim to a minimum
- Creates a chaotic crime scene
- Attacks victim with sudden violence
- Does not use restraints
- May have sex with corpse
- Leaves body at crime scene
- Leaves weapon
- Leaves a variety of evidence.

Profile of Jack the Ripper:

A New Perspective

Here's a little academic morsel to ponder. It was derived from actual events surrounding the notorious crimes that terrified Victorian London and related crime reports. Using the Profile Matrix as a guide and looking beyond the crime scenes, this information offers an alternative viewpoint on this infamous criminal who murdered six to eight prostitutes.

Who

Victims were all lower-class women forced to earn a living via prostitution. Crimes appear to be victim specific. Perpetrator could either be male or female. Crimes reflect *organized* type. Suspect presumed to be male because of sexual bias of the day, but female could have committed the same crimes.

What

There were multiple stabbings, mutilation, necrophilia, indications of cannibalism and necrophilia and some occult overtones. All the killings had the same modus operandi, or MO.

When

Two murders occurred prior to more famous mutilation murders that began in August 1888. It is possible that this first set of killings was experimentation. From then, five murders, the infamous "Ripper killings," transpired over a period of five months — four on very secluded streets, one in the fifth victim's home, all always at night. Two victims were killed in one night, probably because the killer was interrupted while committing the first crime of that night. Despite the belief that the Ripper had committed suicide, another identical murder occurred eight months later in July 1889.

Where

The crimes occurred in the back streets of the poorest, most crime infested, most severely neglected and ignored neighborhoods of London. Victims were attacked in secluded areas, but it was very common for the sound of screaming to be heard, so victim's cries, if any, would have been ignored. The fifth murder in victim's flat would have been ignored as a domestic dispute.

How

Weapon believed to have been used was either a bayonet or a surgeon's knife or a butcher's fillet knife. Blade was extremely sharp, long and narrow.

Why

There are many theories, including one that says a crazed journalist committed the crimes to bring attention to the plight of the poor of Whitechapel. However, the most feasible theory is the idea that the killer was driven insane by syphilis and that prostitutes were killed because the killer believed them to be the source of the disease. If the killer had a mission, it is possible that he or she believed that by killing whores, the disease would be eliminated. Another plausible theory suggests that a female drug addict did the killings, at first for money and then for satisfaction.

CRIME FACT, CRIME FICTION

As a society, we have a need to be entertained. As our society becomes more sophisticated, people find that they are more and more dependent on mass communication and its by-product, mass culture. Essential to mass culture is our folklore, the myths and legends and the facts or history that inspired them. This is where we writers come in because we are both the purveyors of fact and the creators of fiction. We supply the drug that society is addicted to because all entertainment has a "narcotizing effect." It is what the social scientists call the "pain-pleasure principle," as both pain and pleasure are addicting, and entertainment simultaneously produces the experience of pain and pleasure.

As the drug of choice, the majority of people need to be entertained by fictional stories about the evil and the horrible. At the same time, as long as it does not intrude on or interfere with individuals' lives, the public is equally entertained by true crime. In the 1880s and 1890s, the public was terrified and captivated by the horrible reality of Jack the Ripper and the fictional horrors of *Dr. Jekyll and Mr. Hyde* and *Dracula*. Over a century later, the public is still thrilled and chilled by Ted Bundy, Jeffrey Dahmer, and mothers who plot murder to help their daughters win cheerleading competitions. At the same time, this same majority spends millions on the fictional counterparts of these real-life monsters, such as Hannibal the Cannibal.

The media and writers have always been party to a curious love triangle involving the public and the real-life blood monsters. Even the world of fiction has had its share of inspiration from true crime. The era of modern serial killing was born with the Jack the Ripper crimes. One cannot help but suspect that Bram Stoker was so influenced by Jack's crimes of 1888, with their implications of blood drinking and flesh eating, that he adapted a little of these real-life horrors to his character, Dracula, in 1890. By 1897, when *Dracula* was finally published, the Age of the Sex Crime was full blown.

Crime Fact

The ancient Sumerians believed that there are seven gates to the Otherworld where the Old Ones, the Gods of Evil, wait for the time when they can pass through these gates and take over our world, ruling it with eternal evil. This may just be a myth, but it's almost a certainty that the floodgates of madness have flung wide open since the days of Jack the Ripper. Prior to 1888, only a dozen men, women or unknown suspects committed the kind of horrific crime that would earn them a place in the annals of criminal history. However, from 1889 on, almost a year hasn't gone by without one or more serial killers or other kind of terribly vicious, violent criminals being caught and tried somewhere in America, Canada or Europe. It's up to you to decide whether or not there is some truth to that old Sumerian belief. What follows is a list of some of these killers, listed according to the type of crime they committed.

Lust Murder

As mentioned before, lust murder is a form of necrophilia, but it is also the most violent of sex crimes. This type of crime may involve both rape and murder, but most of the time these killers kill only because, to them, killing is the ultimate way to achieve sexual gratification.

Bela Kiss. Bela Kiss is the only serial killer to date to be identified as a killer but never caught. In the years prior to World War I, Kiss began his career as a sex killer with the murder of his adulterous wife. Soon afterward he began to advertise for victims, whom he lured to an apartment in Budapest, killed and then took to his home in the countryside of Hungary for disposal. When war broke out, Kiss was drafted and later was believed to have died in combat. It was only by accident that his crimes were discovered. While looking for fuel for the war effort, Austrian soldiers and local police searched Kiss's house and found seven oil drums, each containing the body of a woman. Nearby, they found the bodies of two dozen more women. Since it was believed that Kiss had died in the war, the case would have been closed, except that a report made by the nurse who tended the soldier listed as Kiss said that the man who died was too young to be the real Kiss. There were no fingerprint records of Kiss and only a very bad photo to go by, but the investigation continued after the war, with Kiss being sighted on both sides of the Atlantic. Kiss most probably went on killing for the rest of his life, and if so, he can be considered the most prolific serial killer of all time. At the pace he was going, and considering that Kiss was wealthy and that criminal investigation was still in its early stages, his body count could easily have reached one hundred, possibly two hundred, by the time a reasonable old age killed him. Nonetheless, no trace of Kiss nor any of the crimes he was suspected of has ever been found.

Carl Panzram. Carl Panzram was the first serial killer to consider the world his own private hunting ground, committing twenty-two murders and over one thousand rapes in America and overseas, and the first to write his own autobiography. He began his murder/rape spree at the age of nineteen. He had just been released from military prison for theft committed while he was in the army, and he wanted to get even with the world. So, Panzram traveled from coast to coast, killing, robbing and raping as he pleased. He was the original enfant terrible. He was a destructive child in an adult body. In 1920, he used the proceeds from his robberies to buy a yacht, on which he raped and killed his crew of ten. Panzram took his one-man crime wave to Europe and then to Africa. In Africa, he killed six more men, this time feeding the corpses to the crocodiles he told his victims he wanted to hunt. He had returned to America and was robbing his way from Massachusetts to Maryland when he was caught.

Finally, while in prison, he committed the murder that would send him to the executioner: He smashed in the head of the prison laundry foreman and was sentenced to death. A reform group tried to save his life, but Panzram wrote President Hoover, demanding his constitutional right to be executed. On September 5, 1930, he got his wish.

Peter Kürten. This was the most horrendous sex killer of all time. He was also the first serial killer to be portrayed in a movie. Kürten was the role model for Fritz Lang's classic film *M*, with the title role played by Peter Lorre. Though it is believed that Kürten, known as "The Monster of Düsseldorf" and "Düsseldorf Ripper," committed over seventy-nine murders and assaults, the real body count has never been established. What makes his crimes even more horrible are the motive and the frequency of his crimes. All of Kürten's crimes were committed during a ten-month period in 1929 with the sole purpose of seeking greater sexual satisfaction with each killing. Kürten began his sex murder career in childhood, but his murderous desires did not explode full force until after he married. He proposed to his bride-to-be by telling her to marry him or he would kill her. He attacked men, women and children using a variety of weapons. This led police to mistakenly believe that there was more than one killer. The crime wave got so bad that army troops were called in to help the police. However, it was a trick of fate that caused Kürten's downfall. For some unknown reason, Kürten let one of his victims go, unmolested. The victim then wrote a letter to the police, and Kürten surrendered without incident. He confessed and he was pleased to be executed. Kürten expressed that he felt his own death on the guillotine would be the ultimate sexual thrill. Only *he* knows if he got his wish.

Blood Monsters

While all serial killers and mass murderers can be categorized as historic vampires, only a few fit the true meaning of vampire. In Rumanian, the word literally translated means "blood monster." The only thing these creatures desired was blood. These cases are what we described earlier as classic examples of "haematodipsia," the sexual obsession with blood.

Georg Grossmann. Many years before Jeffrey Dahmer, Georg Grossmann was the first apartment tenant to turn his home into a slaughterhouse. Grossmann was a petty criminal who later became a livestock butcher. This latter talent became Grossmann's sole source of income as he set about making money out of murder. World War I and the chaotic postwar depression caused great food shortages and terrible hardship for the German people. Nevertheless, Grossmann found a way to help the people of Berlin stay well fed. For seven years, he lured prostitutes to his apartment, raped them, killed them and then cut up the bodies to sell as beef or pork to a starving public desperate for meat. His landlord never cared about Grossman's activities as long as he paid his rent on time. And as long as he killed his victims, he went undetected. Finally, in 1921, one of his victims put up a fight and the landlord called the police. They found Grossmann with a dead woman and butcher knives in hand. All told, the body count was fifty women, and within a week of his trial, Grossmann committed suicide.

Fritz Haarmann. A lot has been written and said about Jeffrey Dahmer. But Dahmer's crimes are insignificant compared to Fritz Haarmann. He was known as the "Vampire of Hanover" because from 1918 to 1924, he killed, ate the flesh of, drank the blood of, and sold the flesh of almost sixty young men and boys. A petty criminal and homosexual, Haarmann would have his accomplice Hans Grans lure young refugee boys to Haarmann's home to feed them. Once the victim finished his meal, Haarmann would attack, biting into the neck to achieve orgasm. In his frenzy for sex and blood, Haarmann would devour the flesh of the neck until the head almost came off each victim. At the same time, he drank the blood. Afterward, Grans would cut up the bodies, and like Grossmann in Berlin, he and Haarmann would sell the flesh to desperate, unsuspecting people who thought they were buying steak. These two also sold the victims' clothes. In 1925, Haarmann and Grans were executed, even though Haarmann tried to get the police and courts to believe he was innocent. He confessed to most of his crimes, but claimed that he was in a trance each time he killed so he should not be held responsible. Grans was buried in a prison grave, but Haarmann's brain was taken for study by a university in Hanover and the rest of his body was cremated, most probably, as some accounts of the time put it, because no one wanted to take a chance of him returning.

Mass Murderers

The massacre of several victims in a single, short, bloody period is an old crime that has seen a resurgence in the past forty years.

This has made mass murder a more common social phenomenon than it had ever been in previous centuries.

Vasili Komaroff. Wolves have had a bad rap down through history. It is true that they are predatory, but the stories about wolves killing people are a myth. Wolves rarely kill people, and they never kill their own kind arbitrarily, like humans do. Thus, it was extremely unfair to label Komaroff "the Wolf of Moscow." It would be more appropriate to call him "the Dimwit of Moscow" because after killing and robbing thirty-three people for a total take of $26.40, he told the police, "I needed money for food and drink." Komaroff stands out in the annals of criminal history, not just for being the most stupid, but also for conducting a brutal crime spree in Moscow in the midst of Communism's bloody infancy. The Cheka, Lenin's secret police, were killing people by the score every day for so-called political crimes. So, it is reasonable to believe that Komaroff's crimes might have just been ignored amidst all the slaughter that was going on. However, while mass murder by the state was praised, private entrepreneurs were not tolerated. On June 18, 1923, Komaroff was executed by firing squad. And because it fit the Communist logic of the day, Komaroff's wife, who was innocent, was executed with him as an accomplice.

Joe Ball. Ball loved his pet alligators so much, he fed them a special diet: people. The owner of a tavern called the Sociable Inn, Ball had an unusually high turnover in waitresses, who also lived at the inn. Ball would tell people that the women just left without notice, and no one paid any attention to the disappearances until relatives of three of the women made complaints to the local authorities. In 1937, the police began to suspect that the local joke about the waitresses becoming food for the gators might be true. However, they never got a chance to question Ball or bring him to trial. When the police arrived on September 24, 1938, and asked him about their suspicions, Ball pulled out a gun and killed himself. Fortunately, the truth about the missing waitresses did not go to the grave with him. The inn's handyman showed the police the alligator's food barrel filled with human flesh and confirmed that this was the fate of the fourteen missing women. The handyman was sent to prison for four years as an accessory, while the alligators lived out a life of luxury in the San Antonio Zoo.

Dennis Nilsen. Dennis Nilsen hated the idea of living alone so much that he never got over his homosexual boyfriend leaving him. So when the next lover tried to leave, Nilsen killed him. From that day on, Nilsen would never be alone again because he killed fourteen more lovers. Sometimes he would set a corpse up in a chair and talk to it as a sort of shy, mute companion. However, this practice made it difficult to lure new victims to his apartment. So when each corpse started to get really decayed, he would cut it up and either hide it or burn it or flush it down the toilet in pieces. After a while, disposal of the bodies became a problem, and Nilsen's crimes were finally discovered by a plumber who, trying to solve the problem of clogged drains in Nilsen's building found pieces of bone and flesh. When the police arrived to inquire about the horrible discovery, Nilsen, in his usual mild-mannered, friendly way, showed them his collection of undisposed body parts, including the heads he kept in the freezer, and made a full confession to all fifteen murders.

Andrei Chikatilo. In 1978, the Soviet State Militia, the police of the former Soviet Union, knew it was faced with a serial killer, but the leaders in the Kremlin had tied the militia's hands and made it a paper tiger. The bodies of innocents who had taken a walk in the woods with a stranger were piling up, but Communist Party policy forbade warnings to the public or broadcast news of the murders because this would have been an admission that the Party was not in control as it had made the people believe. Five Soviet premiers knew of the murders, the KGB knew, the army knew, but the people were left in the dark. The officials had a suspect, and his name was Andrei Chikatilo. However, in the old Soviet Union, the Communist Party used to say that its worker's paradise was free of the kind of violent crimes, especially serial murder, that plagued the capitalist West. However, as we now know the Soviet Union was a mass of confusion, corruption, chaos and inefficiency that helped produce what is possibly the worst serial killer in modern history. Coincidentally and simultaneously, five other serial killers were at work in other parts of the Soviet Union, one a teenager and the son of a high-ranking Party official. This added to the mayhem, and so, ignorant of any danger, innocents continued to take walks in the woods with Chikatilo. After killing his victims, Chikatilo would mutilate them and eat some of their flesh. In 1984, Chikatilo was picked up on suspicion but was released for lack of evidence. Finally, six years and twenty-five thousand suspects later, he was arrested again, but this time, for some unknown reason, he confessed. He was tried for fifty-two murders, but the figure is much higher. At this time, he is awaiting execution, even though he has tried to convince the courts that he is insane. Chikatilo will get a bullet in the back of the head because the Russians say hanging is too good for this monster.

Crime Fiction as It Relates to Crime Fact

In the past two-hundred years, there has been a curious coincidence regarding how literature, in the nineteenth century, and later film, in the twentieth century, has been influenced by crime, sometimes intentionally and sometimes accidentally. At the same time, the perceptions that society has of criminal behavior have been shaped, not by the criminals themselves, but by the reflections portrayed in books and film. With this in mind, we can look into the mirror of art and we will see some excellent examples of true-to-life criminal behavior. In studying how writers and filmmakers have been influenced by criminal behavior, you will come to understand how they, in turn, have influenced the public and our cultural perceptions.

Literature

Edgar Allan Poe gave the world of horror and mystery fiction the first novel involving a serial killer in his *Murders in the Rue Morgue*. However, this classic work was more a reflection of crime detection methods than it was of crime itself. It was during the eighty-seven-year period prior to the appearance of Jack the Ripper that the genre that truly reflected criminal behavior was first created: vampire literature. From 1800 to 1888, beginning with *Wake Not The Dead* by Johann Tieck, twenty major works of vampire literature were published that coincided with a variety of real-life killings. At around the same time, the notorious Marquis de Sade was making his place in history and branding our culture and civilization with the criminal behavior that is based on his name: *sadism*. The Marquis is not only infamous for his perversions, but also for his acts of vampirism — manifestations of haematodipsia — and the authorship of two books, *Justine* and *Juliette*, which contained vivid depictions of bloodlust. In 1819, Dr. John Polidori, the physician of Lord Byron, wrote *Vampyre*. The main character of this work was modeled after his former friend Byron, but Polidori was most probably more influenced by the crimes of that time. Prior to his bitter falling out with Byron and the publication of his book, Polidori was very close to Byron, Mary Shelley (of *Frankenstein* fame), and her poet husband, Percy Shelley. Their favorite pastime was to tell horror stories in front of the fireplace while indulging in opium. Concurrently, Antoine Leger and Andreas Bichel, notorious murderers and vampires, were committing crimes that were having a dramatic impact on European society and mirrored the horror literature that was evolving. Twenty years later, Poe introduced *Ligeia* to tingle the spines of society, and in 1848, Alexandre Dumas wrote *The Pale Faced Lady*.

In the period of 1819 to 1887, the foundations of horror and mystery fiction were being firmly established. This, ironically, coincides with the evolution of modern serial killing. Sex was the underlying theme of most of these books. It was also the motive behind the brutal murders that were portent to Jack the Ripper and all the blood monsters who followed. Curiously, the book that coincides with Jack's crimes was Guy de Maupassant's *The Horla*. This is a tale of demonic possession and vampirism, factors that relate to the Jack the Ripper crimes. Another factor that is related is syphilis. It was a factor in the creation of *The Horla* and could have been a cause of the Ripper murders.

The era of modern crime literature began in 1888, the year of the debut of Jack the Ripper. While crime and mystery fiction had their origins much earlier, the "art imitates life" theme was beginning to emerge. For example, Sherlock Holmes was unquestionably fictional, but in all of Sir Arthur Conan Doyle's stories, the criminals and crimes reflected reality. In later years, Doyle wrote true-crime stories as a serious study of criminal behavior.

In the 1800s, books were the major form of entertainment. Books also served a limited educational purpose, though this purpose was very informal and very indirect. Theater was nothing more than an extension of the entertainment vehicle that books provided. While the majority of mainstream literature and theater reflected the Victorian prudery that dominated Western society for over half a century, a backlash of underground arts was feeding the growing desire for pornography. This forbidden literature was also having a subtle influence on the evolution of horror and mystery literature.

Sex crimes started to increase by the 1860s. The main cause for this rise in crimes of a sexual nature was the iron rigidity of the puritan social standards that had initially inspired the creators of pornography to break the rules. Pornography is much more widespread and available now than it was over one hundred years ago, but there are far fewer rapes committed today. So then, as now, there was little relationship between violent sex crimes and pornography. If Jack the Ripper had been caught and tried, he or she would very likely have tried to claim that pornography caused him or her to murder. This was the excuse Ted Bundy tried to use, but it didn't save him from execution. In 1889, such a claim might have inspired a wave of sympathy, but it's unlikely that it would have saved Jack from the gallows.

Film

With the invention of film and cinema, art got its first real chance to imitate life. By the 1920s, the cinema systematically began to replace books and theater as the chief form of entertainment; however, film only paralleled these media in their ability to informally and indirectly educate.

No matter how innocuous the content of early film was, it still was never free of social value judgments. The same still holds true today.

With the advent of "talkies," the art-imitating-life theme was in full swing. In 1931, Peter Lorre starred as a psychopath in Fritz Lang's *M*. The film, as mentioned earlier, was based on the life of Peter Kürten. Lorre's characterization of a psychopathic child killer is the most famous in cinema history. Lang was fascinated with the psychopathology of violent criminals, and he combined this interest with a strict demand for realism to create an unparalleled terrifying character. Film historians and clinicians have said that the melancholy expression of Lorre, both sinister and pathetic at the same time, combined with his trademark globular eyes bulging in fear as he is hunted by both the police and the criminal underworld gave this character extremely realistic clinical authenticity.

In 1957, Robert Bloch published *Psycho*, based on the crimes of Ed Gein, which Alfred Hitchcock brought to the screen in 1960 as the film *Psycho*. Now everything was changed forever. A new bogeyman had replaced vampires, werewolves and other monsters as the thing that would haunt human dreams. Thanks to Anthony Perkins's terrifying performance as the psychotic Norman Bates, the public's new nightmares are the guy down the street and girl next door with evil hidden in their minds and horrors buried under the floorboards or in the backyard. The perceptions that Norman Bates created are reinforced every time the news features another story of some gardener or carpenter or mailman or nurse who has killed a dozen or more people. Hitchcock also introduced the public to the fictional film version of a Ted-Bundy-like killer in *Strangers on a Train*.

In 1967, the prototype of Hannibal the Cannibal, the professional as madman, was portrayed by Peter O'Toole in *Night of the Generals*. While the character of General Tanz is a Nazi, which personifies a monster already, the concept of such a brilliant serial killer character is a frightening creation. Here we have a sexual psychopath in a uniform, with power and authority. Picture this same character as a police officer or some other powerful authority figure and you have the public's worst nightmare.

In 1968, the groundwork for today's genre of true-crime movies was laid with the film *The Boston Strangler*. This was the first docudrama about a real-life serial killer.

Also in 1968, Rod Steiger portrayed the perfect fictional serial killer in *No Way To Treat A Lady*. Here is a classic model of a sexual psychopath who vents his obsessional hate for his mother on his victims. The character is extremely true-to-life with all the chameleon qualities that exist in real serial killers. He is intelligent and egotistical and never changes his pattern until suitable motivation is provided. Coincidentally, this film debuted the same year that the Zodiac Killer began his reign of terror. And like Steiger, who would phone the police in the film, Zodiac taunted the police with a string of cryptic letters. It is possible the Zodiac took some cues from this movie. Evidence indicates that Zodiac was a film buff and an egotist. This explains why, in 1974, he appointed himself as a film critic. He wrote to the San Francisco police and, in his usual taunting fashion, demanded that his review of the film *The Exorcist* be printed in the newspapers or he would "do something nasty." Zodiac wrote that this film was the greatest "comedy" ever made.

In another coincidence of the same nature, Zodiac popped up in William Peter Blatty's 1983 best-seller, *Legion*, in which the killer was called Gemini. In 1990, Blatty turned his book into a screenplay and directed the movie. Titled *Exorcist III*, this film offered the very unique theory that demonic possession may play a role in serial killings.

The strangest twist of fate is that both books and the first and third *Exorcist* films were surrounded with coincidental serial killer incidents. Both books are set in Washington, D.C., and the films were shot there as well. In the years 1971 and 1972, when the first book was a best-seller and the *Exorcist* movie was just beginning production, young black women were being killed by an unknown killer dubbed the "Freeway Phantom." Concurrently, gay men, thirty-two in all, were being killed by another unknown killer. In 1987, when *Legion* was enjoying the same popularity as its predecessor and the film *Exorcist III* was in development, the "Freeway Phantom" returned, killing several more times before disappearing again. Neither killer has ever been caught.

Accurate Films

Following is a list of films that accurately reflect the realities of crimial thought and behavior. Many others also offer accurate reflections while *very* many others distort the truth for the sake of drama.

1. *Frenzy*—This Hitchcock film, based on a novel by Arthur LaBern, provides a perfect study of a sex killer who exhibits extreme sexual excitement from the strangulation of each victim, hence the film's title.

2. *The Abominable Dr. Phibes*, *Dr. Phibes Rises Again* and *Theatre of Blood*—These films, starring horror master Vincent Price, may be very camp in their use of black comedy, but the serial killer themes and plots are unique and highly inventive. These films are also very accurate in their portrayal of the ritualistic and obsessive nature of serial murder. This serves as an excellent example of how creative the madness of real-life killers can be.

3. *Play Misty for Me*—This film, which was produced by, directed by and starred Clint Eastwood, was the first stalker movie. Here we have a very realistic characterization of an obsessed psychotic whose delusions turn deadly, resulting in a cat-and-mouse game of horror and murder. This is a very credible representation of what happens in real-life when stalkers terrorize their victims.

4. *The Fan*—Here is another true-to-life portrayal of a psychotic stalker; however, this film shows a methodical study of fanta-

sies of love that degenerate into obsessive hatred and murder.

5. *The First Deadly Sin* — Both the film and the book, written by Lawrence Sanders, offer authentic portrayals of madness that leads to a sexual compulsion to kill.

6. *Nighthawks* — This movie is a realistic depiction of a true-to-life terrorist. Forget the idea that terrorists are mad dogs foaming at the mouth. Like many of the real-life counterparts, Rutger Hauer's character is charismatic, intelligent, highly deceptive, and dangerously cool, calm and collected.

7. *Scarface* (1932), *Al Capone* (1959), and *The St. Valentine's Day Massacre* (1967) — Here we have three of the most realistic portrayals of sociopathic gangsters, whose whole lives revolve around power and killing. In the 1959 Capone film, Rod Steiger stays true to history with his characterization of the psychopathic killer/mob leader who is driven into psychosis by syphilis. The 1967 film about the St. Valentine's Day Massacre was the first docudrama-style movie to provide an in-depth study of the social structure and psychological composition of the gangster lifestyle, highly accurate in historical detail.

With all the violence portrayed in books, film and television, the old debate over whether or not there is a cause and effect relationship between the media and violence is an important issue to address at this point. The controversy is so vehement that Congress is on the verge of undermining the whole Constitution to satisfy a society that refuses to take responsibility for the problem and face reality. The fact is that there is *no* conclusive scientific evidence that identifies the media or any specific medium as a cause of violence or contributory factor to violence.

In the 1960s, a Stanford University study showed that children exposed to images of real-life violence were ten times more likely to behave aggressively or violently than children who were exposed to actors and actresses pretending to be violent. The TV/film theory loses more credibility when it comes to the issue of domestic violence and child abuse. All the scientific evidence on this particular subject indicates that children who are witness to and/or are victims of domestic violence are at high risk of becoming abusers or possibly violent criminals when they grow up. As you study the pathology of criminal behavior and violence, keep in mind that it takes much more than the media to produce a violent criminal.

F I V E

SERIAL MURDER

As I mentioned before, writers supply society with its favorite drug of choice—to be entertained by true-crime and fictional mystery and horror—as part of a curious love triangle involving the public and reality. This is why it is not surprising that the favorite subject of both writers and entertainment consumers is serial murder.

The Fantasy

For writers today, the serial killer is the new source of gothic horror. This is the new monster that truly emphasizes the grotesque, mysterious and desolate. From the dawn of time to the late nineteenth century, the vampire legend, a part of every culture in the world, has inspired the creators of human mythology, from writers to playwrights to filmmakers. Cannibalism has even been integrated into the mystic. By romanticizing the vampire lore of central Europe, some nineteenth-century writers were able to capitalize on the dark desires of Victorian society. This is part of the reason why Bram

Stoker's *Dracula* followed *Frankenstein* with such astounding success. Ironically, Jack the Ripper's crimes had more to do with making Dracula a modern fiction icon than anything else. It was the underlying theme of unbridled sexual passion in Stoker's book that caught the attention of and delighted the repressed Victorians. And this was the unspoken truth that so fascinated these same people as they read with horror the details of the Ripper murders, even though these crimes were never acknowledged as sex crimes. Jack the Ripper inaugurated the Era of Sex Crimes, and Dracula and other horror fiction characters pioneered the way for the sexually oriented gothic romance genre. Through crime literature and true-crime stories, human beings, particularly those of Western industrialized society, find an outlet for the "death instinct" within us all, while simultaneously the dark side of our human nature is afforded the opportunity to empathize with these real-life nightmares. Now, the serial killer, the twentieth-century embodiment of Dracula, is the food for human fascination with things dark and deadly. Case in point is the success of *Silence of the Lambs* and Lawrence Sanders's Sin series, as well as the proliferation of true-crime books. As Mary McCarthy said in *On the Contrary*, "Characters in Fiction" (1961), "In violence, we forget who we are." So, as it was for our ancestors who huddled together around a fire hundreds of thousands of years ago, the monster is still a source of escapism.

The Facts

Serial killers are everywhere. They are the waste product of our frustrated, bored, over-stressed Western industrialized society. Worldwide, no one really knows how large the serial killer population is, but here in the United States, the FBI took a shot in the dark in 1991, estimating that there are about one hundred to two hundred serial killers stalking and hunting throughout our cities, suburbs, towns and countryside and along our strategic system of highways. However, the Bureau cautioned that this is a conservative guess at best and that the population of serial killers could be in the thousands. Some Justice Department experts have unofficially speculated that there could be as many as two thousand, while others theorize the number could be five thousand or more. Regardless of the numbers, the thought of even one, let alone thousands, of these monsters running amok in the United States, Europe and Canada is a terrifying thought to many. Just in 1993, over a dozen serial killing cases have either been identified as such or closed, with the killers being brought to justice. In England, the spirit of Jack the Ripper came back to terrify London in May and June 1993. Beverley Allitt, a nurse, was convicted of the murder and assault of thirteen children who were patients on the hospital ward where she worked for fifty-nine days. During the same period, another killer stalked the homosexual community of London and amassed a body count of seven while he taunted the police and the media, saying he would kill one homosexual a week until he was caught. In South Africa, a serial killer has murdered sixteen young, white boys.

Here in the United States, an unemployed gardener named Joel Rifkin was arrested with a body in the back of his truck. Later that night, he confessed to that murder and claimed to have killed seventeen prostitutes in and around the New York City area. When police searched his home, they found boxes of trophies taken from the victims and evidence that indicates his murder spree was an effort to copy and outdo the Green River Killer of Washington state. When Rifkin's neighbors were told of the crimes, they were in shock, telling reporters that he was friendly, helpful and "respectable." They also wondered how such a "nice guy, a sweet, quiet, awkward bachelor who lived with his mother" could be responsible for such horrible crimes.

Just before the year was out, one Lewis Lent, Jr., was arrested for the murder of a young boy in upstate New York. He is suspected of killing several children in the New England and Mid-Atlantic region over the past couple of years. Coming on top of a terrorist bombing and a madman who massacred a bunch of train passengers, this case, along with three others, has increased the climate of fear in a nine-state area, making people afraid of almost everyone and everything around them. This terror factor is one of the many things that makes serial murder the most unusual social phenomenon of the twentieth century. Every day, these recreational killers go about their business of "hunting humans," randomly killing for the delight of it. Sadly, the majority of these deaths will go undiscovered for years, and the victims will be regarded as missing persons.

Hunting Humans

Serial killing is nothing new, but it is the crime of the 1990s because of the increasing incidence and media attention. While the term "serial murderer" was coined in the 1980s to differentiate serial murderers from mass murderers, the problem of serial murders is ancient. Besides Gilles de Rais, Vlad the Impaler and the Beane Family, there was Elizabeth, Countess Bathory, who, in the early 1600s, drained the blood of over six hundred fifty young women just to bathe in it. She truly believed that bloodbathing was the secret of eternal youth. She also drank the blood and was known as the "Blood Countess." The Countess Bathory demonstrates that, prior to 1850, an individual killer could amass a body count in the hundreds and sometimes the thousands. She also reveals that in those days, the women could outdo the men. In the 1670s, Catherine La Voisin killed over fifteen hundred people, and Madame de Montespan dispatched over fourteen hundred innocents. In one year alone, Marie de Brinvilliers killed over one hundred people in France.

While this kind of bloodletting has been around since the dawn of time, the pattern that Western society has come to know as "serial killing/sex crime" is only 123 years old, with the first of these crimes being committed in 1871, seventeen years before Jack the Ripper.

So why did things take a turn for the worse in the late nineteenth century? Sigmund Freud and his contemporaries, as well as several modern clinicians, such as Eric Fromm, have contended that the reason was "sexual repression." As many social historians have indicated, sex was viewed with a healthy attitude prior to the 1800s. However, the historical accounts and the literature of the period have indicated that the society of the 1800s, especially the Victorians of England and America, regarded sex as filthy and shameful. Table legs were covered with long tablecloths so that the thought of bare legs would not stir forbidden passions. This is the social attitude that gave rise to the proliferation of pornography and the birth of the Age of the Sex Crime. The book *The Age of Sex Crime* provides a comprehensive study of this peculiar social environment.

From 1820 to 1860, prostitutes, especially children, were as easy to find as bread and just as cheap. Women and children suffered the worst during the poverty of the early Industrial Revolution, and this made them easy and "available" victims. To avoid starvation and to provide for shelter and gin, any woman would sell her body for today's equivalent of a dollar or more. By 1860, the situation changed with the invention of the typewriter and the development of trades requiring the skills of women. Suddenly, women were able to rise out of poverty without submitting to criminal victimization and advance into the middle-class. Prostitutes were still plentiful, but a whole class of "unavailable" women had emerged. Subsequently, rape increased tenfold, and the term "sex crime" was introduced. In 1871, one of the first documented serial killings, motivated by sex, occurred when a French meat vendor named Eusebius Pieydagnelle killed six women with a knife for the sole purpose of achieving sexual gratification.

Except for Jack the Ripper and a few dozen others, the majority of serial murders occurred after World War II. What is truly amazing is the occurrence of serial killers in countries with sophisticated national police forces or ultrastrict dictatorships. In post-World War II Germany (previously West Germany), which developed one of the most modern police forces in the world, a killer called the "Ruhr Hunter" carried out a murder campaign from 1959 to 1976. He killed eleven children and three adults. With all his victims, he raped them, killed them, and took the bodies home to cook and eat. Even the rigid Communist police states of Eastern Europe and the Soviet Union had almost a dozen serial killers who, in the space of thirty years, killed over three hundred people. Gruesome murders like those in the movie and book *Gorky Park* really happened right under the noses of the Kremlin.

Definition of a Serial Murder

While there are a few similarities, the phenomenon of *mass murder* is vastly different from the phenomenon of *serial murder*.

Mass murderers kill their victims all at once. They choose a killing field and try to take the lives of everyone in sight. They do not hunt, torture and then kill their victims. Well-known mass murderers include Richard Speck, who killed eight nurses in the apartment they shared; Charles Whitman, the Texas Tower Killer, who killed sixteen people by raining bullets down on a college campus; or James Huberty, who killed twenty-one people in and around a California McDonalds in 1984. Serial killers, on the other hand, hunt their victims, and it is this *hunting factor* that is the primary difference between serial murderers and mass murderers.

In a 1988 report issued by the National Institute of Justice, *serial murder* was defined as "a series of two or more murders, committed as separate events, usually, but not always, by one offender acting alone. The crimes may occur over a period of time ranging from hours to years." However, there is some controversy over this definition. Unlike *mass murder*, there is, unfortunately, no singular way to define *serial killing*. Instead, the definition has to be very broad. Therefore, to reduce confusion, let's use the following as a working definition of *serial murder*: any series of murders, committed over any period of time, by either a male or a female, for any motive, and in any location or locations. This definition should encompass any class of victims and take into account any kind of pattern and type of murderer.

Types of Murderers

To understand why serial killers and related ilk commit such horrible crimes, it is important to examine and appreciate the concept that most of the information and misinformation people have ingrained in their minds about criminals, especially serial killers, comes from labels and the misuse of said labels. Researchers are quick to apply labels and therefore typecast criminals, consequently creating labels and descriptions that contradict and conflict. To add to the confusion, the media is always eager to use and infuse new buzz words into the vernacular of our culture. W. Wille, in the book *Citizens Who Commit Murder*, identified ten different psychosocial categories of murderers:

1. Those suffering with acute depression
2. Those suffering with acute psychosis
3. Those afflicted with organic brain disorder (cancer or tumor)
4. Those who are psychopathic
5. Those suffering with passive/aggressive personality disorders
6. Those suffering with alcoholism (includes any drug dependence)
7. Those experiencing hysteria
8. Those children who kill
9. Those who are mentally ill
10. Those who are sex killers.

Another set of Justice Department labels exists that categorizes murderers by their motives:

1. Profit

2. Passion
3. Hatred
4. Desperation
5. Revenge
6. Opportunism
7. Fear
8. Contract killing*
9. Power/Domination*
10. Compassion (as in mercy killing)*
11. Ritual*
    * Motives most often associated with serial killing

Types of Sexual Behavior Involved in Serial Killings

While most serial killers are influenced by a variety of deviant sexual behaviors, some of which are listed below, it is a mistake to typecast these monsters as "sex maniacs," and it would be a mistake to assume that there is a cause and effect relationship because not all deviances lead to murder. It is just important to examine and appreciate how these behaviors influence our perceptions of this class of criminals:

1. Animal torture—This involves mutilation and killing of animals. These acts are usually committed by serial killers in their early childhood as experimentation in sadism and killing. However, this behavior has been known to be exhibited in killers after they become adults. Both Peter Kürten and Jeffrey Dahmer killed animals for sexual gratification when they were teenagers. Then they graduated to humans.

2. Anthropophagy—This refers to sexual gratification achieved through cannibalism.

3. Coprophilia—This means one derives sexual gratification from touching or eating human excrement and/or urine.

4. Fetishism—This is a situation in which a person derives sexual gratification from the substitution of an object. This usually involves the mutilation of the victim to obtain "souvenirs" of the murders, as in the collection of heads, sex organs and other

body parts. Dennis Nilsen had closets full of body parts, a refrigerator full of "prizes," and a collection of heads. John Christie collected pubic hairs from his victims.

5. Gerontophilia — This refers to the sexual obsession for elderly victims as the subjects of rape and murder. This was the first pattern of Albert DeSalvo, the Boston Strangler.

6. Lust Murder — This is when one murders sadistically and brutally, including the mutilation of the victim's body, especially the genitalia. Classic examples of this type of behavior are Jack the Ripper and Peter Kürten. Also, Peter Sutcliffe, the Yorkshire Ripper, is a good example, as he went from using a knife to using a screwdriver to using a hammer to murder thirteen women. Changing weapons provides greater sexual excitement. This kind of murder also involves the dismemberment of bodies for disposal, eating flesh and drinking blood.

7. Triolism — This is the experience of deriving sexual gratification from watching a partner have sex with a third person, such as a victim. In the case of serial killings, this occurs with team killers, as in the case of the Hillside Stranglers.

8. Necrofetishism — This involves having a fetish for dead bodies or body parts, as in the case of Ed Gein, the role model for Hitchcock's *Psycho*. Gein collected corpses for a variety of purposes, including the making of clothes out of skin and body parts.

9. Necrophilia — This means to have sex with dead bodies.

10. Pedophilia — This refers to having sex with children.

11. Pederasty — This is the occurrence of anal intercourse, or sodomy, with children, as in the case of Dean Corll, who raped, tortured and killed over twenty-seven boys.

12. Home movies and tape recordings — A lot of killers like to document their crimes so they can derive sexual excitement from viewing the acts. Serial killers Leonard Lake and Charles Ng videotaped their crimes as "home snuff films."

13. Interest in pornography — While Ted Bundy may have "confessed" to being addicted to pornography — a form of insanity plea — it is certain that he lied as part of his plan to avoid the death penalty. Generally, pornography is only a source of fantasies.

14. Rape — This is the most common deviancy among serial killers.

15. Torture — This is another common behavior that is generally concurrent with rape.

16. Sadomasochism — This is the infliction of mental and/or physical pain on others (sadism) or on oneself (masochism). Sadism is very common as a concurrent behavior with rape and torture, but masochism is uncommon. However, there were some serial killers like Albert Fish, a child rapist and killer, as well as cannibal, who enjoyed inserting pins in his scrotum and burning himself. Fish was delighted to be executed, except that the hundreds of pins he had put in his groin short-circuited the electric chair.

17. Voyeurism — This refers to the deriving of sexual gratification by visual observation, for example, looking through windows to watch people undress or bathe or perform sexual acts. The relationship with serial killing is indirect, but it is known that some killers were "peepers" before they became killers.

Social Structure

The media stereotype of the serial killer as an obsessed loner is, unlike many media stereotypes, quite true. Eighty-seven percent of American serial killers are loners, as in the cases of Ted Bundy and Son of Sam. Ten percent hunt in pairs or packs, earning them the label "social killers." Three percent are unknown and may vary in their pattern, killing sometimes as a loner and other times with another person or as a member of a group.

Of the social killers, 59 percent are composed of men acting in groupings ranging from two-man pairs to gangs of a dozen or more. This would include Dean Corll, who hired others to procure victims; two-man teams like the Hillside Stranglers; cults like that of Charles Manson, who is suspected of several other murders; and Robin Gecht, who led a cultlike gang of teenagers that is suspected of killing over a hundred people.

Twenty-three percent are male/female couples, and 18 percent are mixed groupings of varying sizes. The couples include Douglas Clark and Carol Bundy, who killed several prostitutes, and Alton Coleman and Debra Brown, who murdered, raped and robbed over a five-state area in 1984.

Two percent of the loners are female. Aileen Wuornos, who killed seven or more men in Florida, is not as rare as people think. It's just that these female predators are harder to apprehend than their male counterparts because of a sexual bias that blinds most law enforcement professionals to the idea that women are capable of crimes like serial killing.

The Predatory Types

Serial killers can also be classified in the following categories according to their geographical preferences.

Territorial killers stake out a defined area — a city or a county, sometimes a particular street or park — and rarely deviate from their selected game preserve. The National Institute of Justice (NIJ) believes 58 percent of American serial killers fall into this category, including 65 percent of all blacks and 44 percent of all female killers. Son of Sam fits into this group.

Nomadic killers travel widely in their search for prey, driving law enforcement agencies crazy as they wander from one hunting ground to the next. Such was the case of Christopher Wilder, a wealthy race car driver and businessman who hunted from California to New England, abducting women from shopping malls, then killing them. The development of interstate highway networks has enhanced the ability of these killers to prey on communities at will. This makes them a strategic menace. According to NIJ, 34 percent of all serial killers are of the nomadic variety, with 34 percent of black killers and 28 percent of women killers among this group.

Stationary killers are the guy/gal-next-door-type of killer who crouch in wait for victims like spiders in a web. John Wayne Gacy and Jeffrey Dahmer are two of the most famous of this type. This type of serial killer prefers to commit murders in his or her home or place of employment, such as clinics, nursing homes and hospitals. While only 8 percent of all serial killers fit this group, including a small percentage of blacks, NIJ indicates that the majority (28 percent) of these predators are women.

Theater of Blood

When Andy Warhol said everyone will be famous for fifteen minutes, he was not thinking of serial killers and other blood monsters.

When it comes to serial murderers, fleeting moments of glory will not sate their desires. Though it may not be part of their original intent, the idea of being immortalized in the annals of history by the media is a factor that their out-of-control egos revel in. The more they kill, the more this idea of being immortal in memory and spirit becomes part of the power factor ingrained in their motives.

Serial killers are nobodies desperately trying to be somebodies. If, as Shakespeare said, "All the world is a stage," then serial killers are the bit part extras who want to upstage everyone, in order to show how great they are. It is a myth that serial killers secretly want to be caught. They only want to demonstrate their power over society by doing whatever is necessary to come close to being caught. Then, they show how smart they are by evading capture. It is true that many serial killers want attention and some desire fame. However, they want to be anonymously famous. And like all actors and actresses, they have their own roles, which they cast and wrote the scripts for. These roles fall into four categories: those with *visions*, those with *missions*, those who *enjoy killing*, and those who *lust for power/control*.

1. *Vision killers* — These are classic psychotics or at least they claim to be. They say they hear voices that tell them to kill. Many times, the claim is that the voice of God has ordered the crimes, but other times the perpetrator blames the Devil. In the case of the Son of Sam killer, David Berkowitz claimed that his neighbor's dog, Sam, was possessed by Satan and it was the dog who told him to kill. This claim turned out to be a hoax. Genuine psychosis in serial killers is rare, and if they do hear voices, then are most probably the voices of their own violent fantasies and delusions speaking from the dark depths of the shadow side, as in the case of Albert DeSalvo, the Boston Strangler. Psychosis and related visions/delusions can also be produced by drug abuse.

2. *Mission killers* — These killers believe that it is their duty or destiny to exterminate certain types of people as a way of cleansing society. This could be the motive for London's recent killer of homosexuals, as well as other serial killing cases involving homosexuals as victims. In many other cases, prostitutes, or women who have the appearance of such, are the targets. The killer nurses, the "Angels of Death," that prey on their

patients in hospitals and nursing homes, committing what they call mercy killings, also feel they have a mission. These killers can be either psychotic or psychopathic.

3. *Pleasure killers* (also called Hedonistic types) — These are the killers that are typecast as "thrill seekers," those who kill for fun or for satisfaction. This category includes people who kill for profit. This subgroup of "for-profit killers" is solely interested in maintaining a high standard of life, surrounded by comfort, and has no interest in working for the money to support such a lifestyle. So, they kill for it. These would be the "Black Widow" murderesses and killers like John Haigh, who killed six people solely for their money and disposed of the bodies in an acid bath. Another subgroup is the "lust murderers." They kill to indulge their perverse sexual desires, usually subjecting their victims to rape or torture followed by mutilation after the victim has been killed.

4. *Power/control killers* — These are the psychopaths or sociopaths whose desires are generally not sexual but concern deriving pleasure from control and exerting power over life and death. These killers enjoy, in an almost sexual manner, watching their victims beg for mercy and cower in fear. In a sense, the murderers feed off the fear of the victims.

The Disease Cycle

In the life of the violent criminal, especially the serial killer, there has been a constant cycle of violence. These creatures, who have made a career of inflicting a variety of intentional trauma on others, were themselves the victims of trauma. Most of the research on the childhood backgrounds of serial killers shows that many suffered a variety of severe psychological traumas, such as rejection by their parents or being abandoned or neglected. Many also experienced unstable home environments or suffered the loss of one or both parents or were hurt by their parents' divorce or had to endure extreme poverty. Many other killers were the victims of physical trauma, such as child abuse or sex abuse, in addition to suffering emotional harm. Others were adopted and/or illegitimate. Of course, many people suffered the same experiences and never became violent offenders or turned homicidal. So why did these perpetrators become infected with the disease of violence, while others remained healthy?

The reason is *resistance*. This is the same principle at work that explains why some people catch the flu, while others stay healthy in the middle of an epidemic. Just as every human being has physical defense mechanisms or immune systems or varying strength that work to protect him or her from physical illness, everyone has strong or weak psychological defense mechanisms that work just as hard to protect the person from mental illness. These defense mechanisms of the mind are also known as *coping mechanisms*. These coping mechanisms help us deal with the stresses of life, just like our immune systems fight off germs. It seems violent criminals, such as serial killers, lack such coping mechanisms and therefore are unable to deal with the trauma that is inflicted upon them. As a result, when these killers reach adulthood, their minds are so eroded by stress that their thinking becomes distorted and their ability to deal with crisis is little or nonexistant. So when any trauma, major or minor, strikes their lives, this crisis can send them into a spiraling fall that culminates in a continual cycle of violence. In this disease cycle, the killer makes the decision to kill, then proceeds to commit the crime, which is the actual hunting and killing process. Once the crime is committed, the killer reverts to the pretrauma state, which is still a life of distorted thinking, and waits for the next reason to start the cycle all over again.

The hunting and killing process can even have its own cycle. An example of this is the cycle followed by most power/control-oriented killers. First, the hunt begins with a violent fantasy. Second, once the fantasy is developed, the killer then acquires the target. Third, with the target acquired, the target is then abducted. Fourth, the target is raped and/or tortured, then murdered. Fifth, the cycle is complete when the killer is completely finished with the corpse, which may include the taking of trophies, mutilation, or the removal of body parts for perverse use. Then the body is disposed of.

Crime Scene Characteristics

Law enforcement officials pose the following questions when viewing the scene of a murder:

1. Is the crime scene a controlled one?

2. Has the killer committed overkill?
3. Is the crime scene chaotic?
4. Is there evidence of torture?
5. Was the body moved?
6. Is there a pattern of specific victims?
7. Was a weapon related to the crime found?
8. Could the victim be related to the killer?
9. Could the victim have been acquainted with the killer?
10. Did the weapon used produce violent wounds, as with a knife or ax or hammer or other?
11. Is there evidence of aberrant sex, such as sodomy?
12. Is there evidence of necrophilia?
13. Was a weapon or object used for torture found?
14. Was the victim strangled?
15. Is there evidence of forced sexual intercourse (male or female victims)?
16. Is there evidence of object rape?
17. Was the victim blindfolded?
18. Is there evidence of attacks to the face and/or oral sex?
19. Was the body buried to be hidden or dumped to be found?
20. What kind of weapon produced the cause of death?
21. Was the victim mutilated and/or dismembered?
22. Was the victim tied up?
23. Was the victim specially positioned by the killer?
24. Did the killer take souvenirs, such as panties, bras, shoes, wallets, jewelry and/or other personal effects?
25. Does the killer appear to fit in any of the following categories concerning victims and methods of killing?
    - Victim specific — Method specific
    - Victim variety — Method specific
    - Victim specific — Method variety
    - Victim variety — Method variety

As I mentioned before, it is important to not let your ego get in the way as you examine the behavior of violent criminals, especially serial killers. These killers are capable of anything, so don't develop tunnel vision. You may think that all serial killers are crazy, but both psychotics and psychopaths are dangerous. In particular, psychopaths are crazy like a fox. Once you look into the shadows and begin to appreciate that chaos, sadism and/or overkill are the signature, that is, the prominent feature of the crime, then you will have an understanding of the psychotic killer. To understand the psychopath, you should appreciate that these killers regard themselves as all-powerful and all-knowledgeable and they feel they were born to do anything they want.

CULT-RELATED MURDER

For all writers, as well as the general public, this area is filled with more myth than truth and is riddled with propaganda and media misconceptions. This is an area in which you have to keep a very open mind. The subject of Satanism alone is the ultimate paradox. Satanism exists, but a nationwide Satanic conspiracy does not. However, while the cult cops have no evidence to prove its existence, the theory is given credence by another theory that alleges that the Satanists are extremely good at hiding their existence and crimes. All this would make a good Frederick Forsyth novel, but as pseudo-fact, it is dangerous.

Since humans first walked this planet, people have believed in evil and the monsters and creatures that serve it. Humanity even invented Gods of Darkness to explain all the horrible things that happened around them. In the Middle Ages, witchcraft, vampirism, and lycanthropy were blamed for every heinous crime that happened.

Gilles de Rais murdered hundreds of children in the hope that

Satan would reward him and restore all the wealth he had lost. But de Rais was a sexual psychopath who used Satanism as an excuse to commit crimes against children. In the fifteenth century, it was easy to use Satanism as an excuse for murder. It was the original insanity plea, except that it only spared the accused from being tortured before being executed. Thus, de Rais was hanged and burned simultaneously for his crimes. Today, de Rais would most probably be treated like Charles Manson, or if he was lucky enough, he would be institutionalized in a hospital for the criminally insane.

Werewolves were blamed for the crimes of Sawney Beane and his murderous family of cannibals. Gilles Garnier was burned alive for being a werewolf and practicing witchcraft in France in 1573. He killed and ate six children. Peter Stubbe confessed to being a werewolf only after spending some time on the rack. He killed fifteen people, thirteen of whom were children, as part of what he said was a deal with the Devil. For his cooperation with the court, Stubbe was tortured to death, which shows the difference between German and French justice of that period. The seventeenth century saw the end of Satanism and witchcraft as excuses for crimes.

Satanism

Mention Satanism and people start to think of *Rosemary's Baby* or heavy metal music. To set the record straight for writers, researchers, and all other interested readers, Satanism is a Christian scapegoat for all things evil dating from the Middle Ages and the inquisition. All Satanic beliefs are based on Judeo-Christian myths, and the worship of Satan is nothing more than a symbolic rebellion against Christianity, often associated with irresponsibility and attempts to escape guilt. Satan is a Christian invention, and the demons associated with it are myths borrowed by Judaism from pre-Christian cultures, such as Babylon and Assyria.

Satanism is technically defined as the worship of Satan (the Christian Lord of Hell), the Devil, Lucifer, and all the other unholy demons, as well as all things non-Christian. But too often the word is used to label any way of thinking or living that breaks from the social norm. In the 1600s, 1700s and 1800s, Native American religion was branded as a form of Satanism and devil worship, first by Puritan settlers and then by missionaries. In many circles, homosexuals have been labeled as being in league with the Devil, and in 1990, a minister on a national religious broadcasting network labeled Freemasons and Masons as being Satanic cults.

Today, the worship of Satan is out in the open, and the worshipers are without fear of being burned at the stake. Satan worship is now an organized religion. Since Aleister Crowley founded two black magic cults in the early 1900s called the Order of the Silver Star and OTO, two other groups have sprung up. The most famous is the Church of Satan, founded in 1966 by Anton LeVey. The other is the Temple of Set, founded by former army intelligence officer, Dr. Michael Aquino. For the most part, these groups, like Crowley's Order, are involved in exploring the occult for either spiritual enlightenment, self-actualization or increased sexual activity.

At one point, a self-proclaimed cult expert stated that 40,000 to 50,000 human sacrifices have been made in the U.S. each year, but this number has never been corroborated. It's also impossible. This would mean that there are 30,000 bodies that no one in law enforcement is aware of. This does not mean there is no relationship between Satanism and crime, but it has been highly distorted by the media.

Most of what the public knows about Satanism is based on fiction or media misconceptions. Every time cats or dogs disappear, bunches of pets are found mutilated, or pentagrams (five-pointed stars associated with devil worship) show up painted on the sides of schools or in alleys, people start thinking there is a Satanic cult operating in the area. Some talk-show hosts even have the public believing in a nationwide Satanic underground, but there is no proof that anything like this exists beyond the realms of fiction and grocery store tabloids. Just a few years ago, a leading Fortune 500 corporation was accused of being involved with the Devil because some fundamentalist Christians said the company's logo contained Satanic devices.

There are three levels of individual involvement in Satanism. Two are related to crime and murder; the other is not. The latter is the first level, which is made up of the organized groups that have been around for years, such as the Church of Satan and the Temple of Set. Offering more theatrics than actual religion, these high-profile groups lean very much toward obeying the law. To date no member of these groups has been involved with murder or any other violent crime nor has any law enforcement agency found evidence to connect these groups to such crimes. The dogma is more oriented toward socializing, sex and fun, though the groups' leaders and members are seriously interested in the occult and magic. The members of these two groups are not dangerous, however, and Anton LaVey has been involved several times as a police consultant on crimes suspected of having Satanic connections.

The second level of Satanism involves self-styled Satanic groups that are usually organized by teenagers who are solely interested in cheap thrills. While many fundamentalist Christian groups will declare that Satanism is a danger to all society, the danger is not from Satanism itself, but from groups and individuals who use Satanism as a front for crime or as a means of controlling and manipulating others. The most infamous of these "killer cults" is the Manson Family, led by Charles Manson. These groups are nothing more than criminal gangs who use Satanism as an excuse to commit crime and murder or as a means of manipulating others. These groups start on a whim, and except for criminal gangs, they last only until the members lose interest or one or more members are arrested for a violent crime. These people are usually of low or average intelligence, and the only knowledge they have of Satanism is what they see in movies or read in books.

Satanism's third level involves self-styled individuals who have dabbled in or are involved in Satanism to justify their crimes or are team killers who have simply dabbled in Satanism out of curiosity. A high degree of psychosis is involved here, and sometimes Satanism is part of a "visionary" pattern of murder. Zodiac fits this pattern. In other cases, Satanism is used to disguise the murders or throw off the police. A fair number of cases have involved hoaxes and claims that were made as part of an insanity plea or to sensationalize the crimes. Henry Lee Lucas claimed that he and his partner, Ottis Toole, were involved in Satan worship and that they were paid to abduct children to be used in human sacrifice, prostitution and black market sales. This claim is highly suspect, since his other claim to have killed hundreds of people all over the United States and Canada proved to be a hoax. Donald Harvey, who was convicted of killing thirty-two people in three different hospitals, had some common books on Satanism that could have been found in any bookstore, but there was no evidence that he was a practicing Satanist. Robin Gecht and his teenage hoodlems used a homemade brand of Satanism in their terror and murder spree in Chicago in the early 1980s. Real Satanists view Satan worship as a religion, and this kind of behavior does not fit the behavior of serial killers. Satanism involves an organized discipline that would be incomprehensible to most serial murderers.

Children and Satanism

Child sexual abuse is another minefield that has been made more complicated by the fact that there are so many false cases being brought that it's difficult to sort out the truth. Sadly, there are parents, ministers, and even some so-called child welfare advocates who have "coached" kids into making false accusations. One such case involved a person who, in order to protect children from alleged sex abuse, was beating and shocking children to get them to make false statements about being involved in Satanic rituals and being raped by Satanists. According to Kenneth Lanning of the FBI, when cases of ritualistic abuse of children are discovered, the perpetrators are always found to be members of conservative Christian cults. These groups who believe it is God's will to harm children include the Gideons in Florida, the River of Life Tabernacle in Montana, and the Stonegate Christian Community in West Virginia.

Witchcraft

Contrary to popular belief, there is no relationship between witchcraft groups and Satanism. Witchcraft, or Wicca, is the oldest religion on Earth. It is a form of shamanism and nature worship that dates back to the Stone Age. The Catholic Church, in its effort to consolidate its power among the lower classes, invented the Devil 501,200 years later. Satan was already a feature of Jewish mythology and was mentioned in the Old Testament, but other than the story of his temptation of Christ, no one ever made a big deal over the so-called Prince of Darkness.

When Christianity was first establishing itself in Europe, it was the religion of the nobility. The majority of the common people still held onto their belief in the Old Religion. To them, Christianity was not a practical religion because when a person became ill, all the priests would do was pray. At least the Old Religion offered cures. The witches or shamans of the Old Religion were well practiced in medicine and had a good track record in healing the sick and injured, which was a power the Church frowned on. These healing arts gave women a respectable power base, and they were cherished by the communities they lived in. In a sense, witchcraft was a form of feminism. However, the Church saw these women and the Old Religion as a threat.

For centuries the policy of the Church had been one of gradual co-optation, but it was also busy fighting heresy with the ranks of Christianity. From the fall of the Roman Empire to the Crusades, there were numerous Christian sects that sprang up all over Europe and Asia Minor. They believed in a variety of doctrines that disagreed with the dogma of the Church of Rome. In 1258, the Church brought out the Inquisition, and from here the witchcraft hysteria began. In 1486, two priests added fuel to the fire with their book *The Malleus Maleficarum*, and the hysteria exploded. Ironically, most of what the Church called heretical, anti-Christ and Satanic beliefs were philosophies that had been the foundations of early Christianity. After the Reformation began, Christian burned Christian at the stake calling each other's religion "Satanic." Today, anything "occult" gets branded with the label of Satanism. The current opposition toward women in medicine, particularly as doctors, nurse-practitioners and midwives, is based on the medieval viewpoint that female healers are a threat to the proper order of society.

The True Nature of Witchcraft

Mention the words "witchcraft" and "magic" to savvy citizens of the twentieth century and they will suddenly regress to the mentality of twelfth-century peasants with all the incumbent superstitions. To the media, witchcraft practitioners are a bunch of dangerous, irrational weirdos. Psychologists brand them as power-crazed neurotics. However, the psychologists forget that their own science was branded as witchcraft and nonsense just over a hundred years ago. The journalists who have little or no knowledge of history overlook the fact that famous scientists, such as Newton, Galileo and da Vinci, were once regarded as heretics and witches. Today's science was yesterday's magic.

The word *witch*, according to the *Oxford English Dictionary*, is derived from the Old English word *wicca*, which is derived from the Indo-European root word for "wisdom." *Witchcraft* literally means "craft of the wise." Also known as Neo-Paganism, all modern witchcraft has its roots in pre-Christian beliefs of self-actualization. It is a system of nature worship that involves the god of the hunt and the goddess fertility, or Earth Mother. This Old Religion was universal, and the evidence of its practice can be found wherever cave paintings and goddess figurines have been found. The dates and names of ancient pagan festivals have even been incorporated into Christianity.

It is misguided hype that has confused witchcraft with Satanism. Contemporary witchcraft was revived by Gerald B. Gardner, a British civil servant and amateur archaeologist, in the 1940s. He basically founded a new religion centered on worship of the Mother Goddess. In later years, early followers of Gardner, like Alexander Sanders and Sybil Leek, founded their own traditions of witchcraft based on more ancient beliefs. These traditions include Egyptian, Norse, Celtic and Druidic beliefs. Today there are over two hundred thousand members of the Neo-Pagan and Wiccan movements. They are mostly middle-class professionals seeking spiritual enlightenment.

Wicca and the Neo-Pagans worship the all-powerful Earth Mother goddess as a triple deity that represents the three stages of life. These representations are the Maiden, the Mother, and the Elder or crone. Beside her is her consort, the father god, and together they represent the male/female equilibrium of life. Depending on the tradition they believe in (Greek, Roman, Celtic, Egyptian, Norse, etc.), witches also acknowledge a pantheon of deities. In the Celtic tradition, the main deities are known as the huntress and hunter or by their proper names, Dana and Dagda.

This religion practices magic, but *not* through the intercession of demons. This practice is conducted through a harmonious relationship with nature that utilizes the cosmic power that lies within all of us and is the underlying foundation of the universe. Magic does not involve the supernatural, but as Isaac Bonewits defines it, magic is "folk parapsychology, an art and a science designed to enable people to make effective use of their psychic talents." As Harriet Whitehead puts it, practitioners of witchcraft and students of the occult are people who refuse "contentment with the finite world." To them, she states, "The occult world offers to the individual a 'free marketplace' of ideas." In a sense, it is an intellectual paradise. They are eclectic and this alone is not conducive to criminal behavior. This is a major factor that is overlooked by many in law enforcement. In fact, the whole philosophy involved in witchcraft and expressed in the Wiccan Principles of Belief is an affirmation of life and is totally devoid of the ego and power elements that are common in criminal behavior.

Witches value freedom and believe in the autonomy of human beings. They also stress in their doctrines, "Lest ye harm none, do as you will!" Doing harm to others is also held in check by the law of rebounds. This is the belief that all the effects of magic will be revisited on the practitioner threefold and, contrary to popular belief, prohibits human sacrifice. However, witches' beliefs have led many to become involved in the ecology, human rights and feminist movements.

Witchcraft groups are autonomous groups organized into "covens," or "circles," of eight to twenty-six people. There are no leaders. According to anthropologist Margaret Murray, witchcraft is a joyous religion whose practitioners meet twice a month at the new and full moons, for regular meetings called "esbats" and eight times a year for the major solar festivals or "sabbats." These are Samhain (Halloween), October 31; Yule, December 21; Oimelc (Candlemas), February 2; Spring Equinox, March 21; Beltane, May 2; Summer Solstice, June 21; Lughnasadh, August 1; and Fall Equinox, September 21. Samhain is the Celtic New Year and has nothing to do with the contemporary ideas surrounding Halloween. Beltane (also May Day or Lady Day) is the great fertility festival that celebrates the glory of life.

There are three phases of membership in a coven: the neophyte, the beginner who enters the coven; the second degree, the accomplished witch who has mastered certain basic knowledge; and the third degree, the priesthood. According to Margot Adler, the sexual acts attributed to witchcraft rituals are another media exaggeration. She states that the sexual rites are all symbolic. Even though many rituals are conducted in the nude, rarely do men and women of the covens engage in sexual contact of any kind. There are no orgies. When sex is used in rituals, it is usually done as part of private ceremonies conducted by couples.

The Occult

The major reason there is so much hype about witchcraft and Satanism is that there is a lack of understanding about the true nature of the occult. The word *occult* refers to things mysterious, secret or hidden. According to the *Oxford English Dictionary*, a definition dating from 1543 also defines *occult* as "something not understood." This definition was usually applied to the practices of alchemy, astrology, theosophy, necromancy and theurgy.

Even though many of these practices were invented over two thousand years ago in Egypt, Mesopotamia, China and India and practiced for centuries by the general public, Carl Jung (a student of the occult) believed that our understanding of magic and the occult became hidden in our collective unconscious because of Church persecution. Ironically, alchemy and astrology were often condoned by the Church, especially if the practitioners were rich enough to afford the necessary bribes. There were also many Church scholars who practiced magic and alchemy, such as Roger Bacon. The eminent physician Paracelsus established the relationship between chemistry and medicine through his study of magic and alchemy in the sixteenth century. His practice of magic led to his invention of ether and laudanum and to a number of other important medical discoveries. The early foundations of the Christian faith were founded on occult beliefs. This was the Gnostic Church of the first century A.D. and was supposed to be based on the secret teachings passed on from St. Paul to Timothy. A few centuries later, the followers of this early Christianity were burned at the stake as heretics and witches. Other serious students of the occult include the writers Balzac, Shakespeare, William Blake, Keats, Debussy, the artist Manet, Mozart, Plato, Victor Hugo, the Irish poet William Butler Yeats, and Sir Arthur Conan Doyle. Sir Issac Newton practiced alchemy and magic. The great mathematician and geographer Ptolemy was the inventor of modern astrology, and Pythagoras, another great mathematician, used mathematics as a form of magic.

All in all, there is very little in our modern culture that does not have roots based in the occult. As I mentioned earlier, yesterday's magic is today's science, so who knows what the witches and serious students of the occult will yield for the benefit of society tomorrow.

Christian Cults

When there is a cult-related murder or proven ritualistic sex abuse of children or cult violence, the perpetrators are usually from some fundamentalist Christian sect or some other religious group. They are never connected with any truly satanic group or witchcraft coven.

The Jonestown Massacre, the Waco Massacre, the Mormon Murders, and the White Supremacist Movement have accounted for a body count ten times higher than that which is alleged and unproven to have been committed by Satanists. The only non-Christian group involved in a murder of this type is the Black Muslims, in the Zebra killings.

In the 1970s, there was an explosion of cult-related violence. Ervil LeBaron founded a polygamy sect called the Church of the Lamb of God and declared war on everybody who disagreed with him. By the time of his arrest and conviction in 1979, he had killed his brother and over a dozen others. The decade was capped by the mass murder/suicide of 911 people at the Jonestown People's Temple. This massacre followed the assassination of U.S. Congressman Leo Ryan ordered by People's Temple leader Jim Jones.

The standout in religious violence was that of the Black Muslims. For years, their conflicts were internal, with the assassinations of Malcolm X and Raymond Sharieff. However, in 1973 and 1974, the antiwhite rhetoric of the Nation of Islam turned into murder when several members randomly killed a number of white people in San Francisco.

Since the 1980s, several religious groups have been at war with the U.S. government. The Mormons and their practice of polygamy had always been the main source of contention, but the mainstream Mormon Church made peace with the United States back in the late 1800s. However, splinter groups that have established communes in Idaho and elsewhere in the western states have been responsible for several murders and armed confrontations with federal and local law enforcement agencies.

Before Waco, other groups besides the polygamists had engaged in armed confrontations. Foremost among these are the White Supremacists, particularly those churches affiliated with the Identity Movement. These are the CSA (The Covenant, the Sword and the Arms of the Lord), Posse Comitatus, the Church of Jesus Christ Christian-Aryan Nations, and the Order. CSA has been at the center of Neo-Nazi and other ultra-right-wing activities. This church has used its facilities and communes are paramilitary training centers and is one of the key dealers in the illegal weapons trade. The members feel it is their Christian duty to traffic in death and destruction in order to preserve the white race. Gordon Kahl, who has alleged to be the Prophet of God, was the founder of Posse

Comitatus. In 1983, federal authorities shot it out with Kahl and his followers at their fortress-commune in Medina, South Dakota. Two U.S. marshals were killed, and Kahl escaped. Four months later, Kahl was killed while trying to make his way to the CSA commune in Arkansas. In 1984, CSA members were convicted of murder.

In 1985, CSA's founder, James Ellison, and several other church members were convicted of racketeering. Since 1975, the Order, which is suspected to be the military wing of the Identity Movement Churches, has been at war with the American government and Idaho authorities. The Order is suspected of a number of terrorist acts and was connected to the murder of Denver talk-show host Alan Berg. In 1984, Order founder Robert Matthews was killed when authorities laid siege to his house in Washington state. In 1985, the Order member arrested for the murder of Berg and found with the gun that killed him was convicted of assaulting the FBI agents who arrested him. Also in 1985, several were arrested on a variety of charges and ten were convicted of racketeering charges. Their beliefs are an odd mixture of Old Testament scripture and revisionist history.

Like Hassan and his Assassins, these militants have a religious-political agenda that advocates terrorism. Their self-righteous philosophy, called Anglo-Israelism, claims that the Anglo-Saxons are the original descendants of the tribes of Israel and that Yahweh (God) has decreed that the Christian whites are the chosen people. The Identity Movement is extremely racist, anti-black and anti-Jewish. It is allied with the Ku Klux Klan and other racist movements. CSA members believe that God has chosen them to establish a new nation in the Heartland (a "Golden Triangle," according to their founder, that extends from Pittsburgh to Atlanta to Lubbock, Texas, to Scottsbluff, Nebraska) and to defend it as a sanctuary of the white race against the coming collapse of the American government. They believe that they are destined to battle the children of darkness and Satan (i.e., blacks, nonwhites and Jews) when this collapse comes.

At this writing, there are about a dozen or more known and suspected Waco-like cult communes with the potential for an armed conflict/massacre scenario. Besides the CSA commune in Arkansas and some Order communes in Idaho and the Pacific Northwest, the cult with the highest potential for violence and disaster is the commune of the Church Universal and Triumphant, led by Elizabeth Clare Prophet. Members of this commune have built a bunker and are known to be stockpiling guns and ammunition. This cult sees itself as the true church of Jesus Christ and Buddha, and they are preparing for Armageddon.

SEXUAL PREDATORS

Rape and other sex crimes are the number one felonies in America. For writers, this can be a complex and sensitive issue to deal with because there are so many myths about sex crimes. Here we will dispel the myths so that these crimes can be seen and portrayed by writers in a realistic fashion.

Rape is the only crime in which the victim is regarded as the offender, and sex crimes are treated with indifference, often being whitewashed with the label "victimless." At this writing, a number of police departments in Maryland are being condemned for the practice of using polygraphs, which are totally unreliable, to check the credibility of the *victims*. If the victims failed this test, they were branded liars and the cases closed. However, in over 75 percent of these cases of so-called "liars," perpetrators turned up years later who confessed to the cases that were closed, proving that the victims had told the truth in the beginning. Unfortunately, this treatment of victims is common all over the United States. The implementation of special sexual assault units by police departments is a recent innovation, the first of which was pioneered in the early 1970s; there has not been much progress in those twenty years.

Rape Defined

The best way to define rape and sex crimes is to define what they are not, then define the reality. This will then be followed by some myth busting to set everything in its proper perspective. Rape is not an act of passion gone out of control, as many people believe. It is an act of destruction and degradation that is a symptom of a complex psychological disorder. It is also a malicious, violent crime that defines the essence of violence as a disease.

Sexual relations are usually achieved between individuals either by means of consent (negotiation), through pressure (exploitation) or by force (intimidation). The first is the basis of all healthy relationships, and the latter two are the basis of all nonconsenting sexual encounters, i.e., sex crimes.

Rape and *sex crimes* are defined as nonconsenting sexual encounters involving unwilling individuals who are either forced or pressured into sexual activity by persons in positions of power or dominance. In exploitative encounters, the victim is harassed and pressured into having sex. If he or she refuses, that person's social or economic or job status is placed in jeopardy. In forced encounters, the victim is threatened with physical harm or is subjected to physical harm with the accompanying threat of death or more serious injury or there is the implication of physical harm to the victim or others. There may be no visible direct threat, but the victim perceives a genuine risk. A forced encounter can also involve assaults on victims who are incapable of consenting or resisting, as in the case of people who are unconscious or physically or mentally disabled.

Rape is always the act of a psychologically dysfunctional person, but the offenders are rarely insane. This is why rape and sex crimes are such complex issues. It is also the reason that the myths are so appealing. The psychosocial issues are so frustrating to comprehend that the myth is easily more satisfying than reality.

First of all, the worst myth that has to be busted is that rape and sex crimes are about sex. Rape and sex crimes are only about power and anger. The majority of clinical studies of sex offenders reveals that these crimes are motivated primarily by hostile, aggressive retaliatory (not related to rejection reaction) and compensatory needs and not sexual needs.

Myth number two concerns the stereotypes about the perpetrators. The popular misconception of offenders frequently regards them as either lusty males reacting to rejection, sexually frustrated men trying to satisfy pent-up needs, or demented sex fiends with insatiable and perverted desires. Again, the majority of clinical studies show that sex offenders are often either impotent or sexually dysfunctional. This explains why in many cases of rape, there is no evidence of semen. This does not mean that forced intercourse did not take place. Also, intercourse does not have to be part of the rape. The victim can be subjected to sodomy or oral sex, and even in those cases, semen may not be present because the rapist was sexually dysfunctional.

Rapists are also viewed as oversexed or unable to engage in normal sexual relations. Since rape and sex crimes are an expression of power and violence, sex is not a motivational source. So, the simplification that offenders are oversexed is a fantasy. According to federal statistics, one-third of sex offenders are married or have girlfriends (relationships that still do not satisfy power needs) and are highly active sexually with their spouses or partners at the times of the crimes.

Many people think that sex offenders are either insane or just healthy, aggressive young men out to sow some wild oats. Typical sex offenders are profiled as individuals with serious psychological problems that impair their ability to engage in healthy, intimate relationships with other people, male or female. They are usually suffering from personality disorders that make them incapable of displaying any warmth, trust, compassion or empathy. Any relationships that sex offenders do have are usually seriously lacking in mutuality (caring about things in common, likes and dislikes), reciprocity (caring about each other), and any genuine sense of sharing.

As to myths about victims, the worst is the public attitude that rape victims "ask for it" or provoke the assault. It is also a popular misconception that the victims can prevent an assault if they really want to. When you take into account that sexual assault victims include both males and females and range in ages from infancy to the elderly, the idea that the victims are at fault is absolutely without merit. A four-year-old boy or girl is in no way seductive or provocative and neither is an eighty-five-year-old woman in a wheelchair, but these are samples of the 1993 rape victims in the Washington, Baltimore, New York areas, and it is doubtful that they invited their assaults. Sexual assaults have been committed by doctors and lawyers in their offices, with a variety of victims. At this time, there are over a dozen school teachers up on sex offense charges on the East Coast alone. Sex crimes have been committed in the victims' homes, public parks, cemeteries, shopping malls, public rest rooms, churches, alleys, and on main streets, side streets and beaches. Sex crimes have occurred in all places, in all seasons, and at any time of the day, and the victims have ranged from male police officers to female soldiers to elderly hospital patients to severely mentally and physically disabled children. Since sexual assaults are committed using intimidation with either weapons or threats of harm or injury or by use of brute force, it is doubtful that child and elderly victims can prevent being attacked.

The last myth concerns the belief that pornography and sexual explicitness are the causes of rape and sex crimes. Several studies sponsored by the Justice Department, including FBI profiles, show that sex offenders are generally less exposed to pornography and erotic materials than average males.

Forms of Rape

The crime of rape is categorized into three forms:

1. Anger Rape
2. Power Rape
3. Sadistic Rape.

In all nonconsenting sexual encounters, the components of anger, power and sexuality are always present. In these crimes, sexuality is nothing more than the primary tool with which the perpetrator is expressing his or her anger and/or power needs. Sex crimes are, therefore, patterns of sexual behavior that are primarily concerned with status, hostility, control and dominance. Sensual pleasure and sexual satisfaction are generally nonissues and nonexistent in these encounters. The acts of sexual predators are violent, destructive sexual behavior in the service of nonsexual needs.

Anger Rape

Anger rape accounts for 40 percent of violent sex crimes. The assault is characterized by physical brutality. It either comes as a "blitz" attack (a sudden, extremely violent attack) or is preceded by a ruse of some sort that distracts the victim. Once the victim is off guard, the attacker savagely overpowers the victim. The offender is fully conscious of his anger and rage and vents his fury both physically and verbally. The intent is to debase and injure the victim, and the rape becomes the ultimate expression of his contempt. Vicious, brute force is often the attacker's only weapon used to overpower the victim, after which sex is the weapon of degradation. Other acts of humiliation include sodomy, oral sex, and urination or ejaculation or defecation on the victim.

The attacker is generally impotent during the attack. In fact, the anger rapist often regards sex as "dirty," and this makes it appealing as a weapon that he can use to defile and humiliate his victim. The sex act itself is often disgusting to this type of offender; satisfaction and relief are only gained by the discharge of the attacker's anger, not by the sex act. These attacks are short in duration. The attacker strikes, assaults and flees, and there is rarely any premeditation involved. The common theme that appears in these crimes is that these incidents are often motivated by revenge. The attacker often feels that he has been wronged, hurt, put down or treated unjustly by some individual (often a woman), situation or event (often involving a woman). In most cases, the victim is an innocent who had no association with the attacker, but the attacker makes the victim a symbol and transfers his hate for the actual subject of anger to the victim. Since these attacks require a catalyst, they are often sporadic and have no pattern to them.

Power Rape

In these crimes, sexuality becomes a tool by which the attacker compensates for feelings of inadequacy, and the assault serves as an expression of mastery, strength, control, authority, identity and capability. The intent is to capture and control the victim, and only enough force is used to achieve this aim. Verbal threats, intimidation with weapons and /or physical force are used to this purpose. The sex act is only evidence of conquest to the attacker, and the assault often involves the victim being kidnapped or held captive, followed by repeated assaults over an extended period of time. These attacks are usually the result of obsessional thoughts and masturbatory fantasies (unrelated to sexual impulse) about sexual conquest and rape. This type of attack constitutes a test of the attacker's superiority, and the attacker often feels excitement, anxiety, anticipated pleasure and fear. This is part of the thrill of the fantasy, but in reality, the attack usually disappoints the offender, never lives up to the fantasy, and the attacker goes on the hunt again, continually in search of "the right victim."

In these crimes, a pattern is prominent. The attacks are repetitive and compulsive. Several attacks may occur in a short period of time, making this offender a serial rapist. The attacks are either premeditated or opportunistic. The victim generally is the same age as the attacker, and the choice of victim is determined by availability, accessibility and vulnerability. After the attack, the offender may feel so in control of the victim that the rapist may tell his name to the victim, drive the victim to the police station, or do some other defiant act. These offenders feel so secure about their crimes that they feel they can get away with anything, and unfortunately, they often do. This further increases their sense of power and control. The intent of these criminals is to assert their competency and validate their masculinity. The latter is motivated by fears of homosexuality or conflicts with identity. They regard all types of sexuality as threatening, and their pursuit of heterosexual encounters is often driven and compulsive and serves to counter fears of being homosexual. Power rape accounts for 55 percent of sexual assaults.

Sadistic Rape

With this crime, we can find all the factors of power rape and anger rape. Sadistic rapes account for 5 percent of sexual assaults. The offender transforms his anger and desire for power into eroticized aggression that is then vented upon the victim in the form of acts of sadism. The intent is to derive intense gratification from injuring the victim and to take pleasure in the victim's torment, anguish, distress, helplessness and suffering. Usually, the victims follow a pattern in age, appearance and occupation, and they often symbolize to the attacker something he wants to punish or destroy. The crimes are deliberate, calculated and preplanned, with the offender taking great precautions to hide his identity. The victim is stalked, abducted, abused and sometimes murdered. The attacker usually ties up and tortures the victim, often in a bizarre or ritualistic manner, as in the case of the nomadic killer, Christopher Wilder, who blazed a trail of serial murder/rape from coast to coast in 1984. The attacker may cut the victim's hair or arrange it in some style;

he may wash the body or dress the victim to suit some fantasy; and he may force the victim to behave in a certain manner. The victim may be subjected to biting, burns and whipping. Injury to sexual areas of the victim's body, such as breasts, genitals and buttocks, are common, and in some cases, the victim may be object raped with a bottle, stick, knife or other objects as a substitute for the offender's own sex organs. These crimes often accompany sexual homicide, and the offender will often mutilate the victim prior to or after death and have sex with the corpse.

For this type of offender, excitement and sexual gratification are associated with and derived from the infliction of pain and the exercise of power over the victim. Control is all-important, and the offenders often derive further satisfaction from their ability to hide their dark side and to be like chameleons, as in the case of Ted Bundy. For these perpetrators, there is a thrill factor to being an "invisible hunter." The intent is abuse and torture, the means is sex, and the motive is to punish and destroy.

Patterns of Sex Crimes

As with other types of crime, sex crimes can be broken down into categories — patterns that experts have discerned through years of observation.

Gang Rape

The majority of sex crimes are committed by loners. However, there is an increasing trend toward assaults involving multiple offenders. If the attack involves only two, it is called a *pair rape*. The term *gang rape* is reserved for crimes with three or more attackers.

In the majority of gang rapes, the crime is committed against a single victim, though there have been cases of two and three victims in a single incident. Offenders are generally white and range in age from 16 to 34, with the majority being 17 to 27. Victims are generally also white and within the same age range. Contrary to popular belief, rape is a predominately white crime, with the majority of victims being white. Blacks make up a small percentage of offenders and victims, and rarely are the crimes interracial. Gang rape has the same characteristics as single-attacker rape involving power as a motive, but in the cases of multiple attackers, the assailants derive peer support and mutual respect from their acts. The attackers usually target strangers, and a vehicle is generally used in the crime. These crimes are usually premeditated.

Male Rape

This is a subject that little notice is given to because the public prefers to give a blind eye to men who rape men. Instead, the concentration is put on crimes committed against women and children. However, male rape is equally as important as sexual assault against women and children. There is an unfortunate myth that all males are safe from sexual assault once they become adults and that the only way a man gets raped is if he goes to prison. This is regrettably untrue. A male is just as much at risk as a woman. Approximately 2 to 6 percent of all rape cases reported to rape crisis centers involve male victims, and the victim population is most probably much higher; however, there is a far worse stigma attached to male victims than to female. This stigma usually discourages men from reporting being assaulted.

The only times the public becomes aware of male victims is when they are murder victims, as in the cases of John Wayne Gacy, Jeffrey Dahmer and Dean Corll. Unfortunately, the public automatically assumes that the victims were homosexual, otherwise they would never have been associated with their killers. In fact, most male victims are heterosexual and are usually attacked after they have been abducted and rendered incapable of resisting. It is also assumed by the public that men who rape men are homosexuals or bisexuals. However, the average offender is married or has a girlfriend and is sexually active with such at the time of the crimes.

It is generally believed that a man is more powerful than a woman in defending his sexual zones from invasion. However, since attackers employ the same tactics against men as those used against women, the victim's ability or inability to fend off attack is irrelevant. Attackers usually employ either entrapment, intimidation and/or physical force to control their victims. In most cases, a combination of all three along with the use of weapons, drugs and alcohol are used to subdue the victim. In the known cases, one-third of victims were attacked while unconscious, another third were coerced with a gun into forced sex, while the other third were the targets of blitz attacks and were raped after being beaten senseless.

Patterns of Violence

In a recent study of all known cases of rape, the victims were assaulted in the following manners:

- 22 percent were sodomized
- 19 percent were subjected to anal sex and forced to perform oral sex on their attackers
- 7 percent were sodomized and masturbated by their attackers
- 4 percent were subjected to both anal and oral sex
- 11 percent were forced to perform oral sex on the perpetrators
- 7 percent were subjected to oral sex and then forced to fellate their attackers
- 15 percent were subjected to oral sex only by the perpetrators
- 4 percent were forced to masturbate their attackers
- 7 percent were forced to have sex with other male victims while the offenders watched
- 4 percent were fondled and object raped.

The one major difference between attacks on men and attacks on women, other than the types of sex acts, is that male victims are ten times more likely to be subjected to multiple sex acts than women who are usually assaulted with a single vaginal penetration.

In 30 percent of known cases of male rape, the victim was hitchhiking. This is the same high-risk activity that women victims were often involved in. Another 30 percent were assaulted while swimming and hiking alone. Seven percent were attacked on the street, while another 7 percent were attacked in their homes. Four percent were attacked by their employers at their workplaces. John Wayne Gacy lured his male victims to his home with job offers. Offenders are generally between 12 and 41 years old, with the average age being 21. As with the rape of females, the offenders and victims are predominately white. Only 8 percent of offenders and 4 percent of victims were black. Eighteen percent of assaults were interracial. The majority of offenders were strangers to their victims, but many cases also involved friends who raped friends and older relatives who raped younger relatives.

Offenders usually commit these crimes for five reasons:

1. *Conquest and control*—the same power dynamic as in the rape of women
2. *Revenge and retaliation*
3. *Sadism and degradation*—coincides with the murder of the victim

4. *Conflict and counteraction*

5. *Status and affiliation* — usually associated with gang rape.

Child Rape and Rape of the Elderly

Rape crosses all boundaries of age and sex. Because of their vulnerability and helplessness, children and old people, both male and female, are often the victims of rape.

Children are the subject of power rape usually when an adult victim is unavailable. However, the majority of victims are targeted for sadistic rape and murder, as in the cases of Wayne Williams and Dean Corll. In cases of anger rape, the sexual assault is usually used as an additional punishment of an already battered child.

Again, this is predominately a white crime, and the offenders range in age from 12 to 72, with the average age being 35. In cases of power and anger rape, the victims and offenders are either acquainted or related. In sadistic rape, the victims are strangers to their attackers.

The rape of the elderly is almost the same in nature to child rape. Because of the myths about rape, the public believes that the attacks are motivated by sexual arousal and desire on the part of the offender combined with the victim being at fault for doing something that stimulated his or her attacker. Thus, we have this stereotype of a victim that is young, attractive, and dresses and acts in a sexually provocative manner. This stereotype goes up in flames when it comes to child cases or cases of elder rape. The reality of rape is that children and old people are not chosen for their sex appeal; they are chosen because of their helplessness.

Offenders are predominately young, white, single males. The age range is from 12 to 38. As for victim preference, the choice of prey is white women ages 50 to 85.

Of all forms of rape, sexual assault of the elderly tends to be the most violent. In the majority of cases, offenders intentionally inflicted life-threatening injuries, and in many other cases, murder was intended along with sexual assault. In over a third of all cases, offenders clearly intended to injure as well as rape their elderly targets. Only a small percentage of cases shows that the offender only intended to rape. In clinical studies of offender motives, the reason why assaults of elderly women are more violent than of other age groups appears to be that these older women represent authority figures to the offenders, such as teachers, principals or employers. The victims also symbolize people the offender has come to resent and want revenge upon, such as a parent, stepparent or foster parent. The elderly, like children, are the most vulnerable in our society. However, the fact that the elderly are more isolated and, in many cases, in poor health makes them more at risk than children. No one is eager to keep an eye out to protect these defenseless members of society, and as the offenders know, the elderly have been left totally helpless.

Marital Rape

Other than the movie *The Burning Bed* and the Bobbitt case, there has been little attention paid to the issue of marital rape. While many people are acquainted with the brutal statistics of domestic violence in the United States, very few know or realize that many women are raped, as well as beaten, almost on a daily basis. Many of these victims are subjected to rape and sadistic torture up to two or three or more times a day. In other cases, women are subjected to beatings and rape by their husbands and boyfriends and then forced to prostitute themselves or else suffer worse abuse.

Many cases have come to light in recent years of men who forced their wives to engage in sex with friends, family, and any other male acquaintance the husband would want to share his wife with. The attitude of these men is that a wife or girlfriend is a "sex slave," who can be treated like livestock. These men feel they have the power of life and death over these women. It used to be that a husband had spousal immunity from prosecution for "forcing his attentions" on his wife, but increasingly, states are abandoning these laws. Now a wife has a right to say "no."

As to motive, offenders generally hold the following views:

1. *Sex is equated with power* — Offenders feel that they have a God-given right to sexual relations with their spouses and that if a wife refuses, the offender sees this as a loss of control. Thus, rape is used as a means of "keeping her in line."

2. *Sex is equated with love and affection* — These offenders regard sex as the only means of expressing closeness. So to them, when their wives refuse sex, they are saying they don't love their husbands anymore. In response to this rejection, the rape becomes a perverse way of saying "I love you."

3. *Sex is equated with virility* — To these offenders, sex with their wives is an affirmation of their manhood. To be denied sex is

to be emasculated. To avoid such damage to their egos, rape becomes the solution to their insecurities.

4. *Sex is equated with debasement* — Punishment is the intent of these offenders, and they use rape as a weapon for teaching their wives or girlfriends a "lesson." The sexual assault may be concurrent with a beating. The wife overcooks dinner, she gets raped. She doesn't do the laundry right, she gets raped. And so on.

5. *Sex is equated with marital success* — These offenders see the rape as a way of making a success of their marriages. Sex is used as a panacea, a cure-all, for a failing marriage.

Women Who Rape

Contrary to popular belief, a woman is just as capable of committing sexual assault as a man. While it is not heard of often, it is not uncommon. Just like few men are willing to report being sexually assaulted by other men, they are just as reluctant to report being assaulted by women. With these offenders, the motive is power. Since the law does not specify the sex of an offender, any form of "forced sexual encounter" is regarded as rape, regardless of whether the attack was committed by a man or a woman. Since society upholds the myth that a man cannot be raped by a woman, a man is perceived to be a "willing" sex partner. However, the reality of rape is that since the sex act is a physical one, a man can be sexually stimulated against his will. When a woman forces a man to engage in sexual intercourse or oral sex at gunpoint, this is rape. Women also rape women, but like men raping men, it is generally not motivated by homosexual desires.

The most common sex crime women commit is the rape of children. In the majority of cases, the offender is the mother of the victim, but there have been many cases of male children being raped by teachers, baby-sitters and health care workers. The motives are the same as with male offenders, and the crimes are usually ones of opportunity and availability of the victims. As to victim preference, boys are commonly the targets of rape because they are less likely to report the incident than girls.

CHILD MOLESTERS AND CHILD MURDERERS

To the public and to most writers, the term *child molester*, like *serial killer*, invokes the worst kinds of stereotypes. Many believe that these offenders are dirty old men in grungy raincoats hanging around playgrounds with bags of candy, waiting to lure children. Others believe that the offender is the dark stranger who takes advantage of the vulnerability of children. And finally, there is the belief that child molesters are perverts who expose themselves or fondle children without engaging in vaginal or anal intercourse. Behind all these stereotypes is the myth that says all child molesters are nonviolent offenders, an unwarranted idea that these offenders never physically harm their victims.

Ritual is the one word that best describes crimes against children. And contrary to popular belief, these rituals are the worst forms of violence because of the lifelong emotional and psychological wounds that are inflicted. This factor voids the belief that these criminals are "nonviolent."

The Child Molester

Crimes against children, especially sex crimes, are absolute proof that violent crimes do not have to involve physical injury, and these crimes are the very essence of what defines "acts of *intentional trauma*." Therefore, the definition of *child molester*, in medical and legal terms, that is used by the Justice Department is "any individual, male or female, who inflicts intentional trauma and engages in illegal sexual activity with children and nonconsenting minors under eighteen years of age." This is the true portrait of a child molester, and like the serial killer, this criminal can be *anyone*.

The Pedophile

In very recent years, the 1980s in fact, the term *child molester* has become passé, and now the media has popularized the term *pedophile*, which used to be exclusively a psychiatric term. *Pedophile* has been defined as "anyone sexually attracted to prepubescent children," and the term *hebephile* has been applied to those who are attracted to pubescent children. *Hebephile* is rarely used because it does not constitute sexual perversion in the view of the psychiatric community. On the other hand, *pedophile* has developed a broad public usage, even to the point of becoming cop slang, as in the terms *pedo case* for a child molestation case and *pedo squad* for the investigative team that tracks down pedophiles.

The *Diagnostics and Statistics Manual of Mental Disorders* (DSM-III-R), which is the clinical bible of the American Psychiatric Association (APA), defines *pedophilia* in the following medical terms, not legal terms:

> 302.20 PEDOPHILIA—The essential feature of this disorder is recurrent, intense sexual urges and sexually arousing fantasies, of at least six months' duration, involving sexual activity with a *prepubescent* child. The person has acted on these urges, or is markedly distressed by them. The age of the child is generally 13 years or younger. The age of the person (patient/offender) is arbitrarily set at age 16 years or older and at least 5 years older than the child (victim).

Note that the key word here is *prepubescent*. However, despite this definition, many mental health and social work professionals apply this overused term to people who have a sexual preference for teenagers. The other important factor is that the definition stresses both the *act* and *fantasy* of engaging in sexual activity with children. This is a psychosexual disorder of the first degree. However, misuse and overuse of the term, along with misperceptions about this disorder, have led to problems in recognizing, investigating and convicting offenders.

It is the "nice guy" syndrome, which is the same cause of misconceptions about serial killers, that clouds the minds of both victims and bystanders. It is also that recurring "label" problem. People make assumptions that a person cannot be a child molester because he or she is "such a good neighbor, church deacon, den mother, good worker, etc." So, these "nice people" escape detection and conviction for their crimes because people do not realize that these offenders can be anything from a convicted felon to a minister, rabbi or priest to a doctor or lawyer or teacher. It must also be understood that child molesters can also have "normal" sexual relations with adults, and the molesters often engage in sexual relationships with adults in order to gain or continue access to their preferred victims: children. It is not uncommon for a child molester to marry or have a relationship with a person who has children so that there is a source of victims.

Two important questions to consider: (1) Are all child molesters pedophiles? (2) Are all pedophiles child molesters? The answer to both questions is *no*. While the terms are used synonomously by the public and the media, there are major differences between the two, even though many pedophiles are child molesters and many child molesters are pedophiles.

The Types of Offenders

The medical model divides sex offenders who target children into two broad categories: situational and preferential. The law enforcement model, however, goes several steps further in an expanded definition of types that fits the needs of obtaining identifications, arrests and convictions. This model was developed by the FBI Behavioral Science Unit.

Situational Child Molesters

These offenders do not have a real sexual preference for children. Their motives for engaging in sex with children are varied and complex, with the frequency of such activity ranging from chronic to a one-time act. The numbers of victims are generally small and the molesters may, at will, change from child victims to defenseless, vulnerable adults and back to children. It is not uncommon for this type of offender to work in a day-care center and then leave that job in order to sexually abuse elderly patients in a nursing home.

Regressed. This type of situational child molester usually has low self-esteem and poor coping skills. He or she targets children as a substitute for a preferred adult sex partner. A stressful or traumatic event can often be a catalyst of child molesting behavior. Victim preference is based on availability. Often this offender will molest his or her own children. This molester usually coerces children into engaging in sex and may or may not collect pornography. If the offender does have a porno collection, it is the homemade variety, composed of videos and still photos of offender and victims.

Morally Indiscriminate. This is a very aggressive offender who lives to abuse others. The sexual abuse of children is part of a general pattern that also includes lying, cheating, stealing, and abuse of friends, family, coworkers and spouse or partner. These offenders molest children because they feel they have a right to do so. Victim criteria involve vulnerability and opportunity. The offender has the urge, sees a child, says "Why not?" and attacks. Force, lures and manipulation are the usual means of obtaining victims, with strangers being the main targets, but it is not uncommon for the offender to be an incestuous mother or father. A pornography collection may include detective and S&M rags and some child porn of teenagers. Impulsiveness makes this person a high risk to any child of any age.

Sexually Indiscriminate. This offender likes to experiment with sex. He or she is willing to try or do anything when it comes to sex. Again, the motive is experimentation, and there may be no real sexual preference for children. The offenders just molest children whenever they are bored. They may experiment with their own children. Sexual encounters with adults will tend to lean toward the bizarre, and it is not uncommon for children to be included in these activities. This offender is generally found among the middle class and upper class of society and will also have multiple victims. Offenders will collect porno and erotica, but kiddie porn will comprise a small portion of this collection. Offenders' sexual history will include sadomasochism, spouse swapping, bondage, and use of the occult for sexual purposes only. They are never active Satanists.

Inadequate. These offenders may be psychotic, schizophrenic (eccentric and out of touch with reality to a minor or major degree), mentally disabled, senile, or a combination of these factors. They tend to be misfits and loners. This offender usually becomes sexually involved with children out of loneliness and insecurity or curiosity and can be considered at risk of committing murder. Children are chosen as victims because the offender finds them to be nonthreatening objects with which to explore sexual fantasies. Victims can be either strangers or known to the offender or related to the offender. Sexual encounters with children are generally the result of expressions of anger and hostility that have built up to the boiling point in the offender. Sometimes the victim is a substitute for a specific adult. Cruel sexual torture is not uncommon, and these molesters may often abuse the elderly—whoever is helpless and encountered first. This offender collects adult porn. Most of the sexually motivated child murderers are this type of offender.

Preferential Child Molesters

These offenders are sexually attracted to and prefer children and fit the clinical definition of pedophile. Their behavior is part of a highly predictable pattern called sexual ritual. These offenders feel compelled to attack children and will do so even at the risk of discovery. They not only have a hunger for children, but they desire many children, which leads them to molest large numbers of children. They usually have age and gender preferences for victims, with boys tending to be the common targets. Among this category are three subgroups of behavior.

Seduction. Here the pedophile actually courts the victims with attention, affection and gifts, just like an adult would seduce another adult. After a while, the victim becomes willing to trade sex for these benefits. Seductive activity involves multiple simultaneous victims and a sex ring, a group of offenders that shares victims. The offender's ability to identify with and relate to children enables him or her to build rings within schools, day-care centers, churches, or neighborhood institutions, such as scout troops. The offender's status as an authority figure is also a factor in the seduction. Children who have already been abused or neglected by others are at high risk of being targets of these offenders' seductions. Seducers are rarely at a loss for a source of victims. Often the seduction creates such a binding relationship that the offender has difficulty "dumping" a victim who becomes too old. The victim often threatens to disclose the relationship if the offender tries to terminate it, and this places the offender at high risk of discovery. At this point, the offender will use threats and/or physical violence to keep the "secret." He or she will also use coercion to hold onto victims to prevent them from ending the relationships before the offender is ready to.

Introverted. This is the source of the dirty-old-man stereotype. However, this kind of offender can range in age from 16 to 80. Generally, these offenders are found among the young. They engage in minimal conversation with their victims, preferring instead to wait around places children frequent and to target strangers or very young children. Sometimes these offenders will just watch the children; other times they will engage in brief sexual encounters. They will also tend to expose themselves at playgrounds and school yards or make obscene phone calls to children. Sometimes they will frequent child prostitutes and will often marry in order to beget children that they can abuse as early as infancy. These offenders definitely prefer children and are also very predictable.

Sadistic. These offenders are the most likely to commit abduction and murder. They only prefer children as victims, and they only gain satisfaction from the infliction of psychological and/or physical pain. There have been cases of seduction molesters who became sadistic molesters, and it is not known if this pattern of behavior is something that already exists in the offender and surfaces for some reason in the offender's criminal career or if the sadism is a need that develops later as part of the abuse pattern.

Combination Offenders

It is not uncommon for pedophiles to have multiple psychosexual or personality disorders or to be suffering from psychosis. A pedophile's sexual interest in children might be combined with other sexual deviations. These may include any or all of the following:

1. Exposure (exhibitionism)
2. Obscene phone calls (scatophilia)
3. Exploitation of animals (zoophilia)
4. Urination (urophilia)
5. Defecation (coprophilia)
6. Binding (bondage)
7. Baby role playing (infantilism)
8. Infliction of pain (sadism, masochism)

9. Real or simulated death (necrophilia).

This list, however, is not complete. We would need a book on this subject alone to cover all the sexual deviations. Also, the combinations of behavior disorders are only limited by the imagination. Preferential molesters may want to experiment with other sexual deviations. Indiscriminate situational molesters may desire to involve children in their chronic experimentations. Child molesters can be psychopathic or paranoid or serial killers of adults. The most dangerous are the indiscriminate preferentials. Having no conscience, it is not beyond them to commit abduction, sadistic torture and murder of children for the fun of it. These offenders can fit into a very broad pattern of multiple behaviors.

Sex Rings

In summary, while a lot of attention has been focused on day-care centers, keep in mind that sex rings may be found anywhere groups of children are being cared for. Hospitals, pediatric nursing homes (hospices), schools, churches, juvenile shelters, community centers and recreation camps can be the hunting grounds of employees who manifest any combination of sexually deviant behaviors. Religious cults and large religious sects are the most prone to harbor and, in several cases, even promote child sexual abuse. There is no conclusive evidence of Satanic cults involved in such abuse, but there are many cases involving Christian groups. There have also been a few cases involving New Age sects. Always remember David Koresh and his child brides. This type of case is typical of the rule, not the exception.

Incest

Of all child sex offenses, this is the hardest to prove. Also, there is no typical pattern of behavior that is specific to incestuous parents. The classic pattern involves the preferential molester who marries a man or woman with children of a desired age and gender. It is also common for the offender to just live with the children's parent, pretending to be a caring boyfriend or girlfriend. There is also the type that befriends a single parent, offering to help as a "parental figure" and as a financial resource. With the increase in single-parent families, this type of M.O. is becoming more common. It is not uncommon to hear of "uncles," and sometimes "aunts," who have no family connection to the child victims, sexually abusing children. Also, offenders may marry in order to be able to adopt or become foster parents. The least common practice is for an offender to beget his or her own children, but it happens.

Often, child sex abuse is not the primary factor in incest cases. These involve incestuous parents who just morally indiscriminate. Since they are devoid of a conscience, they are cunning, manipulative predators. If caught, they turn on the charm and deny any wrongdoing, or, if the evidence guarantees a conviction, they will plead that "they are sick and need treatment." This plea for help is generally an attempt to escape being put in jail, where these offenders run a high risk of being made victims of sexual abuse by their fellow inmates. These morally indiscriminate offenders are suffering severe personality disorders that are more serious than pedophilia. They are dangerous and are considered to be difficult or impossible to treat. To buy into their sympathy ploy is to give them a future license to hurt people.

Female Offenders

Two social stereotypes make female sex offenders very hard to identify and convict. The first concerns the position of women as care givers in our society. In this context, women who are in charge of caring for children can handle children in almost any manner without suspicion. This is reflected in several recent cases of sex abuse in day-care centers. The offenders were all women. In many cases of physical abuse involving mothers or "sitters," sexual abuse may be concurrent. Murder is also very feasible. The second stereotype involves the sexual double standard regarding age and gender that is inherent in our society. If a man has sex with a teenage girl, he is a pervert. However, a sexual relationship between an older woman and a teenage boy is regarded as an achievement of manhood for the boy.

While a number of cases concerned female offenders motivated by sex, other cases indicated a motive involving more serious psychological problems. It is considered rare, if not impossible, to find a woman who displays the behavior seen in male preferential child molesters. However, for a long time, the idea of women as serial killers was dismissed as an impossibility. Such an idea went against all those sacred social myths about women. And like all myths, this one was flushed when several women fitting the profiles applied to male serial killers were identified, arrested and convicted. Contrary to popular belief, any criminal and destructive behavior that a man is capable of can be committed by a woman. Personality disorders are also not gender specific.

Teenage Offenders

This is also a growing phenomenon. Teenage offenders can fit into any category of molesting behavior, but the majority are found to be of the morally indiscriminate preferential type. This group is growing at a very disturbing rate.

Most teenage child molesters are or were victims of sex abuse themselves. When a younger child is molested by an older child, it is common for the case investigation to lead to other older offenders who have abused the older child.

The Pedophile Profile

While there may be more situational child molesters than preferential, the number of victims is higher with preferential offenders. The situational may only molest a handful of children in a lifetime. However, a preferential may account for hundreds or even thousands of victims in a lifetime. Preferentials are also the main type involved with sex rings, child prostitution and child pornography. While all child molestation cases are hard to prove, the preferential offender makes investigation easier by his or her predictable and repetitious behavior patterns. The characteristics of these patterns are identified below. (NOTE: These factors mean nothing by themselves. Even all together, they do not constitute proof. But, the presence of a combination of these factors constitutes the grounds for more intense investigation.)

1. Long-term and persistent pattern of behavior
   - Victim of child sex abuse
   - Limited social contact as teenagers
   - Discharged from military for child molestation
   - Moves frequently and unexpectedly

- History of prior arrests
  1. Sex offenses involving children
  2. Nonsexual types of offenses
  3. Attempts to acquire child victims
  4. Impersonating a police officer
  5. Violating child labor laws
- Multiple victims
- Planned, repeated or high-risk attempts to acquire victims

2. Personal traits
   - Over age 25, single and never married
   - Lives alone or with parents
   - Limited social life
   - Rarely or never dates
   - Married but with "specific intent" or has "special relationship" with spouse
     1. Married to person with minimal sexual needs
     2. Married to strong, dominant type
     3. Married to weak, passive type
     4. Marries as cover or for convenience
     5. Marries to gain access to children
   - Excessive interest in children
   - Has "special friends" who are either teenagers or young children
     1. Socializes only with children
     2. Hangs around places children frequent
   - Few or no relationships with peers. May have close adult friends who are also pedophiles
   - Has victim pattern that indicates age and gender preferences
   - Refers to children as clean, impish, pure, innocent, etc.
   - Refers to children as objects, projects or possessions

3. Well-developed techniques in obtaining victims
   - Skilled at identifying vulnerable victims. Almost like a per-

verted sixth sense, the "hunting sense" of offenders can single out, from dozens of children, that one child who comes from a broken home or has been the victim of physical, sexual or emotional abuse or is suffering neglect. These offenders can be compared with vultures and other scavengers that can sense weakness or death in other creatures that are miles away.

- Identifies with children. Unable to relate to adults, these offenders have been described as "master seductors" because of their ability to *listen* to children. Others have been described as "pied pipers."

- Has access to children. This is one of the most important factors, but has been the source of dangerous stereotyping and paranoia. Not everyone who works with children is a pedophile. Unfortunately, many pedophiles use either employed or volunteer positions involving contact with children to provide access to victims.

  1. Holds parties for neighborhood children

  2. Takes them on field trips

  3. Pedophiles can be teachers, baby-sitters, camp counselors, school bus drivers, physicians, dentists, photographers, clergy, social workers, police, scout leaders, Big Brothers, foster parents, sports coaches, business people who employ teenagers or minors

  4. Those who would never be suspected but should never be ruled out, for example, nurses, Girl Scout troop leaders, private tutors and music instructors

  5. Other types of traditional care givers and adult supervisors of children

- Will use any opportunity to "get the adults out of the way" in order to isolate the children for victimization

- Seduces with attention, affection and gifts. The offender literally seduces the victims by befriending them, talking to them, listening to them, paying attention to them, spending time with them and giving gifts. This is a courtship process, and since the offender becomes a "lover" to the victims, it is easy to comprehend why these victims are not likely to report strangers who molest them. A teenage prostitute who is beaten and raped by her pimp may not leave her tormentor because she fears the likely repercussions, but these victims generally express that their main motive for staying is because the victimizer is "the only person who loves me." These victims have been seduced, which is an area of understanding that has been vastly ignored.

- Skilled at manipulating children. This is an essential factor in the operation of a sex ring. To have simultaneous sexual encounters with numerous victims, the offender will use seduction, competition, peer pressure, psychology, motivation, threats and blackmail. Not all pedophiles have the ability to manipulate children.

- Has hobbies, interests and/or activities appealing to children or teenagers.

- Shows sexually explicit material to children. May also use phone sex services and computers to lower the inhibitions of child victims.

4. Sexual fantasies focusing on children
   - Youth-oriented decorations in house or room
   - Excessive photographing of children
   - Collects child pornography and child erotica.

Pornography and the Pedophile

Not everyone who has pictures of nude children is a pedophile or child molester. There are many innocent reasons why an adult may have such materials. Not long ago a famous portrait artist of children was charged with violation of child pornography statutes because she took "references photos" of her own children to use in her work that hangs in many public galleries. Until just a few years ago, such photographs were perfectly acceptable. However, society's paranoia has changed its definition of *pornography* and *obscenity*.

Pornography is derived from the Greek *porne*, referring to anything akin to prostitutes. Generally it is written or pictorial material that describes or portrays the acts of prostitutes or any sexual activities. This is a description based on definitions from several major dictionaries, but the specific reference to the acts of prostitutes expressly limits the definition of pornography to materials that depict vaginal, oral or anal sex between men and women or men and men or women and women. "Anything of a sexual nature" cannot be included in the definition because it would have to include lingerie ads. To the perverted mind of a sexual deviant, even these ads can cause sexual excitement. To any other person, these are just ordinary photos.

Thus, the collection of a pedophile can include almost anything that will represent his or her most cherished sexual fantasies. They save books, magazines, articles, newspapers, photographs, negatives, slides, movies, albums, drawings, audiotapes, videotapes, video equipment, personal letters, diaries, clothing, sexual aids, souvenirs, toys, games, lists, paintings, ledgers, photographic equipment, etc.

Videotape is the current vogue. Computers are also popular. Already, pedophile rings have been discovered using the latest computer technology to "collect" and distribute sexual fantasy material. CD-ROM and Photo-CDs will most probably be the next tech craze for pedophiles. This will make the task of trying to discover "collections" much more difficult, as the perpetrators will be able to "hide" their collections on CDs. There is no limit to the nightmare scenarios for law enforcement.

Research has defined four categories of collectors of child pornography:

1. *The closet collector* — This offender keeps the collection a secret and is not actively involved in molesting children.

2. *The isolated collector* — This offender is deeply afraid of discovery and, therefore, generally keeps his child molesting activity and collecting a secret between him- or herself and the victims.

3. *The cottage collector* — This offender has a need for peer validation, so he or she tends to share the collections with other pedophiles. This person is also an active child molester and shares in this activity as well. There is no profit incentive.

4. *The commercial collector* — This offender is in it for the money and the kicks. These persons are active molesters, but they also recognize the profit potential in selling pornographic and erotic material to other collectors.

Child Pornography

The working definition of *pornography* that we discussed earlier applies only to material depiction sexual activity between adults. The definition of child pornography is similar but must cover a broader scope. Child pornography is defined as any visual (not written) material depicting sexual activity between adults and children and sexual activity between children and children. It also includes photos and videos of naked children, but these depiction are only pornographic if they are sexually explicit, such as close-ups of sex organs.

This is a gray area that involves both a behavioral definition and a legal definition. Therefore, the intended use of photos of naked children is a very important factor. If an artist uses photos of children for anatomical studies in painting, these photos are not pornographic. However, several states may consider such photos as pornography under their obscenity statutes. This is an area where the law can be blind because it makes gross assumptions that can ruin the lives of innocent people. So, it must be kept in mind that the key element of intent to be aware of is "harm." If there is no depiction of harm to the child portrayed or if there is no criminal intent involving harmful victimization, then the photos or videos are not pornographic.

There are two types of child pornography:

1. *Commercial* — This is your black market stuff that is produced and distributed overseas for commercial sale. Wherever there is a large, active sex industry, such as in Thailand and other parts of the Pacific and Southeast Asia, as well as Latin America, you will find a large child prostitution and child pornography industry. American customers are the chief consumers for these foreign markets, but the smuggling of such materials into this country is usually conducted by pedophiles. Because of the risk, there is not enough profit incentive for American organized crime to be involved. However, Asian crime syndicates that control this market are apt to recruit pedophiles to carry the goods in for them. Because of their sexual and personal interests, these offenders are more than willing to take the risks. Often, pedophiles will disguise their commercially produced material to look like the "homemade" variety, to avoid harsher penalties if caught. However, a good

forensics lab can tell the two apart.

2. *Homemade* — This is material that was not originally intended for sale and distribution. However, the quality can be better or equal to that of the commercial grade material. This is because the pedophile has a personal interest in the quality of the product. It is also one of the biggest black market operations in North America. You won't find these materials in the X-rated shops, but they have been found by police in the private homes and offices of doctors, lawyers, ministers, teachers and other "nice people" who are the pillars of society.

While the overseas sex trade does involve a high degree of child slavery, and such a child sex trade is growing in this country, most victims involved in these films and pictures are victims of seduction or sex rings that used coercion. These are generally prepubescent victims.

Despite the growing number of missing children, abduction is not the general means by which children are involved in the pornography trade. Runaway children and throwaway children who become prostitutes are often involved in kiddie porn. A lot of pornographic materials are made with the knowledge of the victim's parents or are made by the parents for their own use or for sale. Because of the seduction factor, you see a lot of these victims smiling in pornographic materials. There are also more boys than girls involved in pornography because of the market's gender preference.

Another factor involved in child pornography is the long-term impact on the victims. These are hidden crimes that involve the victimization of a child. Many victims try to ignore or repress the knowledge of the harm done to them. However, they often find that they cannot escape the past. The pictures and videotapes are permanent records that are used over and over again, further compounding the victimization. It is not unusual for child victims to commit crimes — including murder — as teenagers or adults in order to recover and destroy the evidence of their molestation.

Child Erotica

This is another gray area. Because child erotica or "pedophile paraphernalia" can be *anything* that serves a sexual purpose for an individual, as in a carrot being perceived as a phallic symbol, such items are not generally illegal. For the pedophile, child erotica can be anything from books on children or children's books to toys to games to pictures of children cut out of women's and family magazines. However, collections of any of the materials noted in the following categories are indicators of possible pedophile activity:

1. Published materials relating to children—books, videotapes, magazines and articles on the following subjects:
   - Child development
   - Sex education
   - Child photography
   - Deviant behavior
     1. Child sex abuse
     2. Sexual disorders
     3. Pedophilia
     4. Man-boy love
     5. Incest
     6. Child prostitution
     7. Missing children
   - Police procedures and detective magazines
   - Nudism, erotic novels and "men's" magazines
   - Newsletters from pedophile support groups and advocates of the legalization of pedophilia, such as the North American Man-Boy Love Association (NAMBLA) and the Lewis Carroll Collectors Guild

2. Unpublished materials relating to children
   - Personal letters
   - Diaries
   - Fantasy writings
   - Manuscripts
   - Phone/address books
   - Financial records indicating purchases of kiddie porn or other materials

3. Pictures, photographs and videotapes relating to children

4. Souvenirs, trophies and miscellaneous items
   - Photos, tapes, video and photo equipment
   - Clothing from victims

- Jewelry and personal items from victims
- Sexual aids
- Notes and letters
- Charts and records of activities with victims (scorecards, etc.)
- Computers and equipment
- Toys, games and dolls
- Costumes
- Alcohol and drugs.

Motivation for, Use of and Characteristics of Collections

Nobody really knows why pedophiles start and maintain collections, but theories do exist. Collecting may help satisfy compulsive, persistent fantasies about children or may validate the pedophile's behavior, which may explain why a lot offenders have many scientific and academic books on the subject. Collecting may also provide a means of obtaining peer reinforcement, or it may be related to the need to cherish memories of the offender's encounters with children. The children may grow up and become unattractive to the offender, but the victims' youth and attractiveness are maintained indefinitely by the photo or tapes.

Since we are unsure of the pedophile's motive for collecting, we are also unsure how a pedophile uses the collection. Perhaps it is used for sexual arousal and gratification, sometimes as a prelude to an encounter with children. It might also be used to lower the inhibitions of victims or to blackmail and coerce child victims into continuing the relationship or even to break off the relationship and maintain the secret. Collections could also be used as currency between pedophiles.

A pedophile collection usually has six major characteristics:

1. The collection is the most important thing in his or her life.
2. It is constant. The pedophile can be compared to a pack rat that feels he or she never has enough.
3. The collection is organized, with tidy, well-kept records.
4. The offender has a desire to keep the collection as a permanent fixture in his or her life. Some offenders have willed their collections to other pedophiles to preserve their collections.

5. The offender will always want his or her activities kept secret, so the collection will be concealed. Secret hiding places can be anywhere in the offender's home or work but generally where the offender can get access, including safe deposit boxes. Hiding places are only limited by the imagination.

6. In seeking validation for his or her behavior, the pedophile will share the collection with other pedophiles.

The Computer

There have been many cases of criminals abusing advances in technology to their own ends, but none is more prominent than the pedophile's use of computers. It is an offender's best friend and helps achieve all the characteristics that facilitate collecting. A computer can be used for validation, organization, maintenance of permanent records and so on. It can also be used to produce and distribute porn and to network with sex rings to find new victims. Whole collections, along with records of thousands of victims, can be stored on a few diskettes that can be concealed anywhere. The computer is a communication tool that helps pedophiles contact electronic bulletin boards. NAMBLA has a very large bulletin board that is over ten years old. Recently, in Maryland, a sex ring operated by county government employees was caught using state computer facilities to transmit and receive child pornography. The abuse of today's technology is only limited by the imagination and skill of the offender. Software advances are moving so fast, especially in multimedia, there are almost no limits to the possibilities or applications for criminal abuse. This includes computer-generated interactive kiddie porn. If you look in any computer magazine, you will see ads for adult computer porn. The future may get worse as computers become less expensive, more sophisticated, and easier to operate and the offender's intelligence, skills, economic means or employment access increases. This means the risk factor will become significantly reduced, thus making this criminal market more attractive to organized crime. There may already be a computer network that is smuggling in child pornography by means of computer communications links.

Child Murderers

Child murder is nothing new. As we previously discussed, several of the most notorious serial killers of the early twentieth century were child killers. Albert Fish was the only exception; he was a pedophile who killed one child. Peter Kürten killed both children and women, and Fritz Haarmann killed teenage boys. More recently, there are the cases of John Wayne Gacy, most of whose victims were teenage boys, and Wayne Williams, the Atlanta Child Killer. In a recent study of serial killers, over 25 percent killed at least one child and 8 percent preferred child victims. One of the most famous team killer cases, Myra Hindley and Ian Brady, killed children for kicks. Why children and teenagers? They're easy prey, but there are other motives:

- Sexual gratification
- Enjoyment
- Monetary gain
- Personal reasons — "an urge to kill"
- Perverted acts — child molestation and necrophilia
- Revenge
- Mental illness.

In 1983, there was an explosion of hysteria over the issue of missing children. Numbers reported ranged from 20,000 to 1.2 million children abducted each year. This prompted an army of nonprofit organizations (NPOs) to pop up out of the woodwork. By 1988, there were so many NPOs that they were actually competing with each other for funding and sometimes fighting over cases. All these groups caused so much panic and confusion that the public became vulnerable to con artists and crooks who use the pretense of looking for missing children as a license to steal. There were even ex-cops who tried to hustle a buck in this new "child safety racket." In 1984, the government set up a nonprofit organization to help with this problem, and in the past ten years, despite ups and downs, such as being burned by the numbers game, the National Center for Missing and Exploited Children remains as one of a handful of nonprofit agencies that is reliable and reputable. In 1989, the Justice Department finally did a complete study of the problem and vindicated the FBI, who claimed all along that the number of victims was much smaller than the NPOs were claiming. The bottom line turned out to be that in five years, only about twenty thousand children disappeared and that the annual rate was only one to two per one million population. This means that only about one hundred fifty children per year are victims of stranger abduction, with teenagers 14 to 17 years old being at higher risk. Besides miscalculations of victim populations, there has also been confusion over the definition of victim categories. Missing and murdered children can be categorized as follows:

1. *Runaways* — These are children who voluntarily leave home or choose to leave because they cannot tolerate their home environments, mostly because of sexual abuse. These children soon become involved with drugs, prostitution and pornography. Once believed to account for 95 percent of missing children, the fact is they account for less than 50 percent.

2. *Throwaways* — These are children who have been forced out of their homes or have been abandoned. The numbers are estimated to equal runaways, and their fate is the same. However, they are more likely to be found dead. This is a very large and often ignored victim group.

3. *Parental and relative abductions* — These children are abducted by a parent or a relative, such as an in-law or aunt or uncle. This group accounts for over 50 percent of missing and murdered children. These children are at high risk of being murdered and/or sexually abused by their abductors. Sex abuse is usually the motive for the abduction.

4. *Children murdered by parents or relatives* — Again, these children are attacked by a parent or relative. This group includes children killed in the process of physical abuse or even as victims of murder/suicides involving entire families.

5. *Stranger abductions* — These include two subgroups: short-term abductions and uncompleted abductions. This crime only accounts for 3 percent of all abductions, but it accounts for 64 percent of all abduction/murders.

On the average, two thousand five hundred to three thousand children are killed each year, with about 15 percent killed by their own parents or relatives. This fact, along with the 1989 Justice Department report, completely dispels the myth that thousands of children are being abducted and murdered by strangers. It is also not true that stranger abductions are on the rise. Children are more at risk at home, with black children at highest risk. Last year, a woman in Maryland burned her home down and killed her six children to cover up the child abuse she was suspected of.

Murderer's Profile

While parents and relatives account for most child murders, only 8 percent of all serial killers kill children exclusively. In general, these offenders sexually assault their victims before or after death. Most of the offenders are male, but over 25 percent are female. Male killers target strangers and females target family. As expected, women use quiet means, such as poison, while men are more apt to use brutal violence. The motive for males is generally sexual gratification, while women are prone to kill children for financial gain or just enjoyment, as many have admitted. In several cases, female killers have insured their own children, children of relatives, and children of neighbors and friends, then killed them to collect the insurance. However, there have been other cases of nurses who killed or attempted to kill numerous children as a means of career enhancement or as "acts of mercy," and in one case, the killer wanted to justify the need for a new pediatric care wing and killed over twenty-five children.

Child Lures

In the majority of cases, the victims are "just snatched" when they are left unattended for a few seconds or a few minutes. In cases involving teenagers, the victims were often overwhelmed by sudden, violent attacks or abducted at either gun- or knife point. However, lures commonly used by child murderers are somewhat similar to the methods used by pedophiles. These methods include:

- Coercion
- Bribery
- Asking for help in finding a lost pet
- Pretending to be a police officer, which is why many offenders prefer to use blue sedans.
- Pretending to be a talent agent
- Pretending to be injured and needing help (this is often used on teenagers)
- Offering employment, as in the Gacy and Williams cases.

In the case of Myra Hindley and Ian Brady, two of their victims were abducted from their homes. While it is rare for abductors to break into homes to take victims, children have been abducted from inside and outside their homes, and there is an increasing trend toward this activity.

The modern child molester/child murderer defies the classic stereotypes. Today, these offenders may look like young church deacons or yuppie stockbrokers, is someone like Arthur Gary Bishop. Bishop was a "good Mormon" — the product of a righteous Mormon family — an avid churchgoer, an Eagle Scout, a Big Brother volunteer and a missionary worker, and he worked as an accountant. Over the course of four years, this nice guy committed several serial rapes of children and killed five boys. The ages of his victims ranged from four to thirteen years old. Using his unsuspicious, upstanding appearance, Bishop found it quite easy to abduct victims in broad daylight in public places. One victim was taken from his home, another from a grocery store while he was shopping with his grandfather.

VICTIMS

Unfortunately, the realm of fiction has produced a mishmash of myths, misconceptions and stereotypes about victims of violent crime. This is an area that writers should be very objective in.

Every time a horrible crime hits the front pages—a carjacking, a drive-by shooting, a rape/murder, an abduction—people ask the universal question: "Why?" With the crime rate soaring to all-time heights, this is a common and reasonable question to ask. Violent crime is such a common occurrence, it appears that no one is safe. However, many people never become victims of crime. So, why do people become victims of crime, especially violent crime? Harold Kushner, the author of *Why Bad Things Happen to Good People*, contends that, while most people tend to blame God and everything else for their misfortunes, such misfortunes, including criminal victimization, are just a reality of life that occurred because some chose to act in an evil manner. In previous chapters, I indicated that violence is a matter of medical ecology. In essence, the answer to the question "Why?" is a combination of factors. As discussed in the chapter on sexual predators, no one chooses to become a victim; they are chosen. They are in the wrong place at the wrong time. People have no control over whether or not they become victims, and it is not because of bad luck or an act of God. They become victims because of the reason stated above and one other important factor: A criminal chose evil as his or her way of behavior.

However, there are three other minor reasons why people become victims:

1. Human error or accident (nonintentional trauma)
2. Temporary insanity as the result of human interaction, as in family quarrels
3. Mental illness.

When you put all these factors together, it is easy to see *how* and *why* people become victims. And just like avoiding any other illness, like the flu, once you know the how and the why, it is just as easy to prevent becoming a victim of crime and violence.

Centuries ago, before the discovery of germs and viruses, medical professionals and most people believed that disease was caused by God's curse, the Devil or just the unknown. Resigned to these ideas, our ancestors believed that they were powerless to prevent the misfortunes of accident and illness. Now, modern medicine and science have given humanity the power to control disease. However, when it comes to the disease of crime and violence, the public and many professionals suddenly regress to the mentality and vulnerability of Medieval peasants. This is why the Satanism craze has gained such momentum. People have to have something or somebody to blame for their misfortunes or the misfortunes of others. This is basic human psychology and is part of the foundation of religion. (This is why it is such a traumatic shock when a priest or minister is convicted of child molestation.) It is also the source of the biggest myth in society: Victims are to blame for the crimes committed against them.

We have all heard people say, "Oh, such and such got what they deserved." This is the general belief in all rape cases, and this myth was touched on in chapter seven. You will also hear this in murder cases. Many times, people will respond to a case by saying that the victim must have done something to get him- or herself killed.

In Maryland recently, a young man with no criminal history

was killed with a sword while trying to prevent a fight between two guests at a party. The man who killed him had a history of violent behavior and *chose* to kill this innocent because he had disrupted the fight. For being a Good Samaritan, the victim was decapitated. People will even blame children if they get killed. However, it is impossible to believe that a child would choose to be a victim.

Ironically, no matter how much evidence shows that the crime occurred because of actions of the criminal, the criminal will be exonerated of at least part of the blame. Somehow, through some irrational process, the victim will be blamed.

Crime victims, especially violent crime victims, fall into three main categories. These categories and their members are arranged, in descending order, according to their degree of risk:

1. Family Members
    - Offender's children — easy access and availability
    - Husbands
    - Wives
    - In-laws
    - Other relatives, especially children
    - Offender's mother
    - Brothers and sisters
    - Grandparents

2. Acquaintances
    - Friends and neighbors — less apt to be on guard
    - Children — vulnerable and prone to be easily controlled by people they don't know
    - Women alone
    - Adult males — easily overpowered when attacked by people they know
    - People in authority
    - Members of same peer group — easy access
    - Patients — vulnerable and defenseless

3. Strangers
    - Young women alone, female college students and prostitutes — chosen because they are vulnerable and isolated

- Children—vulnerable, easily overpowered or manipulated
- People at home, entire families—secluded
- The handicapped and hospital patients—vulnerable, isolated
- Business people—vulnerable anytime, anywhere
- Pedestrians and travelers—vulnerable, can be easily isolated
- Older women alone—vulnerable, physically weak
- Police officers—easily isolated and overwhelmed
- Employees
- Homeless/street people
- Newspaper ad respondents
- Persons of another race.

It is a general fact that murder is a family affair. The availability of weapons has nothing to do with the incidence of domestic homicides. Among all murder and violent crime victims, family is the largest victims' group. Holidays, which are high stress inducers, usually are a factor involved in the motive, and while mental illness is usually the cause of holiday murder and mayhem, it is the opportunity for the victims to be in the wrong place at the wrong time that is a crucial factor. One case involved a child and his mother who were killed by the boy's grandfather. The grandfather was upset that the child took a turkey wing without permission. The mother condoned the child's behavior, so the man punished them both by shooting them. In another case, a woman stabbed her husband to death because she didn't get what she wanted for Christmas. The husband was awake and sober but caught completely off guard by his petite wife's sudden attack.

Carjacking victims are victims because of the make and model car they are driving. Drive-by shooting victims are generally children and are only victims because of the neighborhoods they live in. As we discussed in chapter eight, children are victimized because they are chosen and because of their vulnerability. In a Justice Department study of violent crime victims, the two fastest growing victim populations are male teenagers and elderly victims.

Serial killers choose strangers for a variety of specific reasons.

These reasons are generally associated with a fantasy the killer is trying to live out or a psychotic delusion, such as with a mother fixation.

To Know the Victim Is to Know the Criminal

Quite often, from the time the police begin their investigation of a violent crime to the time of arrest and trial, the most neglected area of information involves the factors concerning the victim or victims. Except for the obvious things, like victim's family and acquaintances and the autopsy, data about the victim's life and thinking is rarely collected. If victim profiles were conducted on every homicide, a lot more serial crimes would be discovered and a lot more serial criminals would be arrested.

A psychological profile or psychiatric autopsy of the victim can be the most important intelligence data in finding the criminal. This kind of inquiry can be very time-consuming, and for that reason is sometimes ignored. This is also the main reason why a lot of questionable deaths are ruled as suicides. A victim's profile should contain the following information:

1. Physical traits
2. Occupation — to include past five years and any special training
3. Medical, dental and psychiatric history
4. Activities prior to the crime, profile of last fourteen to twenty-eight days
5. Histories of marital life and bachelor (male and female) life
6. Educational background
7. Sexual history and preferences
8. Personality traits
9. Life-style information
   - Drug and alcohol use
   - Activities
   - Sports interests
   - Hobbies
   - Residences for past five years
   - Incidences involving civil and/or criminal courts.

The usual autopsy information is not going to be adequate when analyzing the victim's physical traits. Every single detail of what the victim looked like, down to the way the victim parted his or her hair, must be studied. If the victim is female, what kind of nail polish did she use and how did she wear it? Did the victim, male or female, wear earrings? This is very important and so is the birthday. Remember New York's Zodiac Killer, who killed people with specific birthdays? Gay killings follow physical trait patterns and so do the murders of young women, especially college students.

The married life, along with histories of previous marriages, is important. If the victim is single, a history of all relationships is vital. Remember, murder is usually a family affair, which means the spouse, ex-spouse or boy/girlfriend could be the murderer. An excellent example of this was the murdering ex-husband in the movie *Sea of Love*.

Special consideration must be given to employment and education history. Stalkers and murderers are often fellow employees acquainted with the victim. Serial rapists who hunt on college campuses may be students and known to their victims.

The relevance of information about lifestyle, where the victim has lived, psychological and sexual history and litigation history is self-explanatory. Lifestyle tells you everything about who the victim was and how he or she thought. This is the information that makes the victim a human being and not just a statistic. The places the victim lived tells you about lifestyle, family background, friends, acquaintances, and a host of other details that are important to this vital human equation. Psychological history tells you about the victim's life, habits and personality. It is also important to know about the victim's love life. Knowledge of whether the victim was gay, straight or bisexual is critical. Litigation in the civil courts as a defendant or complainant and/or encounters with the criminal courts as an offender or victim tell you a lot, including who the victim's friends and enemies are.

Medical history is critical, especially information about AIDS or venereal disease infection. Contracting AIDS has been a recent motive for murder.

Last, but not least, is the history of the victim's activities for up to twenty-eight days prior to the victimization. This calendar of events can be a gold mine of clues about who the victim had been acquainted with and any significant events that may have been a motive. If the victim was raped and/or murdered, a pattern of stalking may show up. A pattern of vulnerability and availability may show up as well.

How Victims Think

The psychological and emotional impact of trauma on victims and their friends and families is an important factor to consider if the victim survives. Without an understanding of crisis and grief, it is almost impossible to gather useful information. It is also important to keep this factor in mind when gathering information from the victim's family and friends, especially if the victim is missing or dead. This is another ignored area and is the key reason why cops are viewed as callous and insensitive. The inception and adoption of Rape Crisis Units on police departments and Victim's Services by prosecutors are only recent innovations. Unfortunately, these are not the widespread practices in law enforcement they should be.

In victim psychology, the major problems encountered are:

- Rape Trauma Syndrome
- Situational Crisis Response
- The Grief Process
- Post-Traumatic Stress Syndrome (PTSS).

The friends and families are victims, too. Therefore, the term "victims" shall mean everyone related to the crime's victim as family and friends. Imagine a crime victim's family, friends, coworkers, classmates and neighbors as circles in the kill zone of a bomb blast. When the crime occurs, the victim is at ground zero and gets the full physical and emotional impact. From zero, the emotional shock waves rush out with devastating impact. The first victim circle to get blasted is the family. The next circle of people to be hurt includes the friends. The third circle contains the coworkers, classmates, acquaintances and others with casual relationships. The outer circle may be distant from the harm, but the suffering is the same. This circle is that of the community in which the victim lives. Though not acquainted with the victim, the people living within at least a two to five mile radius of the crime will be overwhelmed by fear and will experience minor symptoms of traumatic shock and PTSS. A few years ago, in a suburban community of a midwestern city I was living in, a man was shot and killed when he answered a knock at the front door. His killers were two escaped convicts who just knocked on the door and shot the man as soon as he opened it. They took his wallet and car keys and drove off. The only reason this man became a victim was that he was the only person who was home on that block that night and had a car in the driveway. He died because he answered a knock at the door. The next day, this quiet community was an armed camp. Anyone knocking on someone's door would be greeted by people with rifles, pistols and shotguns. People walked their dogs with handguns in their pockets. Gun sales exploded and people even carried guns to do shopping. It is still that way after almost five years because every new crime in that neighborhood opened up the wound of the original trauma and increased the pain and fear.

General Reaction to Traumatic Crisis

In the Chinese language the word for "crisis" is represented by two pictographs. One is defined as "danger"; the other means "opportunity." When traumatic crises hit victims, they are not only the victims of crime, but they are also in great danger of permanent psychological damage. If the victims of crimes survive their victimizations, those people are in danger of being destroyed by their emotional pain if they do not cope, adapt and grow by learning from the opportunities presented by the crises. These opportunities are those which offer the victims new resources, new coping skills, and new strength to deal with future trauma.

When traumatic crises hit, victims are overwhelmed by a state of emotional instability, a sort of temporary insanity, characterized by intense fear and often painful physical symptoms. The usual coping mechanisms are inadequate, and new ways to deal with this period of dangerous stress must be found. The victims' perception of reality becomes totally distorted, and their lives become a whirlwind of confusion, fear and depression. If the victims learn new problem-solving techniques, face the crises head-on, and resolve any issues that arise, they will grow. However, if the victims let their grief and pain bury them, they will drown in their suffering and ultimately regress into emotional basket cases. They will also be at higher risk of experiencing fatal physical problems. If the victims perceive the trauma event realistically, have adequate situational support resources, such as help from family, friends, peers and community, develop adequate coping mechanisms, such as defense mechanisms like denial, intellectualization and rationalization, then the odds will be in their favor regarding their ability to cope with the crises and adapt to the inevitable changes in their lives.

There are three phases that will occur when crisis hits, even if the victim is psychologically healthy. These phases are:

1. *The impact phase* — This is the acute reaction to crisis. Symptoms are shock, disbelief, dismay, anxiety, unstable emotions, and a severe inability to function. This reaction is immediate and can last for months, sometimes years, depending on the victim's ability to cope.

2. *The recoil phase* — This is the period of outward adjustment to the crisis. The acute symptoms diminish and the victims gradually return to near-normal level of functioning. Routine business of living slowly resumes, even though, sometimes, victims will continue to deny the true consequences of the crises. This is a natural defense mechanism for victims, as they are attempting to protect themselves and others from the "danger." Also, victims' interests may expand to concern for others. This phase begins as soon as the victim comes to term with the acute phase.

3. *Long-term reorganization phase* — This is the period of integration and resolution of fears and pain. This is also the time when victims grow into survivors. They attempt to adapt the crises experiences into their lives, as well as try to understand and resolve the meaning they have found attached to their survival of the crises. Even though these new "survivors" have found strength they never knew existed, it is not uncommon for them to occasionally experience feelings of loss and depression. This is a natural and necessary feeling.

Every time new crises hit, the survivors become victims again and the phases start all over.

Rape Trauma Syndrome

The crime of rape creates a whole host of medical, psychological, social and legal problems for the rape victim and all other victim groups affected by the rape. While these other victim groups will experience the general crisis reaction (GCR) symptoms, the rape victim will experience a more intense pattern of emotional reaction.

This pattern is known as rape trauma syndrome and follows three phases, just like GCR:

1. *Impact phase following rape* — This is the period of acute reaction to the crime. It includes symptoms of anxiety, fear and shock and a feeling of numbness. Victims may also feel guilty, ashamed and humiliated. Later, the victims will display responses to the situation that are consistent with their usual coping styles. These can be expressive — crying, anger, confusion, restlessness — or they can be controlled — logic, calmness, composure. For a long time following the rape, victims will appear to be preoccupied and anxious. Physical symptoms, acute fears and insomnia are likely to be manifested. The victims' ability to function will be severely impaired.

2. *Recoil phase* — The victim gradually adjusts to the impact of the trauma of rape. The symptoms of the impact phase decrease, and victims may begin to deny that anything significant has changed their lives. Function will gradually return, as in GCR.

3. *Reorganization phase* — As more time passes, it is not uncommon for the victims to feel depressed, helpless and preoccupied concerning the trauma. They will also try to come to terms with why it happened to them. As they accept the meaning they find, the victims will gradually return to functional lives.

Sudden Death and the Grief Process

Sudden death as the result of violent crime is the only time when the circles of victims of the crime find themselves at or close to ground zero of a devastating acute crisis bomb explosion. The closer an individual was to the crime victim, the more destructive the psychological impact and consequences will be. Sometimes, the crisis reaction can be fatal. In general, all these victims will experience a more acute version of the five-phase grief process defined by Dr. Elisabeth Kubler-Ross in the 1960s. Even though these responses will be more intense than in other death experiences, any distorted, prolonged or delayed graduation into each phase is considered abnormal, and in those cases, the victims should be directed to immediate help. These phases are

1. *Denial* — Victims will be extremely hostile over the news. They will not want to accept it at all. This is a valuable defense mechanism that allows them to slowly absorb the news. Denying the

death allows those close to the deceased to try to more easily manage the business of living.

2. *Anger*—This surfaces when the victims try to comprehend *why* this death has occurred. They will display hate toward everyone around them, mostly because they are angry that this tragedy befell them and not others. Guilt is not uncommon.

3. *Bargaining*—In accepting this tragedy, the victims will try to reach out for an alternative reality, such as begging God to bring back the dead. A parent may ask for his or her life to be taken in trade for a child that has been murdered. Guilt is prominent.

4. *Depression*—This occurs when the victims begin to accept the death. Because there was no opportunity to say good-bye to the murder victim, those who have been left behind must find their own way to put closure on the event. It is an extremely sad phase, but the sadness and depression over the loss are appropriate and must be respected.

5. *Acceptance*—This is the final phase and the transition period for the victims' return to the business of living. They are saying, "OK, yes it happened. Now it's time to put the loss behind me and move on."

Many sources say that each phase has a defined duration, but in reality, each victim's reaction to a sudden, violent death is different. Some people will pass through each phase in a few days to a few weeks, while others will suffer for months on end in each phase. Still others may pass through the first phases quickly and then spend years in the final two phases. In any event, it can be severely harmful to these victims if well-intentioned people try to rush them from one phase to the next. Each victim has to follow this path at the pace that is most comfortable for him or her.

Post-Traumatic Stress Syndrome

For many years, the public has been under the misconception that Post-Traumatic Stress Syndrome (PTSS) is a psychiatric disorder only experienced by combat veterans. However, the reality is that anyone who has experienced a traumatic crisis will experience and exhibit the symptoms of PTSS. Symptoms that are commonly seen by doctors examining victims of a traumatic event or traumatic crisis include:

1. Prolonged shock and emotional numbness
2. Insomnia
3. Nightmares
4. Abuse of prescription drugs and/or alcohol
5. Trembling
6. Sudden, unexplainable bouts of crying
7. Disorientation
8. Fear and hypervigilance
9. Acute anxiety with occasional panic attacks — likely to occur when the victim is somehow reminded of the trauma or around the time of the anniversary of the trauma
10. Depression
11. Helplessness
12. Loss of control or inability to manage control
13. Gradual change into dependent state
14. Violent bursts of temper
15. Aggression
16. Fatigue
17. Physical ailments
    - Chest pain
    - Heart attack
    - Ulcers
    - Seizures
    - Partial paralysis
    - Arthritic-type muscle pain
18. Delusions and other neurotic behavior
19. Suicidal tendencies related to loss of hope after prolonged experience of above symptoms.

Victims are under the crushing weight of severe emotional pain and deep psychological wounds. These wounds are prone to reopening time and time again. A mother whose daughter disappeared over a decade ago still has an acute emotional reaction every time she smells spaghetti; this was her daughter's favorite food. The girl is believed to be the victim of an abduction/murder. The body has never been found.

For many victim-survivors, there is no ability to put closure on the impact of the event, especially in cases of missing children and abduction/murders with no bodies being found, as with the families and friends of victims of Ted Bundy. A number of his victims are still buried in unknown locations, leaving their families and friends to suffer in limbo. Now that Bundy has been executed, these people may never be able to put their grief to rest. As you can see, a serial killer can destroy the lives of many people with one act of abduction and murder. Multiply this by ten to fifty deaths, and the victims impacted by the crimes can reach into the hundreds and thousands.

The recent murders of Nicole Simpson and Ronald Goldman significantly demonstrate the points noted about victims. While no one really knows who committed the murders, that is, the guilt of a suspect has not been determined by trial and jury, we do know things about the victims: They were not in control of events; they did not cause their own deaths; and there was nothing either victim could have done to prevent this tragedy. They were, unfortunately, victims, according to the formula we discussed earlier.

We know beyond a shadow of a doubt that Nicole Simpson was the victim of domestic violence. This was the dominant factor that set the scene. We know that her victimizer was her husband, O.J. Simpson, the NFL football star, actor, and nationally recognized sports commentator and spokesperson. This domestic violence was the dark side of a well-respected, but now fallen, American hero who is currently charged with double murder. As for Ronald Goldman, he was just a poor, unfortunate, innocent bystander who was in the wrong place at the wrong time. He had no relationship with the primary victim, Nicole Simpson, as the press has implied, and his presence was a tragic coincidence. He died because he unknowingly entered a kill zone to carry out an act of kindness, the return of a pair of glasses belonging to Nicole Simpson's mother.

Once Mr. Goldman entered the killer's zone of control, his fate was sealed, like the majority of other innocents who die every day in America and elsewhere. The only control he had left was to try to defend himself. The same is true for Nicole Simpson, who was in the place she belonged, but was there at the wrong time—the time and place the killer had chosen. The initial coroner's report bears out that both victims tried to defend themselves. Sadly, their efforts could not counter the brutality of their attacker.

We know nothing of the killer, despite the trial in the press. Objectively, only a trial in a court of law and a decision by an unbiased jury will determine the guilt or innocence of the suspect. All we know is what the victims tell us about themselves, what they tell the police about the crime, and what the crime scene tells the police. Combine this information with other evidence and the victims may tell the jury who is guilty or innocent. This is the lesson that victims always have to teach.

T E N

THE CAREER CRIMINAL

There are many reasons why a person chooses to follow a life of crime. Antisocial behavior can have its roots in poverty, child abuse, a broken home environment or drug and alcohol abuse. As discussed before, many people would like to blame everything and everyone, from the victims to Satanism, as the cause of criminality. It is human to avoid the subject of mental illness because it is typically human to blame everything and anything in order to avoid facing reality. Mental illness is a taboo subject in our society because if we understand this illness, we are forced to face our worst fears, our vulnerability, and the fact that we are all capable of criminal behavior.

As we have discussed before, criminal behavior has four basic characteristics: irresponsibility, self-indulgence, interpersonal intrusiveness and social rule-breaking. What causes people to be thieves, bank robbers, muggers, check forgers, art forgers, or any other kind of criminal can be these four characteristics combined with mental illness and any of the following:

1. Poverty
2. Low intelligence
3. Poor parenting
4. Hyperactivity, which can be traced to a medical condition
5. Stimulation seeking
6. Psychopathy
7. Impulsivity
8. Learning disorders
9. Any untreated disability or one not coped with well.

No one is a "born criminal," but add any of the following components of the more than eighteen categories of mental illness listed in the *American Psychological Association's Diagnostics and Statistics Manual IV* to the previous factors and you have the "evolution of a criminal." These categories are:

1. Disorders usually first evident in infancy through adolescence
2. Organic mental disorders, including problems caused by brain tumors and birth defects
3. Substance abuse disorders
4. Schizophrenic disorders
5. Paranoid disorders
6. Psychotic disorders
7. Affective disorders
8. Anxiety disorders
9. Disorders causing or relating to physical illness
10. Dissociative disorders
11. Psychosexual disorders
12. Factitious disorders
13. Disorders of impulse control
14. Adjustment disorders
15. Psychological factors affecting physical health
16. Personality disorders
17. Undiagnosed conditions
18. Other conditions.

With the increase of women in the work force and changing social standards, women are committing as many white-collar crimes as men. These offenders are generally from middle-class backgrounds and have college educations, so this rules out poverty, broken homes and low intelligence. Greed is also out. The only explanation for such behavior is drug abuse, kicks (stimulation seeking) or mental illness. Or it's a combination of all three, though mental illness has the highest probability of being the cause, especially among the middle and upper classes.

To say that money was the motive behind the careers of chronic offenders would be too simplistic an explanation. However, it is part of the answer. Career criminals are basically people who desire money, but, as fits their childish nature, they expect something for nothing. At the least, they will steal. At the most, they will kill. The more they steal, the more the stealing becomes a way of life. Add murder, and killing and stealing become the norm. However, there is no real definition of the behavior of chronic career offenders. Thus, it becomes necessary to define by example because a mere label will not provide a clear understanding of the minds of these people.

The Quiet Criminals

Han van Meegeren was an excellent artist who only yearned for the recognition bestowed on the Great Masters. So, he became an art forger. From 1937 to 1945, he painted five paintings that were sold as original Vermeers, netting a total of over $4 million. He explained his sudden wealth as lottery winnings, but he never got a chance to really enjoy his money. In 1946, van Meegeren was prosecuted as a Nazi collaborator because he sold one of his paintings to Hermann Goering. The only way he could prove his innocence was to confess to art forgery and paint a Vermeer. For this he became a national hero, was found guilty of fraud, and was sentenced to one year in prison. Van Meegeren finally got the recognition he wanted all his life, dying a happy man in 1947. The only thing that van Meegeren killed was the reputation of the art critics who had said he was a mediocre artist but had accepted his fabulous fakes as the real thing. This is classic ego indulgent behavior, but it is not the work of a mentally ill person. It is also not criminal behavior because it lacks evil and the intent to do harm that dominate criminal characteristics.

All van Meegeren did was to allow people to fool themselves.

There was also nothing evil about Thomas Patrick Keating. However, he did feel that he was the victim of an evil, elitist, hypocritical art world. From 1947 to 1976, Keating took his revenge by creating over two thousand paintings and putting them on the market. All were acclaimed to be the original works of over 130 artists, including Rembrandt, Degas, Turner and Renoir. Keating's intent was not to make money, as he gave away most of the paintings; he just took sheer delight in fooling the experts. In 1976, he proudly confessed to his deceptions and was put on trial for forgery. But instead of being jailed, Keating became a hero, and in 1982, he was given his own television art show. In 1983, he was finally able to sell his fakes under his own name, making over $100,000. Like van Meegeren, he died a happy man knowing that he had gotten revenge on the pretentious, highbrow art world that had denied him for many years before.

Among burglars, Henry Edward Vicars was the master artist. Over a period of twenty years following World War I, Vicars committed over one thousand thefts. He worked alone, never associated with other criminals, never used force, never damaged property, and never left a clue to his identity. He also dressed well and was well-mannered. Vicars had all the characteristics of criminal behavior, but while he applied his natural aptitude for burglary, he maintained respect for human life and did not harbor malicious intent. He died as quietly as he lived, while serving a five-year term for his crimes.

Put a crook who works in one of the greatest museums in the world, a con man, and a very talented art forger together and you have the makings of the crime of the century. In 1911, this is exactly what happened. Vincenzo Perruggia, a petty criminal, will go down in the annals of crime history as the greatest thief of all time because he stole the *Mona Lisa*. Oddly though, his motive was simply to humiliate the French, for whom he had a great dislike. His partners, though, wanted to make money. Within days of the theft, Eduardo de Valifierno, the con man, contacted six wealthy American art collectors and offered each the chance to buy the *Mona Lisa*. Each paid the bargain price of $300,000 for what he thought was the original. What each got was a perfect copy painted by Yves Chaudron. Besides proving the impossible could be done, these three also proved that a fool and his money are soon parted. Two years later, for some unknown reason, Perruggia returned the original painting through a third party to the Louvre. Since then, a score of other art swindles have befallen the art world and a number of museums still have fakes on display, but only a few will admit to the existence of these forgeries. The others are too embarrassed.

The Grand Showmen

There are many crooks who just want to make money off other people's stupidity, while others in this category simply want to deceive for the purpose of deceiving. To say that they are master manipulators is a small understatement. These offenders are wonderful at deceiving and controlling people, but mostly, they play on the fact that most people *want* to be tricked or fooled. This is typical human nature and it is why televangelists, quack doctors, faith healers, fortune-tellers, the publishers of supermarket tabloids, and the writers of horoscopes steal millions of dollars from the gullible public every year. As P.T. Barnum said, "There's a sucker born every minute!"

No one proved how right Barnum was better than Victor Lustig did; he spent over twenty years depriving the greedy and gullible of their money. In the 1920s and 1930s, he sold the Eiffel Tower twice to businessmen who believed Lustig's story that the French government wanted to turn the famous landmark into scrap metal. In 1936, his career came to an end when he was jailed for dumping $134 million in counterfeit money onto the American market for gangster Al Capone. It was an ambitious project that spanned almost ten years. Lustig's efforts only failed because 1936 was the year that Frank Wilson, the man who really brought down Capone, became head of the Secret Service and made a major effort to shut down the counterfeiting business. Lustig was an audacious trickster who had ten simple rules, which he called his "Commandments of Con":

1. Be a patient listener.
2. Never look bored.
3. Have the same political views as the victim.
4. Hold the same religious views as the victim.
5. Talk about sex.
6. Avoid the subject of illness.
7. Never pry into the victim's private affairs.

8. Never boast.

9. Never be untidy.

10. Never get drunk.

Spies, from the amateurs to the dedicated government professionals, and traitors are a special class of criminals who have all the characteristics of criminal behavior plus they are under the influence of some mental disorder. The classic case of manipulation, deceit and betrayal motivated by blind devotion to a malicious cause was that of Anthony Blunt, Guy Burgess, Donald Maclean and Kim Philby.

All four were friends and attended Cambridge University together. All four were of British upper-class backgrounds, and they ardently believed in the virtues of Communism. They were also all homosexuals. Two were drunks, and three were so adept at deceit that they maintained convincing lives as married family men. However, besides being members of the Communist party, they were all also members of an exclusive, elitist club called the Apostles.

This club was comprised of people who believed that they were above the normal moral rules of society, and many members were homosexuals. These social and political beliefs gave these four self-righteous men the justification they needed to betray their country, devoid of any guilt, and cause the deaths of hundreds of Western intelligence agents spying on the Soviet Union. From the 1930s to the 1950s, this four-man spy ring was a gold mine of secret information for the KGB.

Despite the open homosexuality of Burgess and the drinking problems of Maclean and Burgess, all four were above suspicion and were able, with each other's help, to obtain important government jobs that gave them access to the most important secrets of the British Intelligence and Defense Services. They also had access to a lot of American secrets that were shared with the British, including the atomic bomb secrets.

In 1951, Burgess and Maclean were under suspicion, and they defected to Moscow together. In 1963, Philby followed them. Blunt was the only one who stayed in England, having retired from government in 1947. He remained above suspicion until 1972, when the government covered up his betrayal in order to avoid scandal. He was allowed to keep his knighthood and was director of a royal art institute. However, his secret became public knowledge in 1979, and he died in disgrace, stripped of his title and honors, in 1983. Burgess died in 1963, Maclean in 1983. Philby died in 1988, just before the fall of the Berlin Wall. Ironically, all of them—including Philby, who was a member of the KGB's inner circle and knew of the impending collapse of the Soviet Union—believed that Communism would bury capitalist democracy. They were so good at deceiving others that they even fooled themselves into believing in a lie that ultimately destroyed their lives.

The Robbers

Except for armed robberies committed by amateur-minded bandits, most robberies of banks and places where jewels and art are stored are relatively nonviolent. Offenders in these situations are after large amounts of money and have little or no intent of taking lives. Many of the thefts are burglaries, a further indication that the offenders want to minimize the risk to themselves and avoid harm to others. Some robbers have even gone to great lengths to dig tunnels into bank vaults or commit commando-like raids with military precision to get a payoff of millions of dollars.

The past forty-five years have seen an amazing number of ingenious multimillion-dollar robberies. The targets have ranged from airline cargo services to museums and banks. The motives have been the usual, ranging from desire for money to financing other crimes to providing a retirement fund for old Nazi war criminals.

In 1950, ex-convict and nightclub owner Joe McGinnis and eleven others pulled off one of the largest robberies in North American history. The Brinks Robbery was the result of months of meticulous planning, including visits to the U.S. Patent Office to study the plans of the safe used by Brinks at its armored car depot in Boston. In seventeen minutes, McGinnis and his team cleaned Brinks out of nearly $3 million, leaving behind almost no clues to their identities. The robbers went undetected until 1955, when one of the crooks felt he had been cheated of his share of the loot. He confessed to the FBI, and the entire gang was arrested. Ironically, the arrests came just a few days before the statute of limitations was to expire. However, the FBI only recovered $60,000 of the stolen money, and the rest has never been traced. During the entire planning and execution of the crime, the intent was simply to overpower the guards and empty the vault. Harming the Brinks' employees was out of the question.

In 1961, Georges Lemay broke the Brinks record when he robbed the Bank of Nova Scotia in Montreal, stealing over $600,000 (some estimate over $4 million), from some 377 safe-deposit boxes. Two years later, the flamboyant playboy was arrested in Florida. However, he escaped and neither Lemay nor the money was ever found.

In England, gangs of professional thieves were called "firms," and they ran their operations with high business standards. On August 7, 1963, two firms joined together in a twenty-four-minute robbery that netted over $10 million. This business merger consisted of Bruce Reynolds, the leader; Buster Edwards, a criminal genius; Gordon Goody, a master planner; Roy James, a race car driver and expert at getaways; Jim Hussey, an amiable guy whose talent was his physical strength; Jimmy White, lock breaker; Charlie Wilson, expert thief; Rodger Cordrey, a train expert; Robert Welch, a jack-of-all-trades criminal; Ronnie Biggs; John Daly, whose job was being Reynolds's good-luck charm; and Thomas Wisbey, the leader of the second firm.

Despite the military precision of the raid, the criminals left behind a ton of clues at their hideout. Within a month, most of the gang was arrested. Only Reynolds, Edwards and White remained on the loose. In 1965, Biggs escaped from prison and is still living in Brazil. Edwards surrendered himself after he and his family grew tired of living in Mexico. White was arrested in 1966, and Charlie Wilson, who escaped from prison in 1964, was arrested along with Reynolds in 1968. The sentences were very stiff, but by the 1970s all were released, having served less than ten years apiece. Of the loot, less than 10 percent was traced, with Biggs living very well in Brazil. Ironically, before this robbery, Biggs was the failure of the bunch, never having much success as a thief. He was the first one arrested after the Great Train Robbery, but he was the only one to elude capture after escaping from jail. He cannot be deported from Brazil because he is the father of a Brazilian child, so even though Scotland Yard knows where he is, it can't touch him. He passes his time as a jazz musician. After their releases, the other career criminals went off in the following directions:

1. Bruce Reynolds, released in 1978, went back to jail in 1984 for selling drugs.

2. Buster Edwards, the genius of the crime, became a flower seller.

3. Gordon Goody was arrested in Spain in 1986 for drug-related charges.

4. Roy James was arrested for fraud, but the case fell through and he is now believed to be living quietly in Spain.

5. Jim Hussey and Thomas Wisbey were sent to jail in 1989 for cocaine trafficking.

6. Jimmy White became a painter and interior decorator.

7. Charlie Wilson moved to Spain and was killed in 1990.

8. Rodger Cordrey went into legitimate business.

9. Robert Welch became a car salesman.

10. John Daly, the good-luck charm, proved to be lucky. But only for himself. He was never convicted for his participation in the theft, and he seems to have dropped out of sight since his release in 1964.

It is doubtful that prison reformed the gang members that went straight, so it appears that their fame as criminals made them think twice before returning to crime. They were the ones with the real brains, and they were smart enough to know that they would always be under a microscope by the police. The rest of the gang, except for Biggs and, it seems, Daly, were too stupid to stay out of trouble.

In 1979, the Great Train Robbery record was broken by an American crew that robbed Lufthansa air cargo of between $10 and $40 million. It is believed that the money was used to finance a drug trafficking operation. About the same time, a group of French mercenaries broke into several French banks by tunneling and used the money to help the Nazi underground organization called the Odessa. The total take is not exactly known because the loot came from safe-deposit boxes. Some estimates say $10 million; others say over $100 million. The motive was political, which just goes to show that not all criminal ventures involve persons with a history of criminal behavior or mental illness. These were professional soldiers and not terrorists.

The Deadly Outlaws

Now we come to the murderous sociopaths of history. All of them came from poverty-ridden backgrounds, but while this was their motive to pursue lives of evil, these criminals were egos out of control who enjoyed killing.

In the late 1800s, the so-called Wild West had its share of outlaws and bandits, such as the Jameses and the Youngers, as well as Billy the Kid. However, the 1930s produced a more violent and evil breed of criminal. Between 1927 and 1935, at the peak of the Prohibition-Depression era, three vicious criminal gangs terrorized the Midwest and parts of the South and Southwest. These were Bonnie and Clyde, John Dillinger and his gang, and Ma Barker and her gang.

Bonnie Parker and Clyde Barrow came from dirt-poor backgrounds, but poverty was not their motive for crime. They just had an intense hatred for authority, and Bonnie was in it for the kicks. Joined by Clyde's brother, Buck, and Buck's wife, Blanche, the Barrow gang raided throughout several southern states until they were killed by authorities, Buck in 1933 and Bonnie and Clyde in 1934. As robbers, they were ne'er-do-wells. The biggest haul they made in the dozen of robberies they committed was fifteen hundred dollars. As murderers, they killed a total of twelve people. For some strange reason, the general public regarded people like this as folk heroes. An explanation for this may be found in the general attitude toward an establishment that had caused the Depression and a host of other social problems. To the public, burdened by poverty, Bonnie and Clyde were the antiestablishment rebels.

John Dillinger was a little more intelligent than his peers. However, he was only smart enough to surround himself with criminals who were smarter than he was. Dillinger became "Public Enemy Number One" because he and his gang robbed over a dozen banks in less than one year throughout the Midwest, Tucson and Florida. In 1934, with a ten thousand dollar reward on his head, Dillinger was gunned down while coming out of a movie theater in Chicago. The death of Dillinger marked the end of an era and the birth of the FBI, which up to then was treated with contempt by other law enforcement agencies.

Ma Barker and her four sons were not a very intelligent bunch, but they were very successful criminal entrepreneurs. They were also vicious killers, killing over ten people. From 1927 to 1935, they raided banks and post offices, hijacked payrolls, and kidnapped wealthy people for ransoms. Their total take was over $3 million. They also died as violently as they lived. One son committed suicide in 1927 rather than go to jail; one was killed trying to escape from prison in 1939; another was killed by his wife in 1949; and the other was killed along with his mother, Ma Barker, by the FBI after a forty-five minute gun battle in Florida.

England has rarely been known for "American-style" violent criminals, but Ronnie and Reggie Kray were the exceptions. From 1954 to 1969, the Krays were the leaders of the most vicious firm in London. As children, they were known as the "Terrible Twins," and while they could be polite and charming, they were constantly in and out of prison for acts of ruthless violence. Ronnie was a classic sociopath, and he idolized Al Capone, another sociopath, calling himself "the Colonel." In 1958, Ronnie was committed to an asylum for mental illness. Ronnie was also a violent homosexual. Both men are known to have killed people just because they wanted to. Their wanton acts of violence caused them to take turns going to prison, but both of them were adept at running their criminal empire so it didn't matter who was in or out. Once Reggie swapped places with Ronnie so that Ronnie could escape, but their mother persuaded Ronnie to turn himself in. It was the only time since being in military prison that the Krays came close to serving time together. In response, a member of another gang got out of line, and Ronnie shot the man between the eyes in front of a crowd of witnesses in a London pub. After Ronnie taunted him over never killing anyone, Reggie stabbed a man to death because the gun he tried to use misfired. No one was prepared to testify against the twins, and because of the fear they generated, the Krays regarded themselves above the law. Their reign of fear and intimidation came to an end in 1968 after sixty-eight policemen raided the Krays' home to serve an arrest warrant based on a two-hundred-page statement about the Terrible Twins' underworld activities. Ronnie and Reggie were brought to trial once before, but the jury was so intimidated, the case was dismissed. This time, though, in the longest and most expensive trial in British history, twenty-eight criminals testified under grants of immunity about the Krays' acts of terror. Even without bodies or any other hard evidence, the twins were each found guilty of double murder and sentenced to life imprisonment, with the minimum sentence being thirty years. In 1999, the twins will be sixty-six years old, but they will likely die in prison before they will ever be granted release.

Ronnie and Reggie were classic examples of *antisocial person-*

ality disorder (APD). But while Ronnie was an extroverted primary psychopath who showed a constant and high level of aggression, Reggie was an introverted secondary psychopath. Ronnie was the dominant partner, but Reggie was the brain and the true business-man of the two. Of the ten factors indicative of APD, the Krays prominently displayed the prerequisite four to be considered se-verely disturbed:

1. Repetitive, easily elicited fighting
2. Problems with holding a job
3. Failure to accept social norms
4. Lack of remorse.

Antisocial personality disorder is the most common disorder seen in career criminals with a history of violence. Personality disorders are chronic, pervasive and inflexible patterns of behavior and think-ing that are very common to the maladaptive minds of the criminal world. These disorders and their symptoms are:

1. Borderline Personality Disorder — At least five of the following factors must be evident since early adulthood (fifteen to eigh-teen years old) for this disorder to be diagnosed:
   - Physically self-damaging behavior
   - Uncontrolled, inappropriate behavior
   - Unstable, intense relationships with people
   - Unstable mood
   - Unstable identity
   - Chronically bored; requires higher levels of stimulation
   - Avoids being alone or feeling alone, will not allow him- or herself to be abandoned by another
   - Unpredictably impulsive regarding sex, drugs or alcohol
2. Paranoid Personality Disorder — At least four of the following factors must be evident since early adulthood:
   - Expects to be harmed or exploited
   - Sees threats everywhere or thinks others regard him or her as inferior
   - Unforgiving, bears grudges
   - Fears confiding in others, thinks information will be used

against him or her
- Easily slighted or angered
- Questions partners about sexual fidelity
- Questions loyalty of others, such as family

3. Schizotypal Personality Disorder—This is similar to schizophrenia. Four of the following factors must be evident:
    - Evidence of odd beliefs separating thinking from reality
    - Ideas of reference
    - High social anxiety
    - Has occasional illusions or odd perceptual experience
    - Peculiar patterns of communication, such as metaphorical, vague or digressive speech
    - Inappropriate or constricted emotional responses
    - Suspiciousness
    - No close friends or confidants other than family
    - Odd or eccentric behavior or appearance

4. Schizoid Personality Disorder—These people are the loners. They are asocial, shy, introverted, and indifferent to emotions or social relationships. At least four factors must be evident:
    - Chooses solitary activities
    - Neither appears to have nor claims to have strong emotions
    - Neither enjoys nor desires close relationships
    - Shows little or no interest in sex
    - Indifferent to praise or criticism
    - No close friends or confidants other than family
    - Shows constricted affection

5. Passive-Aggressive Personality Disorder—With this disorder, people become dependent on partners in relationships, then shows hostility and resistance toward partners. At least five of the following factors must be evident:
    - Dawdling
    - Sulks, is irritable or argumentative when asked to do something he or she doesn't want to do

- Procrastination
- Purposefully inefficient
- Conveniently forgetful
- Unjustifiably protest that others are unreasonably demanding
- Is critical or scornful of authority
- Resents productive suggestions from others
- Believes that he or she is doing a better job than others think he or she is doing

6. Obsessive-Compulsive Personality Disorder — A description of these individuals is workaholics without warmth. Formal perfectionists, they hold work and productivity to be sacred. At least five of the following factors must be evident:

- Puts excessive emphasis on details and lists to the exclusion of an overall perspective
- Perfectionism that interferes with performance
- Constriction of affection and emotion
- Excessive devotion to job and productivity
- Needs to dominate in personal relationships
- Indecisiveness
- Hoards objects, even those with no sentimental value
- Lacks personal generosity unless there is something to be gained
- Overconscientious or inflexible when it comes to matters of ethics or morality

7. Avoidant Personality Disorder — At least four of the following factors must be evident:

- Unwilling to be involved with people unless sure of acceptance
- No confidants or close friends
- Avoids jobs or social activities that are high in social context
- Silent or secretive in social situations
- Embarrasses easily

- Exaggerates dangers of risks and has strong need for a routine
- Has excessive fear and sensitivity to rejection or criticism

8. Dependent Personality Disorder — These people are naive and docile and need to cling to stronger personalities who will make the decisions for them. At least five of the following factors must be evident:
    - Unable to make everyday decisions alone
    - Allows others to make decisions
    - Is overly agreeable
    - Lacks initiative
    - Volunteers in order to gain acceptance or approval
    - Feels uncomfortable or helpless when alone
    - Easily upset or panics over minor losses
    - Is preoccupied with concerns about being abandoned
    - Easily hurt by criticism

9. Narcissistic Personality Disorder — Narcissists have little concern for the welfare of others, but then pretend to care. At least five of the following factors must be evident:
    - Has inflated sense of self-worth with related fantasies
    - Has constant need for attention
    - Becomes emotionally unstable after being criticized or defeated
    - Lacks ability to empathize
    - Assumes others will treat him or her well without the need to reciprocate, feels entitled to "special treatment"
    - Needs to exploit other people
    - Believes his or her own problems are unique
    - Preoccupied with fantasies of unlimited success and power, beauty, brilliance or love
    - Preoccupied with feelings of envy

10. Malignant Narcissist — These are the Hitler, Stalin or Saddam Hussein types. There are four major characteristics:
    - Strongly suspicious, bordering on paranoia

- Extremely inflated sense of self, often grandiose
- Exhibits sadistic cruelty directed toward a "higher goal"
- Absolute lack of remorse

11. Histrionic Personality Disorder—These individuals are fickle and overreactive and tend to be overly dramatic in social situations. At least four of the following factors must be evident:

- Constantly seeks or demands reassurance
- Inappropriately sexually seductive
- Is overly concerned with physical attractiveness
- Expresses emotion with inappropriate exaggeration
- Is uncomfortable when not the center of attention
- Has rapidly shifting and shallow emotions
- Is self-centered and is easily frustrated
- Has a style of speech that is excessively impressionistic and lacks detail

12. Self-Defeating Personality Disorder—These are chronic self-perpetuating victims. At least five of the following factors must be evident:

- Chooses situations and/or people that lead to disappointment, failure or mistreatment, even when better options are evident and available
- Rejects or subverts the efforts of others to help him or her
- Responds to positive personal events with acts of guilt, depression and/or a pain-producing nature, such as having self-induced accidents
- Causes others to reject or become angry at him or her, then feels devastated
- Avoids or rejects opportunities for pleasure or has difficulty accepting personal enjoyment
- Sabotages own plans or activities
- Engages in unsolicited self-sacrifice
- Rejects or is uninterested in people who treat him or her well

13. Sadistic Personality Disorder—These are the ultimate destruc-

tive individuals. This is not to be confused with sexual disorder. Sadists live assertive life-styles with self-righteous manners. They are motivated by power, which is typically displayed in individuals committing acts of spouse or partner abuse and/ or child abuse. At least four of the following factors must be evident:

- Uses violence or cruelty to establish dominance in relationships
- Enjoys demeaning or humiliating people in public
- Enjoys inflicting physical and/or psychological pain on humans or animals
- Disciplines persons under his or her control with excessive force and/or harshness
- Tells lies for the purpose of causing pain and harm
- Uses intimidation, or even terror, to force people to do what he or she wants
- Has little regard for the rights of others and tends to restrict the freedom of those with whom he or she has a close relationship
- Has a fascination with anything involving violence, torture, death and destruction.

WISE GUYS AND HITMEN

They are the octopus whose tentacles reach into every facet of our society. In New York, they get $1.50 for every yard of concete laid and a percentage of the garment industry. They are the American Mafia, the Sicilian Mafia, the Southern La Cosa Nostra, the Russian Mafia, the Corsican League, the international terrorist cartel, the Chinese Triads and the Japanese Yakuza. These make up the face of organized crime in the 1990s. It is multinational and multifaceted, with its money financing everything from cocaine crops in Latin America and opium in Southeast Asia to hotels and restaurants in every major city in the world.

"Wise Guy" Behavior

Contrary to popular belief, organized crime is a relatively new social phenomenon. The two oldest groups are the Sicilian Mafia and the Chinese Triads, whose origins are only one hundred to one hundred fifty years old. The Corsican League, the French version of the Mafia, is the next oldest, and the rest are post-World War II innovations. The Russian Mafia is a Cold War baby born out of the KGB dominance of the black market within the Soviet Union and Soviet bloc. However, it is the mindset of these groups' members and it is the way organized crime was forged by history and social policy of the twentieth century that are of importance to this book.

What we have in these "wise guys" is the antisocial personality disorder described in the profile of the Kray brothers in chapter ten. It should be noted that only 30 percent of all criminals suffer from this disorder. Typically, the average mobster, with the exception of the newer, college-educated members, is of lower-than-average intelligence and is characterized by at least four of the following behavior factors evident since the age of fifteen to eighteen:

1. Problems holding a regular, legal job
2. Constantly and easily provoked into fighting
3. Avoids any form of financial responsibility, spends money like water
4. Inability to plan for future
5. Recklessness
6. Fails to accept social norms
7. Chronically deceptive, has total disregard for truth
8. Demonstrates inability to be a responsible parent
9. Unable to maintain marital fidelity
10. Demonstrates total lack of remorse.

For the most part, all these factors are generally learned behavior, the young offender being motivated by the conduct of the people around him or her. Peer influence and criminal role models are the sources of such motivation. As they grow older, these offenders display the typical narcissistic, amoral and impulsive characteristics of the mobster type we are so familiar with. However, these mobsters exist because the public indirectly condones and supports the activities of organized crime by being voluntary consumers of the illegal goods and services that the mobsters make available. They are businessmen in search of easy money first; they are antisocial personalities second. As mentioned in chapter nine, no one is a born criminal; criminals evolve. No where in the history of humankind has this been more true than with the "evolution" of modern organized crime professionals. The history of organized crime, its development as a unique subculture of our society, tells us how and why mobsters think the way they do. They are a true product of Western social history.

Historical Background for Organized Crime

In Europe and Asia, these mobsters were nothing more than criminal warlords. In America, they took on a new social status. When they came to America in the 1860s, they tried to establish their old ways of extortion within their ethnic communities, calling themselves the "Black Hand," but soon they found that Americans were better sources of revenue. The Black Hand and similar secret societies of criminals were a criminal subculture, and the aim of these criminal brotherhoods was to set up a sort of government of their own on a local level. However, they did not realize that the American government would ultimately play into the hands of organized crime. The American white Anglo-Saxon Protestants, the majority that controlled this country, were the criminals' best customers of prostitution, gambling, drugs and other diversions. The gangs had steadily gained control of these "social leisure services" because there was little or no government regulation. However, from the 1880s to the 1930s, the government steadily became the enemy of the people and America became a criminal's paradise. This is why many mobsters and gangsters became folk heroes.

The federal government made a major mistake when it tried to regulate the public's life-style. For a while, there had been a backlash against the mobs, but then the Feds made drugs illegal, introduced income taxes, and took the country into an unpopular war. When they made alcohol illegal, it was the final straw, and the social order turned inside out. In a sort of coup d'état, the mobs used their organization as minigovernments to usurp control of society. And they did it with almost total public support. Mob law was the law of the land, and when the Depression hit, the criminals were the only ones with steady employment. Organized crime was here to stay.

Prohibition was still in force when the Great Depression hit in 1929. It was not repealed until 1933, but by then, the mobsters had made enough money to become the biggest business and employer in America. In the 1920s, any law-abiding citizen could make a week's wage in less than a day by operating an illegal still. Such activities kept starvation away for many people from 1929 to 1930. The government had failed them, so who else could the public turn to in its time of need but the mobsters?

Because of the poor family backgrounds, it is little wonder that organized crime groups call themselves "families." Prior to World War I, despite their crude feudal system of ethnic loyalty, the criminal gangs that plagued this country were very disorganized. Besides the old style Italian gangs and Sicilian Mafia, the criminal world was dominated by two other ethnic groups, the Irish and the Jews. Born out of the slums and harsh discrimination that Irish Catholic immigrants found here in predominately Protestant America, the Irish came to be a dominant force in both crime and politics from the 1850s on. After the Civil War, large groups of Central European Jews immigrated to America and set up housekeeping with their own brand of criminal business. Their biggest racket was prostitution and exploitation of their own people. By the 1920s, they rivaled the Chinese tongs in the vice trade. The Chinese were very powerful in the crime business, but they were excluded from the mainstream white criminal activities because of their race. In the early days of crime gangs, these groups were not equal opportunity employers. Nonwhites were not welcome. So, while the crime business was dominated by the Jews, Irish and Italians, there was no real organization among their activities. Each city had its own ethnic gangs and these ethnic gangs cooperated with their own kind in other cities, but the different ethnic groups almost never worked together.

What Is Organized Crime?

"Organized crime" does not mean the activities within a gang. It refers to the planned networking and cooperation of the different gangs to work as a business cartel. Originally, the Irish worked with Irish, Jews with other Jews, and Italians ran their own affairs; the idea of everyone working together was "dishonorable" to the Irish and the Italians. However, at the turn of the century, the Italian and Sicilian gangs of the Camorra and the Sicilian Mafia merged. Initially, they were more interested in maintaining their ethnic purity and honor than in making money. But prohibition opened up a gold mine, and the only way it could be exploited was for all the gangs in the different cities to cooperate. The Jewish Purple Gang in Detroit controlled all the smuggling of booze from Canada, so without them, Al Capone and the other Italian gangs were out of business. This cooperation led to mutual assistance in other criminal activities. The only holdouts were the Irish gangs and the old-style mafiosi. During the 1920s however, the Irish gangs lost their power because of this lack of cooperation. As the Italian-Jewish network expanded, the Irish mobsters were gradually killed off, and their activities were absorbed by the new Italian-Jewish syndicate. By 1931, fueled by profits from bootlegging during the 1920s and hoping to take advantage of the economic devastation and political confusion caused by the Depression, Lucky Luciano and Jewish mobster Meyer Lansky organized all the gangs and families into a permanent and more efficient crime syndicate. In an almost bloodless coup, the old-style mafiosi were either killed and replaced or coerced into cooperating with the new order. Murder, Inc., the enforcement arm of the new syndicate, was half Jewish and half Italian. However, it was the Italian "family" structure that was the foundation of future growth. Joe Masseria and Salvatore Maranzano were of the old-style Mafia and were killed because they wouldn't cooperate with Luciano's new order, but they knew that there was strength in unity. Unfortunately, their idea was limited to Italian unity, and so they only formed alliances with Sicilian and Italian gangs. Luciano saw that this limited the overall power base.

Organized crime was born in the devastating poverty of the American slums and its ongoing power base comes from exploiting any new occupants of the slums. The original slums of America were inhabited predominantly by Irish immigrants but not by choice. While it is true that most of the Irish who came here in the 1840s and 1850s were dirt poor, discrimination here in this land of opportunity made their lives just as miserable. However, they soon adapted. They formed gangs to protect their own interests, and, like all residents of the ghettos, they exploited their own people. From profits in crime, they moved into politics. More and more law-abiding Irish, however, took the jobs that nobody really wanted. This is how the Irish came to dominate the police and fire departments in many cities like New York, Boston and Chicago. As the Irish gained in prosperity and upward mobility, they moved out of the slums, leaving the next wave of immigrants to set up housekeeping in the same slums the Irish had left. And for the same reasons the Irish created gangs, so did the Jews and the Italians. When the Jews and Italians moved on, the blacks and Hispanics moved in and picked up on the same criminal activities. Early America was not the land of the free. It was a pesthole of bigotry that condoned, created and exploited poverty. This is the main reason that America has such a major crime problem. It is also one of four reasons why America is the only Western industrialized nation with such a dominant organized crime problem:

1. No one else had Prohibition.

2. No one else had a Great Depression like the U.S. experienced.

3. Others had Hitler, Stalin, and other tyrants in power, but we were stuck with J. Edgar Hoover.

4. No one other industrialized nation has such disgusting, destructive and oppressive slums as America.

In summary, Prohibition made millionaires out of the mobsters. It also forced the ethnic mobs to cooperate, creating a generation of Young Turks ready to take over the jobs and territories of the old mafiosi. The Depression froze everything in place. The mobs had the money to ride out the economic storm, but all the wars and violence of the Prohibition era had taken a toll on the mobs' numbers. The poverty of the Great Depression gave the mobs stability by providing them with fresh blood eager to escape the slums. The reality of our battered economic system is that unless people are talented enough to escape through sports or entertainment or smart enough to gain upward mobility through a good education, they are doomed to pursue the only other avenue of escape: crime.

The other midwife of organized crime in America was J. Edgar Hoover, the tyrannical director of the FBI. Luciano and Lansky had little or no problem expanding their criminal operations because the federal government offered no resistance. Why Hoover and the Feds buried their heads in the ground and even denied the existence of the Mafia and organized crime, no one really knows. Hoover was preoccupied with crushing the menace of Communism, but recent accounts point to the possibility that the mobs knew about Hoover's homosexuality and blackmailed him. This is highly probable, and it just shows how powerful the strength of the new Mafia was. And it still has great power, despite the recent successes by federal prosecutors in sending mob bosses to prison. The reason the power base is still there is because of the "family" structure.

Structure

The Mafia crime families have a special power in their organization that consists of:

1. *The Leader* — This is the boss or godfather or don.

2. *The Underboss* — There are often two; one is called the consigliere or advisor.

3. *The Capos* — These are the middle managers or lieutenants.

4. *The Soldiers* — These are the career criminals who have the opportunity to climb the family career ladder. They are also the lower level of management.

5. *The Non-Made Loyalists* — This group is the source of young talent who take the place of those family members who either move up the career ladder, die or are arrested.

The Jewish mobsters never had such a structure of organization, management and group loyalty. This is why the Jewish mobs that joined the Luciano-Lansky National Syndicate were gradually absorbed by their Italian counterparts and replaced with Italian bosses. Maranzano was right in the lesson of unity he tried to teach, but the only non-Italian student who learned it was Meyer Lansky. When Luciano wanted to abandon the family structure in the 1950s, Lansky pointed out that it was an absolute necessity to keep the status quo that everyone else respected.

This family structure is also a training ground for criminal talent. The best and brightest criminals are even sent to college to learn to be high-tech criminals. In comparison to other ethnic crime groups, except for the Japanese, the Mafia is at least fifty years ahead of everyone else. Their upper and middle management may have taken a major blow and the whole syndicate may be down, but it would be a severe miscalculation to count them out.

The Mafia is a parasitic and exploitive social entity that is very flexible and very good at surviving crises. These abilities are based on what is called a "ladder of troughs." Each management level supports the others in a pyramid fashion, and the wealth flows upward. The boss exploits the underbosses, the underbosses soak the capos, and so on, all so that everyone from the bottom up, can get his or her cut and pay off the boss. In turn, the boss reinvests part of his cut in return for a percentage of his people's action. It is a continuous cycle of deviant profit sharing. The boss finances the operations of his management team in return for 1 percent or more interest per week. The capos then reinvest the money in drugs or loan-sharking for a return of 2 to 3 percent interest per week. The soldiers then make their money by collecting for their superiors the money that is owed plus an additional 5 to 6 percent interest per week that the soldiers are allowed to keep for themselves.

There is no pension plan or golden parachute. The only perks that mafiosi can expect are privilege to operate their respective rackets and the right to be gouged by their superiors. It's the underworld version of the Peter Principle, with the parasites at the bottom hoping that someday they can rise up to a higher level so they can suck a little more blood out of those below them and have a little less drained from them by those on the levels above them. This is why they tolerate being bled for the rest of their lives. Remember, it's nothing personal, it's just business.

In the other groups, except for the Sicilian Mafia, the business structure is very different. The Southern La Cosa Nostra is a loose confederation of crime gangs that are mostly Mafia wanna-bes. The new Russian mafia is a network of old-style black marketeers, ex-Soviet soldiers who have turned mercenaries, and ex-KGB officers who originally helped set up the crime network to profit for themselves while they undermined the West as part of the Communist agenda. Recently, they have taken on some of the structure of the America Mafia. The Chinese Triads are still the feudal secret societies they were over one hundred fifty years ago, but they now control 20 percent or more of the drug trade in Canada and America plus about 15 percent of the illegal sex trade. They are also big in the international arms trade, and they are a major source of the guns that are used in crimes. They are the major reason why any form of gun control is useless.

The International Terrorist Network is the most recent cartel to enter the international organized crime scene. With the New World Order coming about, many terrorists groups have lost their funding sources; so, with the exception of the Islamic groups, these groups have put their talents toward organized crime ventures similar to the old-style Mafia.

The only other exception to this pattern is the Irish Republican Army. The IRA has, for almost fifty years, been financing most of its terrorist activities by operating an organized crime network. IRA members traffic drugs into Holland from America and Columbia.

They rob banks. They operate houses of prostitution. And, last but not least, they operate one of the largest extortion rackets in Europe and North America. The IRA is also a silent partner in the resurgence of Irish gangs in America, particularly in Boston where they have been operating with impunity for over a decade.

Hitmen

The IRA and other terrorist groups are also a source of talent for the current version of Murder, Inc. This is not surprising because there is very little difference between a terrorist and a contract killer. To both, it's a business, but the terrorist has a political agenda.

The original hitman was an unknown shadow figure known as the "Shotgun Man." The Shotgun Man was able to enjoy total immunity because, even though everyone in the Italian community knew who he was, the fear that the Black Hand instilled in the public kept people silent. The Black Hand was a nationwide extortion ring composed of members of the Mafia; the Camorra, a Naples-based criminal society; and the Onorta, a secret society of criminal warlords from Southern Italy. Its members were also freelancers who wanted to capitalize on the Black Hand's reign of terror over the Italian immigrant community. The Black Hand had one rule when it came to its blackmail victims: Pay or die!

It was the Shotgun Man who carried out the necessary killings that kept other possible victims in line. Form 1905 to 1920, almost one thousand people were killed by the Black Hand, and the Shotgun Man accounted for over four hundred in New York and Chicago alone. One time, with his notorious sawed-off shotgun, he killed four men in seventy-two hours, on the same street corner. By the early 1920s, Prohibition put the Black Hand out of business because there was more money and less risk in bootlegging. It is believed that the Shotgun Man retired back to Sicily as a very wealthy man from his murderous enterprise.

The Shotgun Man was the epitome of "murder-for-hire." Criminals have been killing each other and other people for centuries. The reasons have ranged from simple greed to revenge to wanting to prevent a witness from testifying to just for the hell of it. But in the world of organized crime, murder took on a very different motive: It became a business. With cold, ruthless calculation, organized crime soldiers and professional killers have planned and carried out almost countless killings. Many members have been executed with military precision. All have been done either as a matter of policy of mob bosses or for large sums of money. But they were all business.

The murder business has even changed our culture. A whole new set of words are now commonplace in our everyday vocabulary: *hit, rub out, clip, whack, bump off, waste, grease,* and a dozen or more other words that are all synonymous with killing. Of course there is also the word *contract,* which has come to mean murder-for-hire.

During the prohibition years, mobsters just killed people at will, for almost any reason. In the process, a lot of innocent people were killed by stray bullets or bomb explosions. In the 1930s, the Syndicate set forth the "contract policy." This was and still is a ritualistic system of rules devised to control the mayhem that occurred on an almost daily basis during the 1920s. Contrary to popular belief, no one from outside the Syndicate can hire a contract killer from within the Syndicate. Called "enforcers," these soldiers are solely at the disposal of the bosses, who are the only people that can order contracts. A victim of a contract hit is usually someone within the Syndicate, a rival criminal, or someone who is a client of an organized crime family, such as a loan-shark victim, gambler or drug user. These contracts were strictly for mob businessmen to take care of mob business by using mob talent to handle problems requiring executive action.

Murder, Inc.

It may not seem logical that murder could be a "business," but in part, the term *soldiers* best explains why this cold-blooded mentality exists. To the mob bosses, the victim of a contract is *the enemy,* some "bum" who wouldn't pay his debts and had to be made an example of or someone who cheated the mob or an informer or a fellow mob leader who got out of line or rival mobsters involved in a "war." The reduction of victims to some subhuman level gives the soldiers, these sadistic personalities, justification and rationalization to kill the people that the bosses have decreed deserve to die.

Following in the bloody footsteps of the Shotgun Man, mob assassinations were carried out by people like Albert Anselmi and John Scalise, also known as the "Mutt and Jeff of Murder." From 1921 to 1929, these two were the master "mechanics," the leading innovators in the art of murder-for-hire and the highest paid assassins of the Prohibition era. Anselmi and Scalise introduced the use of garlic-coated bullets, which would induce gangrene if the bullets didn't kill the victims, and the technique of the handshake hit, in which the victim's hand was held fast while the assassin's partner dispatched the victim with a bullet in the head. Because they were considered artists by their employers, Anselmi and Scalise often received fees ranging from $10,000 to $14,000. Prior to this, anyone had been able to hire a killer for as low as $2 and as high as $100. However, like most mercenaries, they were only loyal to whoever paid them.

When the Genna family wanted Al Capone hit, Anselmi and Scalise decided this was bad for their business and sold their services to Capone. Capone then used the pair to organize the St. Valentine's Day Massacre. Mutt and Jeff were arrested, but they would never get to trial. Shortly after committing the biggest gangland execution in history, the two super executioners were themselves executed by Al Capone for betraying him to the boss of the Mafia, Joe Aiello. Even if Capone had not beaten the two to death with a baseball bat, it is doubtful that these two wise guys would ever have been convicted. They had already been arrested dozens of times and had always beat the rap. Once they claimed self-defense in the murder of two policemen, and the jury accepted their story of being innocent victims of police brutality. They were acquitted. But Big Al found them guilty of being rats and exterminated them.

Four years later, when Luciano set up the Syndicate, he and his partners realized that the necessity of having a private army of assassins at their disposal that would enforce mob policy. So, in the typical businesslike attitude of organized crime, a special troop of killers was set up to be available to all the crime groups all over the country. This new business was dubbed Murder, Inc. Albert Anastasia was the troop's Lord High Executioner. This business even had its own corporate headquarters at an all-night candy store/malt shop called Midnight Rose's.

During the next decade, these Jewish and Italian killers engaged in the execution of three hundred to five hundred victims according to a very simple set of rules set up by Lucky Luciano and company. Under the rules, the Murder, Inc., soldiers only accepted contracts that had the full approval of the Syndicate's ruling circle. Once a contract was issued, the killer, who was always from out of town, would go to the victim's city or town, kill this total stranger and then disappear, leaving the police with no suspects, clues or motives. Suspicions were available by the truckload, but there was no proof. When total strangers kill other strangers, there is little or nothing to base an investigation on.

Also under the rules, no one could obtain or implement contracts against politicians, prosecutors or reporters. It was wisely believed by the bosses that the execution of such innocents would arouse public anger and force authorities to turn up the heat on mob business, which was, of course, bad for business. Killing the good guys, the bosses felt, would undermine the established system of bribed politicians, judges and police, which is the oil that kept the crime machine running smoothly. The mob has been adamant about these rules, so this policy puts a damper on any theory of a mob connection with the Kennedy assassination. A hit of that magnitude would have required a vote of all the families, and since this would never have been approved, no one would have risked the mob's total annihilation by carring out such an insane plan. Such theories also do not fit the psychology of mobsters.

This murder machine ran until 1940, when Abe Reles, one of Anastasia's lieutenants, was arrested. Facing the possibility of execution, Reles decided to sing. However, after Reles's confession sent seven of the top hierarchy to the electric chair, Reles "fell" out of a hotel window while in protective custody. Murder, Inc. was put out of business only briefly. Within a short while, a new Murder, Inc. was organized, and in 1957, the Lord High Executioner himself, Anastasia, was permanently retired when he was shot to death in a barber's chair.

Typically, the average mob murder victim was simply shot, stabbed or shot and stabbed. However, when the mob wanted to "waste" an informer or other mobsters who stole from the bosses or loan-shark victims who were slow to pay their debts, death came slowly and painfully in a manner called "buckwheats." In the classic psychopathic style of the mob, some victims would be ice picked, shot in extremely painful places and then buried alive. One woman victim was stabbed, her throat was slashed, and she was burned. She was also beaten with a rolling pin, a flatiron and a blackjack. Another victim, Albert Agueci, was found tied up with wire, strangled with clothesline, soaked with gasoline and set on fire. But prior to his death, Albert's killers carved thirty pounds of flesh off his body.

Also, a typical mob method of advertising that no one should cross its members was to cut off a victim's genitals, shove them down his throat and then shoot him.

The Modern Mobster

Today's wise guys are better educated and more businesslike than their predecessors. But they are still vicious sociopaths, even though many are ratting out their leaders. This is contrary to the antisocial personality disorder profile and defines a pattern of increased narcissistic behavior. With this new personality wrinkle developing in mobsters, we are witnessing the evolution of a new, more sophisticated and more dangerous organized crime professional, and the course that society takes will determine the future of society's relationship with the criminal subculture of organized crime. An example would be if drugs were legalized. With a loss of a major source of revenue and the social umbilical cord cut, mobsters would find that the only way to do business would be to alter their personalities to be more socially acceptable. This would lead to the subculture's merger into the mainstream of our society. La Cosa Nostra on the Fortune 500 list is interesting food for thought.

DRUG ABUSE

As a mental illness category, substance abuse is the largest cause of crime and the most pervasive and predominant influence on criminal behavior. Every day, we see in the newspapers and on television or hear the radio of tragic crimes committed by offenders under the influence of drugs and/or alcohol. We also see or hear news of countless other traumas caused by substance abuse. These are the suicides, parasuicides, accidents and acts of just plain stupidity. It took over fifteen years of war in Vietnam to kill as many people as those who die every year as the result of drunk-driving incidents alone.

Add substance abuse to an existing personality disorder, psychosis or neurosis and you have the makings of a walking time bomb. While a lot of people like to use Charles Manson and his "family" as the classic example of drug-fueled homicide, it is a mistake to blame drugs and alcohol alone. The drugs only helped them commit their crimes with greater brutality. They would have committed the same crimes whether high or sober.

There is nothing new about the relationship of drugs and crime. In chapter one, we discussed the history of the Assassins, whose name originated in the word *hashish*. But the current drug problem has a more recent foundation. In 1803, morphine was invented from the refinement of opium, but it did not become popular for doctors to use until the 1820s. By the 1850s, morphine was the drug of choice, so when the Civil War broke out, the opportunity for better pain management was available, as was the danger of creating a population of drug addicts that exceeded 400,000.

Prior to morphine, laudanum was the most popular concoction for pain relief and cough suppression. This potent combination of opium and alcohol was even used as a sedative and tranquilizer. It could be bought for pennies a bottle and was given in large doses during the Mexican War and Civil War.

In 1874, Bayer Pharmaceuticals invented heroin. In the 1890s, it was sold in forms and quantities that made it as easy to obtain and use as aspirin is today. By 1910, it was estimated that there were over 500,000 new addicts as the result of this "miracle pain reliever." World War I and Prohibition increased the hard-core drug addict population in America to four million. Prior to that, America was a "drugged culture" that condoned the use of narcotics for almost any reason.

Cocaine was invented in its refined form in 1850, and by 1890, it was being used as the primary ingredient in hundreds of elixirs and potions. In Europe, from England to Russia, a concoction of wine and cocaine was the most popular drink. Sigmund Freud even advocated its use, saying he saw no evidence of addiction. It was also the most widely used stimulant known, and it was much abused by doctors. They used it for treating mental illness, alcoholism and morphine addiction. Doctors also used it themselves, and in turn many doctors in Europe and America were addicts. The most famous use of cocaine was in the 1886 introduction of the soft drink, Coca-Cola. This was the cause of the first cocaine epidemic until cocaine was banned as a food and drug additive in 1906. In 1914, drug control laws came into existence, and taxation and prohibition came in 1924. After these events, the popularity of hard drugs dropped off until a resurgence of use came in the 1960s.

America is a drug-addicted culture, not only because of its history of legalized drug abuse and liberal acceptance of alcohol, but for two other important reasons. First, despite its Puritan heritage and Victorian prudery, America is a free and generally permissive society. Second, America is an impatient society that is inundated with numerous ads and media pressures that advocate taking a drink or a pill to solve our problems, any problem, quickly. This attitude is also reinforced by physicians who are quick to medicate for any reason. This was the problem that created so many addicts during and after the Civil War and has created hundreds of thousands of prescription drug addicts now. Complain of pain, and many doctors will medicate you instead of trying to find and treat the cause of the pain. Since 1863, when doctors and nurses kept their patients quiet with morphine, things haven't changed much, except for the variety of drugs that are now available.

Alcohol Abuse

Alcohol abuse may be declining, but the statistics speak for themselves:

- There are 100,000 alcohol-related deaths per year as of 1990, and the number is rising
- Annually, there is $12 billion in lost productivity costs, costs to the criminal justice system, health care costs and other social costs annually
- One in eight people is an alcoholic or has had trouble with alcohol
- Long-term alcohol abuse causes severe degeneration of the brain and central nervous system
- Alcohol is a factor in over half of all suicides, homicides, domestic violence, rapes, and other acts of intentional trauma
- There are twenty-five to thirty million people who are children of alcoholics
- There are six million children of alcoholics under eighteen years old who have an extremely high risk of becoming alcoholics themselves or suffering some major mental illness
- About 100,000 children, ages ten to twelve, regularly abuse alcohol.

Contrary to popular belief, alcohol is not a stimulant. It is a depressant that first reduces inhibitions of the higher brain functions, which in turn causes a rush-like sensation. This is where the misconception about alcohol being a stimulant comes from. After the inhibitions are broken down, the depression of the lower brain functions sets in. The legal definition of drunkenness is .10 percent blood alcohol. Blood alcohol level and behavior are related as follows:

- From .03 to .05 percent, inhibitions are broken down

- At .10 percent, behavior can become reckless. However, people with low tolerance for alcohol can experience the same behavior changes at lower levels

- At .20 percent, physical coordination and function becomes severely impaired and behavior become uncontrollable

- At .25 percent, a person is "falling down drunk."

Women and Alcohol

A 1990 study of women and alcohol shows that women have a lower tolerance for alcohol than men do because of a stomach protective enzyme that breaks down alcohol. Men produce 30 percent more of this enzyme than women, so this means women absorb one-third more alcohol directly into their blood systems, and women who do not have a history of alcoholism are still at risk of severe physical and mental impairment, as well as severe liver damage. Women with a history of alcoholism do not produce this enzyme at all and, therefore, generally experience major damage to the brain, central nervous system, liver and stomach. The behavior of women with low or zero levels of this enzyme, called alcohol dehydrogenase, can be so severely impaired to the point of experiencing alcohol-induced psychosis. It is also is not uncommon for alcohol to cause or aggravate personality disorders, which explains why women commit more crimes under the influence of alcohol. Women are also more prone to sleep disorders and volatile temper and mood swings.

Stages of Alcohol Dependence

Alcoholism develops in the following stages:

1. *Prealcoholism*—Alcoholics begin with social drinking and weekend drinking, with slow, gradual increase in alcohol tolerance and drinking frequency. Drinking is used as an escape from anxiety, mild depression and boredom.

2. *Initial alcoholism*—Increased depression is accompanied by loss of self-esteem over inability to control drinking. Drinking

pattern is marked by increased tolerance and frequency of use and gradual shift toward solitary abuse of alcohol. Blackouts and memory impairment are common.

3. *Chronic alcoholism* — Total loss of control is manifested. Alcohol impairs nutrition, which in turn affects mental and physical health. Symptoms include impaired thinking, hallucinations, paranoid behavior and central nervous system dysfunction, such as tremors and seizures.

Polydrug Abuse

Take alcohol and prescription and/or street drug abuse, mix them together in one person and you have a psychotic who has not lost touch with reality. However, his or her behavior at work or school and personal relationships have deteriorated to the point of almost total dysfunction. Motivation is also severely impaired. Polydrug abusers are masters of manipulative deceit.

Prescription Drug Abuse

Heavy use of legally available substances has been a facet of our culture since the American Revolution. There has not been a time that a large portion of the American public has not been physically and psychologically dependent on some form of narcotic or narcotic/alcohol mixture or other pharmaceutical. First there was opium and laudanum, then there was morphine, then heroin, then barbiturates like Verinol (a nerve tonic/sleep aid introduced in 1903). In 1914, the Harrison Drug Act made the majority of these drugs illegal unless obtained by prescription. In 1970, the Controlled Substances Act put further prohibitions on these drugs, but it seems that the more something is forbidden by the government, the more it is desired by the public.

Despite the restrictions and controls placed on medications, Americans continue to overuse drugs. Minor tranquilizers, now called antianxiety drugs, such as Valium, Xanax, Librax and Tranxene, are among the most commonly prescibed drugs in the United States. Generally, the assumption had been that these drugs were not addictive, but the Betty Ford Clinics have proven that notion to be a myth. However, thousands of doctors, with no credentials in diagnosing and treating psychiatric disorders, continue to create more addicts with the millions of prescriptions that are issued regularly. Barbiturates, such as phenobarbital and Seconal, are also heavily abused. Not only are they prescribed too often for legal consumption, but they are also popular among heroin and cocaine abusers. Barbiturates are strongly physiologically addictive and are the common cause of many accidental deaths and suicides. Psychotic behavior is common. Another widely abused group of drugs, which were made popular by the weight-loss craze, are amphetamines. Invented in 1887, these drugs did not enter into the mainstream of abuse until Benzedrine inhalers were introduced in 1931 to treat nasal congestion. During World War II, amphetamines were used to keep soldiers awake on the front lines and to treat fatigue and shock, sometimes with fatal and disasterous consequences. Chronic use often causes psychotic and paranoid behavior, which may be acceptable in Japanese kamikaze pilots, who were given large doses before completing their missions, but this behavior is totally unacceptable in combat troops, who were given regular doses as a matter of policy.

Nonprescription Drug Abuse

Much has been said about cocaine, but few know that while it was popular with the Incas over five hundred years ago, cocaine didn't become a drug of popular social abuse until the 1860s. Up until 1914, pure cocaine was readily available. What passes for "coke" these days is only 85 percent pure before it is cut for street distribution. However, crack cocaine can sometimes be 90 percent pure, though generally, it is about 60 percent pure. Cocaine is highly addictive in any form, and prolonged abuse causes nervousness, delirium, impotence, malnutrition, anemia, extreme paranoia and depression. Toxic psychosis is also common, but besides the psychological problems, there are numerous physical dangers, such as liver damage, heart damage, stroke, seizures and death, as in the tragic case of the young actor River Phoenix, who also ingested heroin and tranquilizers.

Opium, known as the "plant of joy" to the Stone Age peoples of Asia Minor and the ancient Sumerians, has been a part of human culture for over six thousand years. Besides its use to ease pain, physicians once used it to treat epilepsy, snake bite, depression, and a host of other ailments. It was also widely abused in a variety of leisure fashions. The invention of morphine made opiate use more popular. The invention of heroin in 1874 and the invention of the hypodermic needle around 1870 opened the door for the current addiction problem our society faces today. Since opiates are highly addictive, both physically and mentally, the crime cycle that is inherent with addiction to them is actually caused by the withdrawal symptoms and the fear of these horrible symptoms, rather than the drugs themselves. The drug causes a feeling of great euphoria, but once addicted, the addict must keep a certain blood-serum level or he or she will start to experience traumatic withdrawal symptoms. To avoid this pain of nausea, vomiting, tremors, cramps, convulsions, sweating, diarrhea, shortness of breath, and sometimes heart problems that can be fatal, an addict will do anything to get more drugs. This includes robbery, burglary, even murder. Once the drug of choice among the lower and lower-middle classes, heroin has now gained a lot of popularity with the middle and upper classes.

LSD and PCP Abuse

LSD and PCP are two of the most dangerous behavior-altering drugs in existence. LSD is a hallucinogenic drug that was developed in 1938 by a Swiss chemist. It is an extract from the rye fungus called ergot. At one point, the Nazis thought about using it as a chemical warfare weapon, but since the German general staff had a fear of such weapons, stemming from the horrors of World War I, none of the chemical weapons Germany developed were used. However, the victors of World War II had no such moral convictions. After the war, the CIA and KGB, as well as agencies of other governments, carried out extensive secret testing on numerous human victims to find out LSD's usefulness as a brainwashing agent and chemical weapon. In 1954, author Aldous Huxley advocated that the public try the psychedelic experience. Later, in the 1960s, researchers, such as Dr. Timothy Leary, promoted LSD as the key to religious experiences. The drug counterculture eagerly embraced it. However, instead of discovering Heaven, the people who used this drug discovered Hell.

LSD is very quick acting. It is also very potent, and as little as four-millionths of a gram can cause the brain to distort time and other sensory perceptions. LSD will unlock the user's deeply repressed memories, fears and anxieties; cause a severe lack of coordination; and cause severe nausea, vomiting, convulsions, panic attacks and psychotic episodes. The long term danger of LSD is the "flashback syndrome," which can cause the victims to suffer the same usage symptoms at any time in their lives without taking the drug again.

PCP was developed as an animal tranquilizer in 1965. Later, it was discovered to be too dangerous, so it somehow graduated into a popular street drug. When used, this overpowering psychoactive drug affects the entire brain, acting as a depressant, a stimulant, an anesthetic and a hallucinogen all at the same time. The effects are extremely dangerous and unpredictable, causing slurred speech, convulsions, coma, panic attacks, psychotic reactions, flashbacks, and heart and lung failure. Despite these dangers, people still snort, sniff, smoke, eat and inject PCP because they think it will be fun.

Recently, a derivative of PCP called ketamine hydrochloride, has made its debut as a street drug. It is a powerful anesthetic that was introduced during the Vietnam War and is also used as an animal tranquilizer and anesthetic. It is now not only abused for leisure purposes, it is also used to commit crimes. Since 1986, prostitutes have used it to knock out victims they intend to rob, and rapists have found it useful for doping victims to avoid using force. Not only is the victim rendered unconscious and vulnerable to attack, the drug also impairs the victim's memory, and he or she usually comes to consciousness unaware of having been victimized.

Motivation for Drug Abuse

It is one thing to explain the cultural factors behind drug abuse and another to descibe the ways that drugs alter behavior, but neither of these explains why people abuse drugs even when the abusers are fully aware of the dangers.

The explanation may be found in the root of drug abuse: poverty. In any society burdened by the pain of major social problems, people are naturally going to desire some sort of escape from that pain. This is bound to lead to widespread addiction, especially among the poor but also among any of the middle and upper classes of people who condone the use of drugs.

When most of the addictive drugs were developed, it wasn't the criminals who created the markets of abuse. It was the governments and private businesses who were motivated by easy profits that sanctioned the mass distribution of such drugs, and it was the cultivation of an almost endless consumer market. This is what happened when the British started exporting opium to China. It had been popular in India, where it was abused on a large scale by the poor of that British colony. Consequently, a market among the poor of China was created by making them addicts. By 1830, the traditionally isolationist Chinese were hooked on it and began importing it in bulk.

When the Chinese government tried to stop the British export of opium in 1838, the British merchants and government retaliated by declaring war. By 1842, the British won the "Opium War," the Chinese were forced to pay $21 million as "war reparations," and China was doomed to become an impoverished nation of addicts. By 1914, over one-half of the Chinese population was addicted to opium.

When the Chinese tongs took up residence in Europe and the United States, they took to supplying opium to the "white devils" that had poisoned their country. It was the Chinese who set up the link between prostitution and drug addiction by setting up opium dens in every city and exploiting the white women who came there looking for cheap thrills. These women were casually addicted to heroin and/or opium, and when they wanted more, they had to earn it by becoming prostitutes. In 1930, there were over one hundred such places operating in Washington, D.C., and Baltimore alone. However, when the Chinese were forced out of this business by government pressure, the new Luciano/Lansky Syndicate took over, with the Chinese helping to supply the drugs.

By 1935, the Mob was running its own narcotics operation, and today the Chinese control only 20 percent of the heroin trade. The Sicilian and American Mafias control 60 percent and the rest is managed by the other organized crime groups.

In 1914, out of the entire U.S. population, one out of four hundred persons was an addict. By 1990, the addict population was one out of one hundred. The narcotics trade has gone from a multi-billion-dollar legal trade controlled by the pharmaceutical industry to a mega-multibillion-dollar racket run by a bunch of murderers who don't care if the product they sell kills its users.

T H I R T E E N

TERRORISTS

Terrorists are often misrepresented by gross stereotypes and major misconceptions. Not all terrorists are ignorant, unintelligent, foaming-at-the-mouth Arabs. Of all the different types of criminals, terrorists are the most cunning. In essence, terrorists are the ultimate predator, the great white shark of criminals.

Contrary to popular belief, terrorism did not begin in 1964 with the founding of the Palestine Liberation Organization. The earliest foundations are those established by Hasan and his Order of the Assassins who were covered in chapter one, but to understand the origins of modern terrorism, we have to go back 190 years to the Napoleonic Wars, when the French Army occupied Spain. The Spanish employed terrorist tactics, and from this point on, all national liberation movements would follow this illustrious example.

This was also the first time a doctrine of cooperation was established during a joint campaign involving an organized group of irregular resistance fighters and a regular army. It was used again during the American Civil War and found new life during World War II.

In between those two wars, the first real "armies of liberation and resistance" were organized by the American Indians. In fact, the fathers of modern terrorism were Commanche Chief Quanna Parker, Lakota War Chief Crazy Horse, and the Apache leaders Geronimo and Cochise. These great warriors organized one of the first campaigns of nationalist/ethnic liberation against an oppressive colonialist/imperialist government, which was the American government of 1866 to 1908. Other anticolonial liberation wars that followed, beginning in 1946, employed this pattern set by Native Americans.

Modern European and South American terrorism has its roots in the Nationalist and early proto-Communist agendas of the early nineteenth century, such as the Irish Fenian movement, the Italian Risorgimento movement; the Young Germany and Yound Poland movements; the Latin American Wars of Liberation of 1810 to 1817; and the Mexican Revolutions of 1812 and 1864. The First and Second Boer Wars in what is now South Africa are the only original standouts of nationalist movements. The Soviets of Lenin and Stalin and their successors did not invent terrorism; they only refined the activities of old political criminal groups.

The Boer Wars marked the third time Europeans fought Europeans using tactics of irregular warfare. There was no real Boer army, just organized bands of Boer farmers who conducted highly efficient raids, with large scale battles in between. These wars saw the invention of several acts of criminal conduct that Western governments are now so familiar with. The Boers introduced the "terrorist bombing," the "hijacking" and the "commando raid." The British introduced "counterterrorism," "pacification" and the "concentration camp," which caused the deaths of twenty thousand Boer women and children. The Nazis only copied the British in both motive and operation. The only refinement the Nazis made was the addition of death camps, which were different from the concentration camps established in the 1930s to detain political prisoners.

What Is Terrorism?

There is no one definition of *terrorism*. A study of references on the subject written in the past sixty years will give you over two hundred definitions. However, there are only five major terms regarding *unconventional warfare* that are appropriate. These are:

1. Guerrilla warfare
2. Resistance/commando warfare
3. Low-intensity warfare
4. Insurgency warfare
5. Special operations warfare.

In 1980, the U.S. State Department adopted a "description" of what terrorism is composed of, but it was not a definition:

> *Terrorism* is the threat or use of violence for political purposes by individuals or groups, whether acting for or in opposition to established governmental authority, when such actions are intended to shock, stun, or intimidate a target group wider than the immediate victims. Terrorism has involved groups seeking to overthrow specific regimes, to rectify perceived national or group grievances, or to undermine international political order as an end in itself.

In 1987, the U.S. State Department published a more specific definition:

> Terrorism—premeditated, *politically* motivated violence perpetrated against noncombatant targets by subnational groups or clandestine state agents, usually intended to influence an audience. "International terrorism" is terrorism involving the citizens or territory of more than one state.

Since the key words in both statements are "political" and "audience," or "target group," in essence, terrorism can be defined as "political theater." It is the only type of crime and class of acts of human destructiveness that is so premeditated that there are a script, actors, a stage and an audience. Why do you think it was so easy to do a made-for-TV movie about the hijacking of the ocean liner *Achille Lauro* and the bombing of the World Trade Center? The terrorists already wrote the script, and the media gave these killers what every terrorist hopes for: *mass publicity*. Madison Avenue ad agencies would kill to get ratings like those that terrorists get. Ironically, the strategy that terrorists use to spread their messages is identical to those used to promote Nike shoes, Hanes underwear, and Coca-Cola. There is no difference between the communications concepts, except that people get killed when terrorists advertise.

Still, there is no consensus on a real definition of what terrorism is. Politicians have their own definition, journalists have theirs, academians have theirs, and psychiatric professionals have theirs. The public's definition depends on which side they support. It has often been said in the Middle East that a "terrorist is one person's hero and another's criminal." At one time, a majority of the Israeli government was wanted for acts of terrorism against the British, when Great Britain governed Palestine. This included Prime Ministers Begin and Shamir. Begin was the one who helped blow up the King David Hotel, killing a bunch of innocent British tourists. However, he condemned the Palestinians for similar actions. The former terrorist Shamir is now the peacemaker who has embraced his enemy Yassir Arafat, who is now the terrorist turned politican/peacemaker. So, as you can see, the business of terrorism is not just political theater, it is a political soap opera that can border on the absurd.

For our purposes in this chapter, we will use the following as a working definition: Terrorism — all acts of politically or religiously motivated violence intended to change, through fear and intimidation, public and/or government policy and which are justified to the perpetrators and are heinous crimes to the targets and victims.

This just about covers all types of terrorism from pro-life zealots who shoot doctors and burn clinics to Islamic fanatics to the IRA to the KKK and neo-Nazi Skinheads to the acts of our own government in retaliatory response to acts of terrorism by foreign groups or governments. All terrorists consider themselves soldiers. George Washington and his officers were patriots to the residents of the American colonies, but they were terrorists to the British, especially our guerrilla fighters like Ethan Allen and Francis Marion, the Carolina Swamp Fox. In a way, Begin and Arafat are George Washington to their people, but until a month ago, they were bitter enemies to each other. All violent religious militants, such as the Hezbollah (Party of God/Islamic Jihad), consider themselves to be "soldiers of God," though it is doubtful that God condones this behavior.

The Elements of Terrorism

Is terrorism a *crime*, an *act of war*, or an *act of political necessity*? Since there is no way to realistically define or classify terrorism, it is best to identify terrorism as a special classification of human destructiveness delineated by its three main categories:

1. Goals
2. Strategies/objectives
3. Operations/organizations

All these characteristics make terrorism a special type of intentional trauma. Terrorism is the use of criminal actions as weapons and tactics of war, which makes terrorism different from other criminal activities. The crimes that are committed are part of the overall operations. Terrorism is an act of war, even though there is no apparent "war" being waged. And it is definitely an act of political necessity. So, simply put, terrorism is a highly premeditated act of intentional trauma.

Goals. Regardless of the motives, either social or religious, the goals of all terrorism are *political*. This sets the terrorist apart from the criminals and mentally ill to which the terrorist is often mistakenly compared. In the minds of the terrorists, they see themselves as victims who must right great social or economic wrongs, for which the ruling authorities are to blame. Terrorists see that only violence, as a tactic of last resort, will make target governments accede to righting the alleged wrong. For terrorists, their goals are the moral imperatives that justify the use of any means to attain these goals. However, it is important to note that terrorist acts are not justified by the doctrines that most terrorist groups subscribe to. All Muslims are prohibited from committing suicide; so, the suicide bombings that Shiite terrorists have committed are in direct violation of their fundamentalist Islamic beliefs — the same beliefs for which the Shiites are waging this "holy war against Western evil."

Strategies/objectives. The objective is simple; it is to terrorize the enemy government and intimidate the public. Unlike conventional warfare, there is no intent to destroy the enemy, only to use the fear and public dissatisfaction created by terrorist violence as leverage to obtain the mandated political goals. Thus, the strategy and the tactics are the use of fear and publicity for maximum psychological effect.

In most cases, the fear experienced by the public is greatly unjustified and exaggerated. However, the threat that exists is overpowering, as exemplified by the hundreds of thousands of American tourists who were afraid to travel to Europe in 1985 and 1986. This fear is instilled in the public by both the terrorists' acts and the publicity that the news media is manipulated into giving. This is the heart of "terrorist theater."

No other weapons better serve the terrorist's cause than the reporter, the microphone and video camera. All victims, all target locations, and the timing of violent acts are chosen in the same manner as an ad agency advertises a client product. The World Trade Center bombing and the subsequent TV movie had the highest global ratings of any media event in 1993.

Crucial to all terrorist operations is the component of the premeditated use of the threat of violence. Terrorist activity is composed of crimes — murder, assault, hijacking, kidnapping, arson, sabotage and other heinous acts — and are not legitimate acts of war, but we are not talking about conventional warfare. This is "unconventional" warfare that pits irregular troops against innocent civilians and the military and law enforcement agencies employed by the target government.

As a matter of operational organization, terrorist groups are paramilitary criminal gangs. In peacetime, there is no justification for terrorist acts. However, in wartime, as in the case of the Vietnam War, both sides employed terrorist tactics as part of their military operations. As Viet Cong irregulars carried out murder and sabotage, so did the American Special Forces as part of their antiterrorist campaign. This is what Operation Phoenix was all about. The only difference between us and them was the level of brutality and the constant use of mass murder that the Viet Cong embraced.

Operations/organizations. Terrorists always work in predatory groups. Some individuals have acted alone in terrorist acts, but this is rare. Like organized crime groups, terrorists are a subcultural element. Members derive self-esteem from the group and not the cause. Thus, peer approval becomes the primary motivation for the individual to commit crimes, and the goals of the group take a backseat. They operate either in small groups or in small units directed by the central organization, such as the PLO or IRA, that are organized into brigades that are subdivided into cells. There is also no allegiance to any particular country. Terrorists are not only a subculture, they are a subnational element within a country. As in the case of the Tupamaros of South America or the Italian Red Brigade, terrorists are a cancer that grows with the body of a nation, with the exception of state-sponsored terrorism, such as in Libya, Iran and

Iraq. All terrorist groups need sponsors, hosts or a parental relationship with a country or a larger group in order to operate and survive.

The Mind of the Terrorist

As stated earlier, terrorists are neither insane nor morally depraved. These gross misconceptions and stereotypes are a way of "dehumanizing the enemy." This is a typical defense mechanism that helps people cope with terrorist violence. It also helps the public avoid facing the real issues that drove these people to commit terrorism. In other words, as long as you think the enemy is a rabid dog, it's easier to kill it instead of trying to make peace with it.

It is very easy to slap on the labels of "antisocial," "psychopath" or "evil entity," but these overly simplistic descriptions of terrorist behavior ignore the political, economic and social environment factors that contribute to the creation of the individual psychopathology of the terrorist. Like all intentional trauma, terrorism is a matter of medical ecology. Terrorists are a product of their own individual psychologies interacting with their environments. However, they are not victims of society, unless they are fighting to overthrow a tyrannical dictatorship or military junta, as was the case with Fidel Castro and his campaign to overthrow the government of Cuba's Batista in 1958, or in a war of liberation, as in the case of the Algerian FLN. In the case of any brutalized, impoverished populace, the use of terrorism to gain freedom is perfectly acceptable. To the British, the Boston Tea Party was a terrorist act; to the American colonies, it was an act of liberation from despots. As you can see, how the behavior of those who commit acts of unconventional warfare is viewed depends upon whose side you support.

The Typical Terrorist Profile

1. Most terrorists are male, but there is a large proportion of females in their ranks, and the women are often more cunning and deadly than their male counterparts.
2. Terrorists usually begin their careers around age twenty to twenty-five.
3. Terrorists are generally single and come from middle- or upper-class families.
4. The average terrorist has a college education and has a history

of being a campus radical or of being involved in student protest movements. Many are college dropouts, which demonstrates their dissatisfaction with society. College campuses are where many terrorists begin their careers by joining or being recruited by terrorists groups. Some groups have started as college protest groups.

There is no terrorist personality type, but there are certain traits that are common to those prone to political violence:

1. Low self-esteem among follower types, not among the leaders
2. A desire to take high risks
3. Feelings of not being able to control one's life
4. Places unrealistic demands upon self
5. Tends to raise expectations, rather than lower them when confronted with failure
6. Unable to cope with rejection or failure
7. Feels life is controlled by external forces
8. Externalizes bitterness over failure and desires to take wrath out on "the enemy" that is allegedly responsible for the problems in the terrorist's life
9. Deep feelings of weakness, self-denigration and self-hatred, which they project onto the society being attacked
10. Single minded; has same organized hunter/killer traits as most serial killers, especially mission-oriented killers
11. Sees society as the "bad enemy" that must be punished — especially common among terrorist leaders
12. Idealizes self; sees self as "good person who has been victimized — especially common among terrorist leaders, who exhibit a grandiose self-image that projects confidence and purpose and attracts followers
13. Extroverted, narcissistic and aggressive behavior, more prevalent in leaders than followers, with a further disposition toward sadistic "appreciation of 'work' "
14. Followers usually drawn by leader's charisma, not the cause; tendency among followers to use group to compensate for feelings of inadequacy
15. Ability to control impulsivity and apply reflective thought to

actions – a sign of mental stability
16. Restrained, able to suppress need for gratification until goals are obtained
17. Inconsiderate, self-centered and emotionally cold
18. Sometimes displays sociopathic traits, e.g., lacks remorse or is easily provoked to violence, but most often displays either ambivalence or abhorrence toward harming people, sometimes even going to great lengths to avoid killing people.

The Group Mentality

Regardless of the psychological makeup of individual terrorists, terrorism is still a group activity which compensates for the individuals' lack of self-identity and provides these individuals with security and certainty. Basically, there is little difference between a terrorist cult and a religious cult. These groups tend to be counter-culture, and the activities tend to be beyond the limits of behavior that society condones. This is why both entities tend to attract people who have a grievance or feelings of deprivation. In essence, one might describe terrorist groups as "violent political cults" that offer their members an explanation of the causes of their mutual problems and propose a remedy. In the case of many Islamic fundamentalist terror groups, terrorism is a family affair. The primary motive of the kidnapping of Westerners in Lebanon was to exchange them for Lebanese relatives who were being held in European jails.

An identity crisis can be the motive for people joining a terrorist group. Irish Catholics who join the IRA and adopt Marxist ideology are substituting Marxism for the Christian faith they are in crisis over. Basque separatists are searching for their own national identity, just as Palestinians are seeking political autonomy. In other cases, members look to the group as a substitute for the family that they are in crisis over. People join terrorist groups or cults to fulfill personal needs or because of social obligations to family or community or religion or ethnic identity. However, they stay in these groups and conform to group demands because of the individual's personal commitment and the pressure of peers from within the group. Many seek to enhance their self-image through dedication to a mission, a need to sacrifice, and any self-justification that they can derive from the group. Others seek to enhance their standing within their own family or community. Admiration of peers and family is a key factor with many IRA members, as well as other ethnic terror groups.

Other key factors are money and power. With the loss of outside support from the Communist bloc and some wealthy Arab nations, many terror groups are engaged in organized crime activities and drug trafficking. With the billions of dollars that members can have access to, monetary wealth and its inherent power are major motivating factors.

Another factor that is essential to group cohesion is the group ideology, which is holy gospel to each member, dictates what is good behavior for members, and submerges and destroys the individual's identity. The individual's morality is drowned and is substituted by the group's morality. Killing may be abhorrent to the individual, but if the group says it's okay, that person will slaughter as many innocents as the group says to. Violence is seen by the individual as politically justifiable, strategically necessary for the group's goals and, therefore, morally essential.

Also contrary to popular belief, terrorism is an act of rational, sane choice. Since these groups are smaller than the enemy they oppose, turning to extreme violence is the most appropriate choice for the group to achieve its political goals. To gain independence for Algeria from France, the Arab FLN (Front de Liberation Nationale) had to resort to terror tactics to defeat the militarily superior French colonial forces. Thus, terror tactics are the wake-up call that is used to force the enemy to address the grievances of the group. Killing innocent civilians also puts pressure on the opponent to make a deal to stop the killing.

The idea that terrorist acts are compulsive is only partly right. Terrorism is part of the cycle of violence that relates to the problem as one of medical ecology. Once a group begins the use of violence, it sets in motion a cycle that continues in response to the actions of each side. If the opponent reacts to the first wave of terror acts by attacking the group or its supporters and resources, the next wave of attacks by the group is retaliatory. The harsher the crackdown, the more violent the retaliation used. However, this escalation of violence is gradual. Each wave of violence by both sides, including the decision to use violence initially, is preceded by intense planning, organization and a strengthening of group cohesion. Also, those who actually engage in violence are those members who have been with the group the longest. The rookies are generally given the nonviolent jobs of administration and logistics, such as bookkeeping, courier assignments, publication production, supply management and even secretarial duties. Once the escalation begins, the compulsion factor comes into play. This factor is controlled by the group's psychology and not by external forces or reality. The characteristics of the group's psychology are:

1. The illusion of invincibility
2. Excessive optimism
3. Excessive risk taking
4. Presumption of moral superiority
5. Single-minded view that the enemy is evil
6. Intolerance of any kind of opposition, from within the group and from without.

David Koresh and his Waco cult were classic examples of terrorist group psychology. However, the environment that brought about their shift toward violence was not an oppressive one; it was an environment of liberal religious tolerance and policies of government noninterference. This is why other groups are growing and moving closer to another Waco-type conflict. They feel they can get away with murder because this liberal climate gives them a false sense of security and invulnerability. Thus, to fully understand the full spectrum of terrorist behavior, you have to appreciate the following motivational and contributory factors:

1. Social dissatisfaction
2. Political disaffection
3. Economic deprivation
4. Personal crises and conflicts.

Strategy, Tactics and Victims

Currently, there are over five hundred terrorist groups in operation worldwide. Only the PLO has turned toward peace, but small splinter factions do not agree with the recent peace treaty with Israel and vow to continue the cycle of violence that Arafat and the majority of the PLO leadership have broken from. Within Israel, peace with the "old enemy of Zionism" has created Jewish factions that are threatening acts of terror against both Jews and Arabs.

Strategy

Terrorism is both a strategic initiative and a system of tactical operations. Terrorists do not undertake random acts. Consider the bombing of the World Trade Center in New York. This act was part of a global strategy that was planned for a long while and was timed to take place for maximum fear and publicity. The fact that the terrorists were caught is not a factor. It is highly likely that their arrests were part of the plan. This strategic element and threat to national security are what make terrorism different from random crime. The strategy involved depends on the political agenda:

1. The IRA is Marxist but is concerned with making money and liberating Northern Ireland.

2. The Marxist groups in Europe are interested in organized crime and perhaps initiating another Russian revolution or world Communist revolution.

3. The PLO is now a peacemaker, except for factions bent on the destruction of Israel.

4. Those with an agenda of ethnic autonomy are the ones to watch because they have the most to lose by not bringing worldwide attention to their cause.

5. The Islamic fundamentalist groups are just out on a "holy war" against *all* non-Muslims and those within their faith who will not conform, as in Egypt.

6. The neo-Nazis and right-wing extremists are out to destroy democracy for the "good" of the people.

In the 1990s, we have a major political void in the sponsorship of terrorism. The Soviet Union is dead and out of the terror game. The Soviet bloc countries are now democracies and are also out of the game. East Germany is gone and definitely out. Libya is more concerned about being bombed by America than bombing America through terrrorism, so they're out, too. Kuwait is out because of the conflict with Iraq, the new alliance with America and its European allies, and a distant relationship with Israel. So, with the New World Order firmly entrenched, the World Terrorist Network (WTN) has had to find new "friends" to help its various assorted causes. China is in; Iran is very in; Iraq is distantly in; Syria is still in, but may drop out soon; and some new-found friends among the Mafia and other organized crime groups mentioned in chapter eleven are in for the

money. They each have their own agendas, but only Iran, as a terrorist sponsor, has an immediate threat potential. The strategy we will
see unfold in the coming years will be based on who is sponsoring,
who needs the most exposure for their cause, and the political situation of the time.

Tactics

The operational tactics of terrorists depend upon the group
and the resources at its disposal. Generally, this will mean any act
that intimidates innocent civilians is a good tactic. When ground to
air missiles fell into the hands of the IRA ten years ago, every air-
liner flying to Europe was at risk — and still is. But, so far, this tactic
does not interest the IRA, as it may upset the applecart they are
operating. They are more interested in parading machine guns in
full view of British troops during IRA funerals, which demonstrates
that even the strictest gun control laws, even those administered
under martial law, are absolutely useless. Terrorists and criminals
can get weapons of any type, anytime they want to. At one time,
drug gangs here in the United States were supplied with weapons
from Cuba that were made in the Soviet Union.

The most common types of terrorist tactics are armed attacks.
Bombings, arson, murder, hijacking and kidnapping are the usual.
Targets can be anyone or anything, but generally the targets have
more of a "symbolic" value than as hard targets. At other times, the
targets are hit purely to gain leverage, as in the taking of hostages.
Extraordinary tactics are generally directed at increasing financial
resources. These include bank robbery, extortion, blackmail, ransom
and drug dealing. The IRA is very big on extortion, robbery and
drugs. They also run a string of brothels in Holland and Germany.
Tactics also depend on the operational environment or theater of
operations, which is where the terrorists have concentrated their
agenda, as in the PLO operating in areas close to Israel.

With resources and sponsors closing down, future terrorist
strategies and tactics will have a far greater potential for mass destruction. Such tactics would include:

1. Computer hacking and manipulation of computer services

2. Nuclear terrorism

3. Use of biological weapons

4. Use of chemical weapons.

With the current instability of the Commonwealth of Independent States (CIS), the former Soviet Union, and their need for hard cash, the possibility of NBC (nuclear, biological, chemical) weapons falling into the hands of terrorists is very great. The future possibilities of terrorist tactics and strategies are only limited by the limits of the human imagination.

Victims

The majority of victims of terrorism are innocents. Only a small percentage of killing during the past thirty years have been hard-target assassinations, and most of these were local opponents of the IRA, PLO or Italian Red Brigade. The innocent majority, such as Christmas shoppers in downtown London, are *symbolic targets*. Almost every year, there is a "seasonal" attack designed to force the British to get out of Northern Ireland. However, the slaughter continues, because both sides are stubborn. To the terrorists, these atrocities assert the message of their cause: An armed struggle is a moral imperative against the oppressive order. The innocents are dehumanized into "the enemy." The victims' responses are identical to the patterns described in chapter nine, except with these types of traumatic crises, the victims' circles are expanded to include the entire country. Almost everyone who visits New York or London wonders if a bomb is going to go off, and almost every airline passenger thinks for a brief moment about the possibility of hijacking. And let us not forget the Lambs of God, who terrorize innocent doctors, bomb and burn buildings, and murder anyone that is opposed to their zealous views. They do this all in the name of God. In their minds, God and Jesus Christ are the precipitators of terrorism and are as motivational as Yassir Arafat. But God gave them a choice, and they chose evil.

WOMEN WHO KILL

Whenever people think of murderous women, gross stereotypes come to mind, such as Lizzie Borden, who has mistakenly been viewed as the classic "hysterical" killer, a poor wretch who suffered from "female problems." However, recent evidence shows that Lizzie was a victim of incest who murdered to end a horrible cycle of sexual abuse of her and her sister.

While history is rife with cases of female murderers, these cases became more frequent during and following the Roman era. Prior to the "civilizing" of Europe by Rome and the advent of Christianity, women held an almost equal standing in the ancient societies of Europe. In some societies, they held a status higher than men. They were queens, warlords, property owners and religious leaders, and they were even responsible for the training of the male warriors, as the skills and wisdom of women was considered superior. As the new emerging societies of the West gradually stripped women of power and position, the murder rate among women increased.

Many scholars, mostly male, only took notice of the increase in homicides committed by women during the 1970s. This increase was, of course, attributed to the women's liberation movement. However, the phenomenon goes back to Roman times. The main reason that women killers receive less attention is the societal perception of women as nurturers and care givers. It is almost impossible for many people, even when confronted with the evidence, to accept the idea of women as "killers." Female killers most often come to our attention when the murders are of a domestic nature, but this only reinforces the veil that blinds us to the true nature of homicide committed by females. Known female serial killers are few because they are almost impossible to detect. There may be thousands more out there. They are not as rare as law enforcement believes. Women serial killers are invisible to the public, because they are quiet killers. Female mass murderers are, however, rare. Women also do not usually go on wild killing sprees. However, there have been a few cases, but in these cases, the killers were suffering from severe psychosis at the time of the murders, which would explain their unusual behavior.

Contrary to popular belief, women serial killers are just as, and sometimes more, lethal that their male counterparts. They are also more efficient, which is why they are able to maintain such a low visability for long periods of time. Of women who commit serial crimes, there are three categories:

1. Black widows

2. Nurses

3. Terrorists and assassins.

Black widows are those who kill husbands, children, relatives, boardinghouse tenants and employees. The nurses are the "angels of mercy" or "angels of death" who target those they care for. Terrorists and assassins are those who kill for nonpersonal reasons, such as political or murder-for-hire, and their victms are total strangers. The women who comprise these three categories are not anomalies nor aberrations in female homicide patterns; they are just ignored because they don't fit our social labels and they are a minority among murderers. The actual body count is unknown and an estimate is incomprehensible. Of the known female killers, the body count averages eight to fourteen victims per offender, which is a higher than the average of eight to eleven victims for male killers.

Characteristics

Female serial killers are generally young and intelligent. Their average age is thirty-two, which is just a few years older than most of their male counterparts. Their killing careers average about ten years before discovery, but the range has been anywhere from a few months to over thirty years. Their occupations have included the following:

- Homemakers
- Nurses
- Career criminals
- Professional housekeepers/caretakers
- Farmers
- Waitresses
- Business owners
- College students
- Disaffected debutantes.

Despite a high proportion of lower-class black women who commit domestic killings or economic crimes, most female serial killers are white and middle class or upper class. Only one known woman serial killer was black and middle class.

While spouse/partner abuse is now a socially acceptable reason for killing, the women who commmit serial crimes do not generally kill their abusers. These women are predominately victims of a variety of abuse, from sexual to emotional, but the motives for their crimes are generally not related to abuse.

Victims and Hunting Techniques

The media and academic sources have, since 1970, tried to portray female multiple and serial killers as a "new breed of murderesses," who kill strangers, but there is no data to support these claims. In over one-fourth of all cases, women killed family, friends and acquaintances, but those same women also killed strangers in equal numbers. A slight trend toward targeting strangers has appeared.

The types of victims, in order of preference, are:

1. Strangers

- Children
- Patients not in the killer's care
- Pick-ups in stores, businesses and on streets
- Victims at home
- Hitchhikers and travelers
- The elderly, especially women
- Police officers
- Politicians
- Prostitutes

2. Family
   - Husbands
   - Children
   - In-laws
   - Mothers

3. Acquaintances
   - Friends/peers
   - Boyfriends and lovers
   - Children
   - Elderly men
   - Elderly women
   - Neighbors
   - Employers
   - Landlords
   - Patients in killer's care.

As with their male counterparts, women killers always prefer to prey on the weak. When the victims are family, husbands are at the top of the hit parade. Such was the case of Nannie Doss, who at the age of thirty, felt the "urge" to kill and went on a murder spree that lasted over twenty years, beginning in the 1930s. She liked to kill, and her victims included four husbands, her mother, two sisters, three of her own children, one grandson and one nephew, for a total body count of twelve, but there were other mysterious deaths in her community. Nannie loved romance novels, and she insisted she killed for romance. The meager insurance payoffs seem to bear out this motive. Her mode of killing was to give her victims large doses of rat poison in stewed prunes.

When female killers murder adults, they generally choose men, but when they go after children, there seems to be no gender preference. Their hunting grounds, in most cases, are place-specific. However, because of the phenomenon of serial killers who roam the country killing victims, either at random or of a specific type, has only recently been discovered, there may be dozens or hundreds more of these wandering murderers. There have only been six known cases of female traveling killers, and the cases were originally attributed to men. It is the invisible nature of women killers that may hide more crimes. Only 20 percent of these rovers are known to have hunted within a specific state or city, and only about 5 percent are known to have worked as team killers with a male partner. The place-specific women killers always use the same killing grounds, such as their homes, nursing homes and hospitals. Because hospitals have such notoriously bad security and death verification procedures and will let almost anyone work for them regardless of the person's background, there could be countless numbers of people being killed in hospitals. Even if a hospital suspects murder, unless it can be proven conclusively, the administrators will generally dismiss the suspect under a cloud and cover up any wrongdoing. The same is true with nursing homes, where people are dying all the time.

Methods and Motives

In ancient Rome and in ninth-, tenth- and eleventh-century Normandy, poison was the weapon of choice among women. It was known both a "widow maker" and a "king or queen maker." The second wife of the first emperor of Rome was so eager to see her son became emperor that she spent several nights putting poison into each piece of fruit in her paranoid husband's private orchard. He had good reason to be paranoid, as she had killed his son, her stepson, and had tried to kill the emperor at least three times, all by poison. Eight hundred years later, the women of Norman nobility solved the divorce problem and inheritance problem with liberal applications of arsenic. It was one of the few ways that women could maintain a political power base. Today, poison is still the most popular murder method with women killers. The most common methods of murder are:

Poisoning	50% of all cases
Shooting	3%
Bludgeoning	3%
Stabbing	3%
Torturing	3%
Suffocating	3%
Neglecting	3%
Drowning	3%
Combining above	29%

Male killers have traditionally used violent means because these methods fulfilled some sexual need, but only a handful of the female killers are known to have been sexually stimulated by killing or to have had relations with their victims. This naturally leads to the great question: Why kill?

- Money
- Enjoyment
- Revenge
- Sex (minor motive)
- Perverted acts (minor motive)
- Drugs
- Cult/terrorist involvement
- Cover up other crimes
- Children a burden
- Inadequacy as a parent
- Combination of the above motives.

As you can see, these motives greatly differ from those of male killers, but the motives still do not explain what makes a woman kill over and over again. For centuries the explanations have been:

- Possessed by Satan or other demons
- Hormonal changes
- Premenstrual syndrome (PMS)

- Female problems, other than PMS
- Maternity.

Recent research has found evidence that female killers, like their male counterparts, are products of their environments, and this accounts for the reason that women are committing more and more economic crimes. However, many researchers overlook the fact that women are just as apt to suffer the same psychological disorders as men. Just as there have been few cases of women serial killers, there are also few women who are treated for severe mental disorders. Women are more apt than men to seek a mental health professional, so they are less likely to reach the dangerous stage. However, some women are too proud or too stubborn or too bound by social constraints to seek help for mental problems. This would explain why so many female killers come from middle-class and upper-class backgrounds. Recent studies by the Center for Disease Control show that women suffer more stress-related illnesses than men and are more prone to alcoholism and drug abuse as a result of the enormous stress of twentieth-century life.

Psychosis is found in the majority of cases of women who kill their children or other children. Ironically, many of these cases could have been prevented because almost half of the women had told others, prior to the murders, that they feared they would kill. They reported this to friends, family, physicians, police and social service agencies. But because of the social blindness to the idea of women killing, these "pleas for help" were ignored.

Stress and psychological trauma are the only related factors linked to women and crime. Studies done in the late 1980s show that the more stress a person experiences, especially a woman, the more likely he or she will "burn out" and suffer major psychiatric problems. Add to these stresses any personal traumas, such as child sexual abuse, childhood physical or emotional abuse, spouse abuse or other traumas, and you have the makings of a serial killer/multiple murderer/mass murderer. In fact, the majority of cases show a biographical history of severe child abuse, sex abuse, prostitution, neglect and unstable marital relationships.

Other characteristis of female killers:

- Insincere
- Amoral
- Extremely impulsive

- Able to dominate other people with manipulative charisma and superficial charm
- Lacks any form of conscience
- Lacks insight
- Unable to learn from mistakes
- Irresponsible
- Unpredictable
- Volatile
- Flagrant disregard for truth
- Above-average intelligence
- Extremely self-destructive
- Prone to take frequent high risks
- Able to mimic "normal" behavior when necessary
- Always blames others for failures
- No life goals.

It should be noted that, their male counterparts, women killers are unlikely to possess all these traits or constantly display any one trait. Instead, women are more likely to have cyclical bouts of behavior extremes, a female version of the Dr. Jeckyll and Mr. Hyde syndrome. They love to kill, and they live to get away with as much crime as time and circumstances permit.

As team killers, women are generally followers, as in the case of Myra Hindley and Ian Brady, British child murderers in the 1960s. But in some other cases, women were the dominant partners. In Missouri recently, a farmer brought home a homeless man to help him and his wife with a cattle theft plan that the wife had organized. The homeless man was grateful for the shelter and food, so he agreed to sell the cattle for his benefactors. However, once the transaction was complete and the wife had the money in hand, she thanked her helper by shooting him in the back of the head and cutting up his clothes to make quilts for the church charity sales. Her husband buried the corpse, and in obedience to his wife, he recruited another victim. It is believed this woman killed at least eight men, perhaps as many as twelve.

The Assassins

While women who kill as amateurs may go undetected and ignored for years, there are ten times as many dedicated professionals who advertise their killing. These are the female terrorists, who are also emerging as the core element of a new-wave Murder, Inc. To Western male academic and security professionals, these women are a source of horror and fantasy. These female killers defy the stereotype of expected behavior in our society, and they are an affront to the prejudices that people hold dear.

Contrary to widely held misconceptions, women became terrorists because of the equality of opportunity that is available. The motives of female terrorists vary, but the dedication to duty remains the same for three reasons:

1. They are pursuing dreams of a better life for people
2. They desire to help people in need
3. They desire to change social and governmental policies.

Women see themselves as soldiers of their cause. They have taken up armed revolution because of their political beliefs, but the women are often more idealistic than the men. Frustrated by earlier attempts at affecting political or social change by peaceful means or traumatized by the injury or death of a loved one who suffered at the hands of the establishment, these women feel compelled to join with the men who share their same beliefs. The only difference is that women terrorists are more ruthless and persistent than their male colleagues.

Western academians have tried to push the notion that most female terrorists are followers who have fallen into bad ways because of misguided loyalty to a lover who is involved in terrorism. However, this stereotype does not hold water considering that many of the founders of the left-wing terror movement of the late 1960s and early 1970s were women. Also, among the new-wave alliance of German, French and Italian terrorism, 70 percent of the leadership is female. While many women have joined terror groups as followers, a large percentage of these followers graduated to leadership roles in a very short time. They certainly were not motivated by sex. The female-as-follower theory also fails to explain the women who become mercenaries of terrorism and later organize terror movements, as in the case of Inge Viett, one of the founders of the new

Red Army Faction and Action Directe, pro-communist groups begun in West Germany. The all-female ultrafeminist terror group known as either Red Zora or Revolutionary Zora is an autonomous faction of the Revolutionary Cells terror movement. This is a highly personal group that is marxist oriented and seeks to redress the wrongs that oppress women and to put an end to sexism and racism.

In the early 1970s, women like Margherita Cagol, cofounder of the Italian Red Brigade; Ulrike Meinhof, cofounder of the German Red Army Faction (RAF); Magdalena Kaupp of the RAF and French Action Directe; and Barbara Balzarini, a principal organizer of the Red Brigade and founder of the separate terror group called Communists for the Liberation of the Proletariat, or COLP, all provided inspired leadership and displayed brilliant organization talents. Balzarini was also one of the people that killed Italian Prime Minister Aldo Moro.

This type of high-dominance woman can choose *good* and become a military professional, law enforcement professional or other career professional or choose *evil* and become a terrorist. These women challenge the misconceptions of what is appropriate behavior for women and redefine the roles of women in the future development of our society. Strategically, it is necessary for women to assume their natural position as leaders, builders and creators or else society will have to deal with an increasing role of women as professional criminals and terrorists.

In the days of the Cold War, the KGB and its Soviet bloc intelligence colleagues saw a great strategic value in the tactical advantages women bring to the terror game. Just as female serial killers are invisible to society, so are female terrorists. An attack by a woman is generally unexpected. So is a woman delivering a bomb. Here is a description of one of the most devious tactics in use by terror groups: Either the woman will appear to be pregnant and have children in tow or she will just give the impression of a mother on a shopping trip with her children. With the pregnancy trick, the "child" is the bomb, which is "delivered" in a nearby rest room, and the woman dons another disguise and leaves. Everyone is fooled until it is found out later that the "saint with the children" was the bomber. Also, when you see a man and a woman on the back of a motor scooter or motorcycle, you automatically think romance and let down your guard. This is what the Red Brigade (RB) expected when such "killer couples" would ambush people the RB wanted to punish, with the woman doing most of the shooting. Since the 1980s, with the help of the KGB, the East Germans, the Cubans, and the Libyan Secret Service, a major portion of the women killers who avoided death and prison became professional contract killers who sold their services to the different terror groups or the government sponsors of terrorism. With terrorism moving into organized crime, there will be an increase in the activities of women terrorists/contract killers.

Since a terrorist group is like a family of sorts, it is not hard to see the role of women as nurturing types, organizing and protecting their surrogate families. This is why Inge Viett has been considered a "godmother of terrorism," along with several of her other sisters in terror.

Of the women who are involved in terrorism because they are following their lovers, they are mostly low-level operatives who are considered expendable by the boyfriend and the group. Even the women leaders consider such followers as nothing more than fodder for their cause. These followers are exploited as decoys, bait, sexual bait, couriers and human bombs. In 1986, Nezar Hindawi, a Palestinian terrorist, put his pregnant girlfriend on an El Al flight from London to Israel. He told her he would marry her in Israel, but he had packed a trousseau that insured he would never marry her and that would destroy the plane as part of his latest terror venture. Fortunately, the suicide-to-be was caught before she got on the plane with a bomb she honestly had no idea she was carrying. Many a holiday shopper in London has been the victim of a "prambomb" or a "dollbomb" or a "shopping bag or gift package bomb" that was delivered by a woman who was assisted by children. Gender and gender-specific activities almost always blind security, police and military authorities, and this is why women have such an excellent tactical advantage.

With the death of Communism in Russia and the rest of Europe, neo-Nazis and neo-Fascists have been quick to take advantage of the ensuing political chaos and confusion. A recent study of the right-wing extremist groups in England, France, Germany, Russia and Italy shows that almost 28 percent of their memberships are women. There are even female Skinheads. The females' involvement is mostly based on family relationships; many are married to terrorists and 28 percent are the sisters of group members. They are all middle class and upper class, they have professional careers (20 percent are teachers), and they are highly intelligent.

As if the world doesn't have enough problems, there are a growing number of female-led religious cults who are espousing murder and mass suicide in the name of God. Recently in the Ukraine, many cult members belonging to a group called the Great White Brotherhood were arrested before they could carry out their Waco-type plans. Their leader is a woman named Maria Devi Khristos, aka Marina Tsvygun, who claims to be God. So far, her prediction that the world will end has not come true. Here in America, the women of the religious right are the most zealous and the most dangerous. They may not actually kill doctors or bomb clinics, but they certainly have the power to manipulate men to do the dirty work.

PSYCHOLOGY IN THE COURTROOM

Every writer has heard of the insanity defense, but contrary to popular belief, it rarely works. There is also a whole host of issues involving the subject of dealing with mental health problems in the criminal justice system that occasionally even confuse the legal professionals who regularly confront them.

The Defendant's Mental Health

In criminal law, there are two standards of evidence; either the prosection must prove guilt by the standard of "beyond a reasonable doubt," or in a case with an insanity plea, the defense must meet the lesser standard of "clear and convincing" evidence that the defendant was insane. In cases involving the mental health of the defendant, there are also other questions that arise.

Is the Defendant Competent to Stand Trial?

The state of a perpetrator's mental health is determined by the standard set by the Supreme Court in the case of Dusky vs. U.S.,

1960: The perpetrator must "have sufficient present ability to consult his lawyer with a reasonable degree of rational understanding — and whether he has a rational as well as a factual understanding of the procedings against him." In other words, the defendant has to be able to comprehend the trial and the sentence he faces if found guilty and be able to cooperate with his attorney in the preparation of the case. If a perpetrator is so out of touch with reality that he does not know what is going on around him and he does not know who or what he is dealing with, he can be considered unfit to stand trial. However, the standards can vary in some states.

Until 1972, a person could be confined indefinitely until he or she was fit to stand trial. However, the Supreme Court ruled in the case of Jackson vs. Indiana that pretrial confinement and evaluation for competency must be limited to a "reasonable period of time." If the offender is not fit, the state can institute civil commitment proceedings. With the advent of antipsychotic drugs, there has been increasing controversy over forcing defendants to stand trial under the influence of these drugs. They may make the offender lucid — less confused, less delusional — but the side effects are grogginess and passivity. These drugs may also destroy any hope of an insanity defense because the drugs will eliminate the genuinely crazy behavior that a jury would need to be aware of.

In the cases of offenders who are mentally disabled, competency is based on whether they have adequate intellectual ability and evaluation of the following factors:

1. Person's history of adaptation
2. Person's level of common sense
3. Any already-observed ability to cooperate with an attorney.

A mildly disabled defendant probably will not stand trial, though exceptions do occur. In more severe cases, the defendant definitely will not stand trial. However, regardless of how unfit a person is to stand trial, for whatever reason, any confessions made to police are still valid and admissible as evidence.

Is the Defendant Responsible for His or Her Acts?

The standard here is whether the offender displayed criminal intent at the time the crime was committed. In other words, did a guilty state of mind known as "mens rea" exist at the time of the alleged crime? If the defendant is found to be "insane," he or she is not legally responsible for the crime. If a person is insane at the time he or she committed a crime, the law says that person cannot be punished in the manner a sane person would be.

The Insanity Defense

The insanity defense is rarely used in criminal cases because it requires that the accused admit to being guilty. If the defendant is not found to be insane, punishment according to law is certain. If the defendant is found to be insane, civil commitment to a mental institution for treatment is assured, and this confinement can be longer than any prison term. Defense attorneys, therefore, are reluctant to enter insanity pleas for their clients.

The insanity defense originated in 1843 in England as a result of the M'Naghten case. Daniel M'Naghten claimed that the "voice of God" told him to kill the Prime Minister, Sir Robert Peel. However, M'Naghten, mistakenly killed Peel's secretary. M'Naghten was acquitted, which infuriated Parliament, enraged Queen Victoria, and forced the courts to come up with a reasonable definition of insanity. The result was called the M'Naghten Rule, which states that

> to establish a defense of insanity, it must be clearly proved that, at the time of committing the act, the party accused was laboring under such a defect of reason, from disease of the mind, as not to know the nature and quality of the act he was doing; or if he did know it, that he did not know what he was doing was wrong.

This standard has been widely criticized for being too narrow in scope, but throughout the U.S., either this antiquated rule or a variation of it is the sole standard in determining insanity.

In 1962, the American Law Institute (ALI) formulated and adopted the Model Penal Code, which has become a very influential concept for the insanity defense:

> A. A person is not responsible for criminal conduct if at the time of such conduct as a result of mental disease or defects he lacks sufficient capacity either to appreciate the criminality of his conduct or to conform his conduct to the requirements of law.

B. "Mental disease or defect" does not include an abnormality manifested only by repeated criminal or otherwise antisocial conduct.

With this standard, jurors, not expert witnesses, can make a reasonable decision as to whether the defendent is insane or not. It is also a helpful standard because it prevents psychopaths from using the insanity defense.

In 1984, Congress passed the Insanity Defense Reform Act in reaction to the acquittal of John Hinckley, Jr., as "not guilty by reason of insanity" for the attempted assassination of President Ronald Reagan. In one sense, this was a step backward, but it also caused a few steps forward. In stepping back, the act eliminated the "inability to conform one's behavior" component of the ALI concept, making the standard as narrow-minded as the M'Naghten rule. However, progress was made by limiting the weight of evidence presented by expert witnesses. They can only present evidence on the mental state of the defendant and opinions on that evidence. The expert may not offer any opinion regarding whether the defendant is insane or not. The act also requires automatic civil commitment if the defendant is found "not guilty by reason of insanity," and the act requires that the defense carry the burden of proving insanity, instead of the traditional burden of proof being the responsibility of the prosection. In addition, the standard of proof was raised from "preponderence of evidence" to "clear and convincing." Unfortunately, the jurisdiction of the act is limited to federal trials. In state trials, it is only a model for change of the state's laws governing trials.

Attempts at establishing additional rules have been made over the years, beginning with the "irresistible impulse rule." This rule has been unpopular with both the courts and the psychiatric professionals because it is difficult to differentiate between irresistible and resistible impulses. Only a few states accept this rule. In 1984, the Supreme Court limited the application of this rule to compulsive gambling and addiction disorders. The only times that lower courts have allowed this rule to be used as a defense have been in cases of command hallucinations and cases of severe obsessive-compulsive disorder. In theory, other disorders could use this rule, but juries rarely give it credence.

"Guilty but mentally ill" is a recent innovation that gives juries a way out of difficult decisions, and it has received a lot of attention. However, the application of this rule requires that the trial be split into two phases. The first determines guilt or innocence and the second phase determines if a plea of insanity is valid, if the defendant chooses the option of entering such a plea.

"Diminished capacity" allows the level of the offense to be reduced by showing that mental illness prevented the defendent from forming the required intent. It's an updated version of the intoxification defense, but the use of this defense rarely works.

In cases involving the voluntary use of drugs, an insanity plea will not be valid; however, if someone commits a crime while under the influence of drugs that the defendant was unaware of having taken, a plea of temporary insanity is usually found valid. Another situation in which this plea is found valid is in cases involving drug-induced mental illness that continues long after the effects of the drugs wear off. This precedent was established in 1979 in the case of New Jersey vs. Stasio: "Insanity is available (as a defense) when the voluntary use of the intoxicant or drug results in a fixed state of insanity after the influence of the intoxicant or drug has spent itself."

In cases involving psychopathic disorders or antisocial personality disorders, the insanity defense is not valid. In death penalty cases, a person can be found competent to stand trial, found sane and guilty, and found to be "incompetent to be executed." There is a long-standing precedent for not executing the insane. The five reasons are as follows:

1. The defendant cannot effectively participate in appeals.

2. Such an execution is cruel and unusual under the Eighth Amendment.

3. There is no deterrence factor served.

4. It does not serve the interests of justice.

5. It prevents the condemned from making a final religious peace.

In 1986, the Supreme Court upheld the Eighth Amendment factor in the case of Ford vs. Wainwright and set a precedent that prohibits states from executing the insane. The general view is that while a person may be sane at the time of the crime and his trial, the impact of being sentenced to death may induce mental illness.

In an odd twist of fate, one of the country's leading experts on the insanity defense attempted in 1990 to use this plea in his own defense when he was tried on charges of conspiracy to commit murder-for-hire. He hired an undercover policeman to pose as a hitman to kill his wife. The jury did not believe the plea because they did not accept the idea that the doctor was mentally ill on each of the various occasions that the police recorded his request to have his wife killed. There were also other elaborate plans that demonstrated that the doctor was sane throughout the entire series of events leading up to his arrest.

Battered Wife Syndrome

The FBI estimates that from two to four million incidents of women being physically and sexually abused occur every year. That's one out of every ten women who share households or relationships with males. The FBI also reports that a wife is beaten every eighteen seconds in this country. With this many women subjected to virtual slavery, degradation and torture, it is not surprising that a number of these women have turned the tables and killed their abusers. They are also in fear for their lives, as domestic violence accounts for almost 50 percent of all homicides and 20 percent of all police officers killed in the line of duty. However, the criminal justice system that should have protected them from abuse failed them again by refusing to accept as evidence a well-established trauma disorder known as Battered Wife Syndrome (BWS).

Using such poor excuses as "equality of choice," "respect for privacy," and "even-handed consideration of the evidence," the police, courts and state legislatures have ignored the criminal atrocities that millions of women must endure every day at the hands of abusive "loved ones." Instead, these women, who have been driven insane by constant brutality, are not allowed to use BWS as a defense to murder. It is a valid form of insanity plea that in essence says that women killed in "self-defense" and therefore should be acquitted. When evidence of the syndrome is allowed in court, conviction is rare—about 10 percent of all cases. The rest are either acquitted or convicted of lesser charges and placed on probation.

Unfortunately, Battered Wife Syndrome is only admissible unconditionally in seven states and conditionally in five states. The rest don't care or have poor excuses to disallow the evidence. Men are getting away with murdering their wives and girlfriends for a variety of reasons, but women who kill to save their own lives are rotting in jail, mostly for violating a social taboo: Women are not supposed to kill.

Battered Wife Syndrome is evidenced by three stages:

1. Tension in relationship builds and small incidents of verbal and physical insults occur.
2. Escalation to more intense violence occurs, resulting in the woman suffering serious injury.
3. The cycle of violence is reinforced by loving remorse that the abuser manipulates the victim with.

The stages are repeated over and over, often increasing in the intensity of violence inflicted on the woman. She submits, hoping to avoid further violence, but is gradually traumatized into passivity. The violence continues until the woman is either dead or dumped by the abuser, the abuser is jailed, the woman runs away, or the woman kills the abuser.

Civil Commitment

When the courts have found it necessary to commit people with questionable mental health, they exercise two forms of power:

1. *Power of the state to care for those in need* (Parens patriae) — Exercised to protect individuals from harming themselves.
2. *Police power of state* — Exercised to protect society from persons deemed dangerous.

These forms of civil commitment are governed by state statute, but in most cases, the precedent set in 1975 in the case of O'Connor vs. Donaldson sets the requirements for commitment. This means that there must be proof of both the existence of mental illness and an indication that the person is dangerous to self or others. Recently, the trend has been to use "imminent dangerousness" as the principal standard for involuntary civil commitment.

In 1979, the Supreme Court held in Addington vs. Texas that the Constitution requires "clear and convincing proof" in all civil commitment hearings. There are two types of commitment procedures:

1. *Formal* — This involves a request by a third party to have the court commit an individual. Decision is made by judge based

on expert evidence. A jury is optional. Confinement, if decided upon, is until the patient is no longer under the influence of the disorder.

2. *Informal* — This is an emergency commitment that does not involve the courts. A person acting in a bizarre manner can be taken by police to a state institution or family can request police to do this or in most states, two health professionals can order a temporary informal civil commitment. Confinement is limited to one to three days, with longer periods requiring a formal hearing.

Recent trends of abuse of civil commitment have led to a mountain of lawsuits. In Texas, mental health facilities were confining people without just cause in order to defraud insurance companies of benefit payments. The lives of thousands of people have been ruined in the process. Other abuses include the use of coercion, which a 1987 study indicates occurs in 50 percent of cases of "voluntary" commitment. In 1990, the Supreme Court ruled in Zimmerman vs. Burch that persons wrongfully committed can sue mental health professionals. This has made the courts and mental health professionals reluctant to proceed with any form of involuntary commitment unless there is clear and convincing evidence. Most states now require hearings and other safeguards, but abuses still continue.

The Issue of Dangerousness

While there is no real definition of "dangerousness" and the matter varies from state to state, the recent trend for mental health professionals has been to play it safe and protect society from harm, rather than be held liable in a civil suit for releasing or not confining a possibly dangerous person.

This trend began soon after the 1976 California case called the Tarasoff case. A psychologist at the University of California-Berkeley mental health clinic was sure that his patient, a Mr. Poddar, was going to kill a Ms. Tarasoff because she rebuffed Poddar's romantic advances. The campus police were called and requested to pick up Poddar for evaluation, but after talking to Poddar, the police felt there was no problem. The police were wrong, the doctor was right, and Poddar killed Tarasoff. Her family sued the clinic. As a result, the court held that the clinic was liable because it failed to take responsible action to protect the victim. This meant that the clinic had "a duty to warn." On appeal, the liability was upheld and the court added that the clinic also had a "duty to protect."

This has opened a Pandora's Box of legal and ethical problems. Soon after the Tarasoff decision, many states passed legislation making therapists liable for their actions or lack of actions. Some states have even stipulated that therapists are liable for not acting on vague or general threats expressed by patients. A few states have stated in their laws that therapists are not liable *if* they take appropriate action, such as warning the victim and calling the police. Ethically, there are no limits set on where to draw the line that voids the patient-therapist relationship. Considering that therapists can misread the entire situation 60 to 70 percent of the time, of every ten patients who display aggressive tendencies, six to seven who will talk harshly but never act are at risk of unwarranted civil commitment proceedings. With the current abuses of the mental health system, it is easy to see why over 50 percent of the people in mental hospitals really do not belong there. Safeguards exist, but they are not always effective, and it is the public that suffers.

Predicting the behavior of an individual has been a very controversial subject since 1974. Therapists have been thrust into the role of crime prevention to avoid civil liability. However, there are two situations that warrant the use of prediction and emergency commitment:

1. When a clear and present danger exists
2. When suicide is imminent.

In August 1986, and again in 1991, postal workers went on a rampage, killing twenty-two people in three separate incidents. Each of the attackers made clear threats of violence and were out of control; the victims who died were in fear for their lives and had requested protection; there were weapons available to the persons who made the threats; and danger was clearly evident since all three who made the threats had motives to kill. However, despite all the warning signals, nothing was done to stop these easily preventable mass murders. Had police and mental health professionals intervened, they would have been 100 percent right in detaining for emergency commitment Patrick Sherrill, Joseph Harris and Thomas McIlvane, who, except for Harris, killed themselves.

Also in 1991, George Hennard put his threats in writing, and a few months later he drove his truck through the front door of Luby's Cafeteria in Killeen, Texas, and killed twenty-two people and then himself. In all these cases there was a clear and present danger, and all the killers had a history of emotional problems and violence. So why didn't anyone pay attention to the flashing warning lights?

The following list of warning factors in predicting aggression has been used by the criminal court system since 1981:

- Young
- Male
- Disadvantaged, comes from a lower economic background than victims
- Disadvantaged socially or racially
- Less educated than victims
- Low intelligence
- Unstable school history
- Unstable work history
- History of substance abuse
- Prior history of violent behavior
- Prior history of suicide attempts
- History of family violence
- Has displayed histrionic or antisocial personality traits
- History of cruelty to animals
- Had rejecting or depressed father
- Suffered recent stress or emotional trauma.

If all of these killers had been committed before they killed, psychologists would have found the following numbers of warning factors (from the above list) that were present in the killers' backgrounds:

- Sherrill — 10 out of 15
- Harris — 9 out of 15
- McIlvane — 10 out of 15
- Hennard — 11 out of 15.

They were also suicidal. The only difference between them and regular suicides is that they wanted to punish the people they hated before they killed themselves. In many cases of mass murder, serial murder and murder/suicide in general, the killers fit the pattern of suicidal tendencies.

Suicide

In all cases of human violence, important factors are obscured by social myth, and suicide is the most hidden in falsehoods.

False. Suicides happen without warning—Suicidal people always leave clues. Fifteen percent leave notes when they die. Eighty percent communicate their intentions before they die. Harris left a note; Sherrill, McIlvane and Hennard all warned others of their intentions.

True. Suicide is related to severe depression—Loners with a history of severe clinical depression are at high risk of suicide, as are psychopaths, psychotics and schizophrenics. Sherrill had a history of depression and so did Hennard.

False. Suicide runs in families—There is no evidence of this, but a proneness to depression can be hereditary. Depression can lead to suicide, which perhaps explains the pervasiveness of this myth.

True. Suicide occurs in all social and economic levels of society—Mental illness does, too. Hennard was upper middle class; Sherrill was poor.

False. Writers, artists and cops are the most prone to suicide—Ironically, the profession with the highest suicide rate is physicians. But any job with a high degree of stress and frustration level is going to push people to violence either against others or against themselves.

Prediction Factors

The following prediction factors indicate a predisposition for self-destruction:

- History of suicide attempts
- Statements of a wish to die
- History of refusal to deal with crises
- Suicide of parent or other role model, though again, the trait is not passed on genetically
- Feelings of failure

- History of family instability and parental rejection
- Recent personal crisis or emotional trauma
- Displays inability to see a way out of situations that are causing a great amount of emotional pain
- Loner
- Unable to handle grief and loss
- History of panic disorders
- History of sleep disturbances
- History of substance abuse
- Shows symptoms of clinical depression — hopelessness, inability to experience pleasure, apathy, loss of resources.

Finally, there is the issue of whether easy access to lethal means, especially guns, is a prediction factor. This is generally false because mental illness is the real cause of death. Even if you deny suicidal people access to weapons, they will still find a means to kill themselves. In England, it's Tylenol. In Japan, it's poison or anything sharp. In the Soviet Union, with strict gun control, it was poison and hanging. In America, the highest rate of suicide is among the young, who favor hanging and poison. Though guns are used, poison, drugs and hanging significantly outnumber gun deaths.

Attempts to Fool the Courts

Quite often criminals will try to deceive the courts, but they will not necessarily be intent on an insanity plea; they just want to see how much they can get away with. Also, not all the offenders who fool or try to fool the court-appointed psychological experts are previous offenders. Many are people who have never been arrested for a crime, but they have a history of family violence, the hidden crimes of spouse abuse and child abuse that rarely come to the attention of the law until someone is killed or so badly injured that health care professionals bring in the police.

When someone who is known as a responsible, upstanding citizen suddenly commits a crime against an acquaintance or family member, we often hear the case referred to as a "crime of passion." Generally, these are crimes within a family, allegedly committed in the midst of a heated argument. However, behind the mask of respectability is a blustery, inflexible and childishly impatient person who is quick to lose his temper if people don't do as he demands. Thus, there is little difference between this "good citizen" and a common criminal.

A close examination of this so-called crime of passion will reveal that the perpetrator and victim had a long history of conflict. The perpetrator feels frustrated, bitter and disappointed concerning the victim, and there are constant arguments and violent fights that result in assault on the victim. The perpetrator builds up more and more resentment, desiring all the while to destroy the victim. When the murder is committed, this sudden act of violence comes as a complete surprise to everyone but the immediate family. Unfortunately, the families of such victims are too ashamed to reveal the dark secret of family violence that resulted in murder.

If the case is taken at face value, the perpetrator simply appears to be a "nice guy" who just suddenly snapped. The crime will be judged to have occurred as the result of temporary insanity, and the perpetrator will be acquitted. However, a close examination of what is behind the mask will reveal a person who is no stranger to violence and is very good at deceiving people, keeping up a squeaky-clean public image. Once the mask is ripped off, it is not hard to prove that the murder was the result of *habitual* violence directed at forcing the victim to submit to the killer's total control. In the master-slave relationship common in domestic violence situations, the killer has already decided that if the victim does not obey, she must be destroyed. Once the image of murder is fixed in the perpetrator's mind, it is not long before the fantasy becomes reality. If the jury knows these facts, it will generally render a verdict of guilty.

Just as so-called "crimes of passion" have hidden motives and obscured premeditation, so do so-called "senseless crimes." These are the random crimes that, on the surface, appear to be nothing more than robberies and muggings with no apparent motives. However, there is a motive and it is not financial. At some point in time, the perpetrators decided that they wanted to commit a crime, any crime, just for the thrill, for fun. These criminals are excited by every facet of the crime, including their own trials.

As discussed earlier, so-called "impulse crimes" are not recognized by the courts as valid for insanity pleas. Also, juries rarely accept the offenders' stories that they are victims of uncontrollable impulses. Habitual, yes. Uncontrollable, no. Close examination will always reveal that those criminals labeled with the term "impulse disorder" are totally in control at the times of their crimes and they are very calculating, often taking great precautions to avoid detection. These people may be mentally ill, but they have consciously made a choice to commit crimes and therefore are *responsible* for their acts. These criminals know that their acts are wrong, and they are completely aware of the consequences.

The American Psychiatric Association defines kleptomania, pyromania and substance abuse as "impulse disorders," along with other problems, including some sex crimes. Jeffrey Dahmer tried to convince the jury he was a victim of his "urges." However, there was not only a great amount of premeditation in his uncontrollable acts, there was also a pattern of criminality in his behavior before he became a killer. Drug addicts often offer a similar defense. When they are caught, they try to convince people to believe that they are victims who will benefit from treatment. They will also say that they "desire" to be helped. Freud would agree, but the courts don't. In most cases, these offenders desire drugs and crime. Unfortunately, many therapists fall for the criminal's con game, and as experts, they plead for the criminal that he or she wanted to get caught and that the crimes were part of a desperate plea for help. The offender *does* want help — help to continue his or her criminal behavior.

In a case of serial murder, mass murder or other bizarre crime, the public's first reaction is that the criminal is "crazy." So it is perfectly logical that, when caught, the criminal tries to perpetuate this falsehood. The more intelligent the criminal, the more he or she will try to outsmart the police, the lawyers, the courts, and especially the court-appointed experts.

Kenneth Bianchi, one of the Hillside Stranglers. at one time posed as a psychologist and ran a phony therapy practice, so he knew enough about psychology to know what kind of con game to run on the doctors. He got the idea of using the latest and most popular psychiatric label to feign insanity. He chose Multiple Personality Disorder (MPD). He fooled the first doctor; the second doctor was so convinced that he wrote a book about Bianchi's MPD. As James "the Amazing" Randi (magician, illusionist and fraud buster extraordinaire) has stated many times, people *like* to be tricked and fooled. It's human nature. The more extraordinary the lie, the more some may buy into it. And therapists are only human and just as vulnerable to being hoaxed as anybody else. However, in Bianchi's case, the expert for the prosecution knew how people could trick the experts, and his tests showed that Bianchi's MPD was a fraud. Confronted with the fact that the prosecution knew he was trying to trick everyone, Bianchi recanted his story of MPD and gave up any further attempts at deception. With the game at an end, he started cooperating with authorities.

Kenneth Bianchi was just one of many who tried to play the psychiatric con game. Many others have gotten tips from their lawyers, and still others were very creative on their own. David "Son of Sam" Berkowitz claimed that the devil had possessed a neighbor's dog, named Sam, and that the dog was ordering him to kill people. Later, Berkowitz told authorities that he had lied about his mental illness. Other ways that criminals have tried to fool the experts:

- Claims to hear or speak with Satan or some demon
- Claims to be possessed by a demon
- Claims to be God's messenger or to hear the voice of God
- Feigns delusions of persecution
- Claims people are trying to kill him or her
- Claims being confused and disoriented
- Claims to have amnesia
- Malingers
- Acts irrational
- Attempts suicide
- Fakes epileptic seizures
- Mumbles to self
- Stares into space
- Pretends to hallucinate
- Commits self-mutilation
- Pretends to be out of contact with reality
- Exaggerates already existing medical conditions and blames illness, such as epilepsy, as cause of crimes.

Bibliography

Adler, Margot. *Drawing Down the Moon*. New York: Viking, 1979.

American Psychiatric Association. *Diagnostic and Statistical Manual of Mental Disorder—III—Revised*. Washington, DC: American Psychiatric Association, 1987.

Brussel, James A. *Casebook of a Crime Psychiatrist*. New York: Dell, 1968.

Caputi, Jane. *The Age of Sex Crime*. Bowling Green, OH: Bowling Green State University Press, 1987.

DiCanio, Margaret. *The Encyclopedia of Violence*. New York: Facts On File, 1993.

Dobson, Christopher and Ronald Payne. *The Never Ending War*. New York: Facts on File, 1987/1989.

——.*The Terrorists: Their Weapons, Leaders and Tactics*. New York: Facts on File, 1982.

Evans, O'Brian, Cohen and Fine. *Encyclopedia of Drug Abuse*. New York: Facts on File, 1990.

Florescu, Radu and R.T. McNally. *Dracula, A Biography of the Impaler*. New York: Hawthorn, 1973.

Frayling, Christopher. *Vampyres*. London: Faber and Faber, 1991.

Fromm, Erich. *Anatomy of Human Destructiveness*. New York: Harper & Row, 1975.

Gaute, J.H.H. and Robin Odell. *The New Murderers' Who's Who*. New York: IPL, 1991.

Geberth, V. *Practical Homicide Investigation*. New York: Elsevier, 1983.

Glut, Donald. *True Vampires of History*. New York: H.C. Publishers, 1971.

Hazelwood, Robert R. and John E. Douglas. "The Lust Murderer." *FBI Law Enforcement Bulletin*. April 1980.

Hicks, Robert D. *In Pursuit of Satan*. Buffalo, NY: Prometheus Books, 1991.

Janke, Peter. *Guerrilla Organizations*. New York: Macmillan, 1983.

Leyton, Dr. Elliott. *Hunting Humans*. New York: Pocket Books, 1988.

Mascetti, Manuela Dunn. *Vampire*. New York: Viking Studio Books, 1992.

Melton, Gordon J. *The Encyclopedia of American Religions*. New York: McGrath, 1989.

——.*The Encyclopedic Handbook of Cults*. New York: Garland, 1986.

Musto, Dr. David. *The American Disease*. New York: Oxford University Press, 1988.

Nataf, Andre. *The Occult*. New York: Chambers, 1991.

Newton, Michael. *Hunting Humans—The Encyclopedia of Serial Killings*. Vols. 1 and 2. New York: Avon Books, 1992.

Posner, Gerald. *Warlords of Crime*. New York: McGraw-Hill, 1988.

Ressler, Robert, A.W. Burgess and J.E. Douglas. *Sexual Homicide*. Lexington, MA: Lexington Books, 1988.

Sifakis, Carl. *The Encyclopedia of American Crime*. New York: Smithmark Publishers, 1992.

Szaz, Thomas S. *Law, Liberty, and Psychiatry*. New York: Macmillan, 1963.

Twitchell, James B. *The Living Dead: The Vampire in Romantic Literature*. Durham, NC: Duke University Press, 1985.

Vachss, Alice. *Sex Crimes*. New York: Random House, 1993.

Vandome, Nick. *Crimes and Criminals*. New York: Chambers, 1992.

Walker, Leonore. *Battered Women*. New York: Harper & Row, 1979.

Warlaw, Grant. *Political Terrorism*. Cambridge: Cambridge University Press, 1989.

Wilson, Keith D. *Cause of Death*. Cincinnati, OH: Writer's Digest Books, 1992.

Wilson, Colin. *Written In Blood*. Vols. I, II and III. New York: Warner Books, 1989.
Wilson, Colin and Patricia Pitman. *The Encyclopedia of Murder*. London: Arthur Barker, 1961.
Wilson, Colin and Donald Seaman. *The Encyclopedia of Modern Murder*. New York: Arlington House, 1988.
—.*The Serial Killers*. New York: Carol Publishing Group, 1991.
Wilson, Edward O. *Sociobiology—The New Synthesis*. Cambridge, MA: Harvard University Press, 1975.
Wingate, Anne. *Scene of the Crime*. Cincinnati, OH: Writer's Digest Books, 1992.

Index

Abominable Dr. Phibes, 64
Achille Lauro hijacking, 182
Action Directe, 203
Aiello, Joe, 168
Al Capone, 65
Alcohol abuse, 173-175
Algerian FLN, 186, 189
Algueci, Albert, 169
Amphetamines, 176
Anastasia, Albert, 168-169
Anger rape, 96
Animal torture, 72
Anselmi, Albert, 167-168
Anthropophagy, 72
Antisocial Personality Disorder
  (APD), 151-157
Aquino, Michael, 83
Argument-motivated murder, 44
Assassins, women as, 202-205
Assassins Cult, 11-12
Assyrians, 9
Avoidant Personality Disorder,
  154-155

Babylon, 9
Bacon, Roger, 89
Ball, Joe, 58
Balzarini, Barbara, 203
Bank of Nova Scotia, 148
Barbiturates, 176
Barker, Ma, 150-151
Barnum, P.T., 145
Barrow, Clyde, 150
Bathory, Countess, 69
Battered Wife Syndrome (BWS),
  211-212
Beane Family, 16, 69, 82
Berg, Alan, 91
Berkowitz, David, 76, 220
Betty Ford Clinic, 175
Bianchi, Kenneth, 6, 219-220
Biggs, Ronnie, 148
Billy the Kid, 150
Bishop, Arthur Gary, 126
Black Hand, 160, 166
Black Muslims, 90
Blood monsters, 56-57
Blunt, Anthony, 146-147
Bobbitt, Lorena, 30-31

Boer Wars, 181
Bondage, 110
Borden, Lizzie, 194
Borderline Personality Disorder, 152
Boston Strangler, 73, 76
"Boston Strangler, the," 63
Boston Tea Party, 186
Bow Street Runners, 16-17
Brady, Ian, 123, 125
Brinks Robbery, 147
Brinvilliers, Madame de, 69
Brown, Debra, 74
Brussel, Dr. James, 39-42
Bundy, Carol, 74
Bundy, Ted, 6, 21, 46-47, 54, 62, 73, 99,
  139
Burgess, Guy, 146-147
Burke and Hare, 18
Byron, Lord, 60-61

Cagol, Margherita, 203
Calabro, Carmine, 44
Camorra, 161, 166
Cannibalism, 8
Capone, Al, 145, 151, 162, 168
Career criminals, 141-157
Career deadly outlaws, 149-157
Castro, Fidel, 186
Chikatilo, Andrei, 59-60
Child lures, 125-126
Child molesters, 105-126
  bondage, 110
  coprophilia, 110
  exhibitionism, 110
  female offenders, 112-113
  inadequate situational, 108-109
  infantilism, 110
  introverted preferential, 109
  masochism, 110
  morally indiscriminate situational,
    108
  necrophilia, 110
  pornography, 116-122
  preferential, 109-110
  profile, 113-116
  regressed situational, 108
  sadism, 110
  sadistic preferential, 110
  scatophilia, 110

seductive preferential, 109-110
sex rings, 111
sexually indiscriminate situational, 108
situational, 107-109
teenage offenders, 113
urophilia, 110
zoophilia, 110
Child murderers, 122-126
lures, 125-126
profile, 125
Child rape, 102-103
Children and satanism, 85
Chinese Triads, 158, 165
Christian cults, 89-92
Christie, John, 5, 73
Church of Jesus Christ Christian-Aryan Nations, 90
Church of Satan, 83
Church of the Lamb of God, 90, 193
Church Universal and Triumphant, 92
Clark, Douglas, 74
Cocaine, 176
Cochise, 181
Coleman, Alton, 74
COLP, 203
Competence of defendant, 206-207
Computer pornography, 122
Computer profiling, 46-52
Conflict and counteraction, 102
Conquest and control, 101
Controlled Substances Act, 175
Coprophilia, 72, 110
Cordrey, Rodger, 148
Corll, Dean, 21, 73, 74, 100, 102
Corsican League, 158
Courtroom psychology, 206-220
attempts to fool court, 217-220
competence of defendant, 206-207
insanity defense, 208-211
responsibility of defendant for actions, 207-208
Covenant, the Sword, and the Arms of the Lord, the (CSA), 90
Crazy Horse, 181
Crime, defined, 32
Crime scenes, 78-80
Criminal behavior, defined, 34-35
Criminal mind, outlining, 35-38
Crowley, Aleister, 83
Crucifixion, 10
Cult-related murders, 81-92

Cycles of disease, 77-78

Dahmer, Jeffrey, 27, 54, 56-57, 72, 75, 100, 219
Daly, John, 148
"Dangerousness," 213-216
Death of a thousand cuts, 10
Decimation, 10
Dependent Personality Disorder, 155
DeSalvo, Albert, 73, 76
Diagnostics and Statistics Manual of Mental Disorders (DSM-III-R), 106
Dillinger, John, 150
"Diminished capacity," 210
Disease, violence as, 28-29
Disorganized types, 48-50
Doss, Nannie, 197-198
Douglas, John, 43
Doyle, Sir Arthur Conan, 61
Dr. Phibes Rises Again, 64
Dracula, 5, 54
Drug abuse, 171-179
Dumas, Alexander
Durrant, Theo, 21, 28

Edwards, Buster, 148
Ego, 29-31
Elderly rape, 102-103
Ellison, James, 91
Elveson, Francine, 42-44
Esteem needs, 24
Exhibitionism, 110
Exorcist, 63-64
Exorcist III, 63-64

Fan, The, 64
Farley, Richard, 45
FBI Behavioral Science Unit, 39-42
Felony murder, 44
Fetishism, 72-73
Fiction, 60-65
Fielding, Henry, 16-17
Film, 62-65
First Deadly Sin, The, 65
Fish, Albert, 123
Flogging, 10
Ford vs. Wainwright, 210
Forsyth, Frederick, 81
Frenzy, 64

Gacy, John Wayne, 5, 21, 75, 100, 101, 123, 125
Gang rape, 99-100
Gardner, Gerald B., 87
Garnier, Gilles, 82
Gecht, Robin, 74, 84
Gein, Ed, 73
Genna Family, 168
Geronimo, 181
Gerontophilia, 73
Gideons, 85
Gilles de Rais, 13-14, 69, 81-82
Goldman, Ronald, 139
Goody, Gordon, 148
Gotti, John, 5-6
Great Train Robbery, 148-149
Great White Brotherhood, 205
Greece, 9-11
Green River Killer, 46, 68
Grief Process, 133, 136-137
Grossmann, Georg, 56-57
"Guilty but mentally ill," 209

Haarmann, Fritz, 57, 123
Haigh, John, 77
Harris, Joseph, 214
Harrison Drug Act, 175
Harvey, Donald, 84
Hasan ibn-al-Sabah, 11-12, 180
Hebephile, 106
Hennard, George, 214-215
Heroin, 177
Hillside Stranglers, 6, 74, 219-220
Hinckley, John, Jr., 209
Hindawi, Nezar, 204
Hindley, Myra, 123, 125, 201
Histrionic Personality Disorder, 156
Hitmen, 166-170
Holmes, H.H., 20-21
Home movies, 73
Hoover, J. Edgar, 162
Huberty, James, 20, 45
Human behavior, 23-38
Human sacrifice, 8
Hungerford Massacre, 46
Hunting humans, 68-70
Hussey, Jim, 148

Identity Movement Churches, 91
Immaturity, 25
Impulse disorders, 218-219

Inadequate situational child molesters, 108-109
Incest, 111-112
Infantilism, 110
Insanity defense, 208-211
Insanity Defense Reform Act, 209
International Terrorist Network, 165
Introverted preferential child molesters, 110
IRA, 165-166, 185, 188, 191, 192
Irish Fenian movement, 181
Italian Red Brigade, 185
Italian Risorgimento movement, 181

Jack the Ripper, 5, 19-20, 51-54, 61-62, 67-68, 73
Jaeger, Susan, 41-42
James, Roy, 148
James Brothers, 150
Japanese Yakuza, 158
Jewish Purple Gang, 161
Jones, Jim, 90
Jonestown Massacre, 90
Jung, Carl, 89

Kahl, Gordon, 90-91
Kaupp, Magdalena, 203
Keating, Thomas Patrick, 144
Khristos, Maria Devi, 205
Kiss, Bela, 54-55
Komaroff, Vasili, 58
Koresh, David, 1, 111, 190
Kray, Ronnie and Reggie, 151-152
Ku Klux Klan, 91
Kurten, Peter, 27, 56, 72, 73, 123
Kushner, Harold, 127

Lake, Leonard, 73
Lambs of God, 190, 193
Lansky, Meyer, 162-164
La Voisin, Catherine, 69
LeBaron, Ervil, 90
Lecter, Hannibal, 5
Leek, Sybil, 87
Legion, 63-64
Lemay, Georges, 148
Lent, Lewis, Jr., 1, 68
Lepine, Marc, 45
Lestat, 5
LeVey, Anton, 83, 83-84
Librax, 175
List, John, 45

Literature, 60-62
LSD, 177-178
Lucas, Henry Lee, 84
Luciano, Lucky, 162-164, 168
Lufthansa air cargo, 149
Lustig, Victor, 145
Lust murders, 54-56, 73

M, 62
Maclean, Donald, 146-147
"Mad Bomber, the," 39
Mafia, 158-170
Malcom X, 90
Male rape, 100
Malevolent, 3
Malignant Narcissist Personality
    Disorder, 155-156
Manson, Charles, 74, 82, 84, 171
Maranzano, Salvatore, 162, 164
Marital rape, 103-104
Maslow, Abraham, 23
Masochism, 110
Masseria, Joe, 162
Mass murderers, 57-60
Mass murders, 45
Matthews, Robert, 91
Maupassant, Guy de, 61
McGinnis, Joe, 147
McIlvane, Thomas, 214
Meegeren, Hans van, 143-144
Meirhofer, David, 42
Middle Ages, 11-12
Mission killers, 76-77
M'Naghten, Daniel, 208
Model Penal Code, 208-209
Montespan, Madame de, 69
Morally indiscriminate situational
    child molesters, 108
Mormon Murders, 90
Moro, Aldo, 203
Morphine, 177
Muderers, types, 71-72
Murder, Inc., 162, 166, 168-169
Murder types, 44-46

Narcissistic Personality Disorder, 155
National Center for Analysis of Violent
    Crime, 41
National Institute of Justice (NIJ), 75
Nation of Islam, 90
Nazis, 181
Necrofetishism, 73

Necrophilia, 27-28, 73, 111
Neo-Pagans, 87
New Jersey vs. Stasio, 210
Ng, Charles, 73
Nighthawks, 65
Night of the Generals, 63
Nilsen, Dennis, 58-59, 73
Nomadic killers, 75
Nonprescription drug abuse, 176-178
No Way to Treat a Lady, 63

Obsessive-Compulsive Personality
    Disorder, 154
Onorta, 166
Opium, 176
Opium War, 179
Order, the, 90
Order of the Silver Star, 83
Organized Crime, 158-170
Organized types, 48-50

Palestine Liberation Organization,
    180, 185, 190, 191
Panzram, Carl, 55-56
Paranoid Personality Disorder,
    152-153
Parental and relative abductions, 124
Parker, Bonnie, 150
Parker, Quanna, 181
Passive-Aggressive Personality
    Disorder, 153-154
PCP, 177-178
Pederasty, 73
Pedophilia—see Child molesters.
Peel, Sir Robert, 18, 208
Perruggia, Vincenzo, 144
Philby, Kim, 146-147
Physical needs, 23
Pieydagnelle, Eusebius, 70
Play Misty for Me, 64
Pleasure killers, 77
Poe, Edgar Allan, 60-61
Police, 16-19
Polidori, Dr. John, 60-61
Polydrug abuse, 175
Pornography, 73, 116-122
Posse Comitatus, 90
Post-Traumatic Stress Syndrome
    (PTSS), 133, 137-140
Power/control killers, 77
Power rape, 97-98
Predatory killers, 75

Preferential child molesters, 109-110
Prescription drug abuse, 175-176
Profile matrix, 47-48
Profiling, 39-52
Prophet, Elizabeth Clare, 92
Psycho, 62
Psychopath, 26-28
Psychotic, 26-28

Rape, 74
    defined, 94-96
    forms, 96-99
Rape Trauma Syndrome, 133, 135-136
Red Army Faction, 203
Red Brigade, 203
Red or Revolutionary Zora, 203
Regressed situational child molesters, 108
Reles, Abe, 169
Responsibility of defendant for actions, 207-208
Revenge and retaliation, 101
Reynolds, Bruce, 148
Rice, Anne, 5-6
Rifkin, Joel, 1, 5, 31, 68
"Right Man, the," 12-13
River of Life Tabernacle, 85
Rome, 10-11
"Ruhr Hunter," 70
Runaways, 124
Russian Mafia, 158-159, 165
Ryan, Leo, 90
Ryan, Michael, 46

Sade, Marquis de, 60
Sadism, 110
Sadism and degradation, 101
Sadistic Personality Disorder, 156-157
Sadistic preferential child molesters, 110
Sadistic rape, 98-99
Sadomasochism, 74
Sanders, Alexander, 87
Satanism, 82-85
Scalise, John, 167-168
Scarface, 65
Scatophilia, 110
Schizoid Personality Disorder, 153
Schizotypal Personality Disorder, 153
Sea of Love, 132
Security needs, 24

Seductive preferential child molesters, 109-110
Self-actualization needs, 24
Self-deception, 25
Self-Defeating Personality Disorder, 156
Serial killers, 46
Serial murders, 66-80
Sex factor, 31-32
Sex rings, 111
Sexual behavior in serial killings, 72-74
Sexually indiscriminate situational child molesters, 108
Sexual predators, 93-105
Sharieff, Raymond, 90
Shelley, Mary, 61
Shelley, Percy, 61
Sherrill, Patrick, 214
Shotgun Man, 166
Sicilian Mafia, 158, 161, 165
Simpson, Nicole, 139
Simpson, O.J., 139
Situational child molesters, 107-109
Situation Crisis Response, 133, 136-137
Social killers, 74-75
Son of Sam, 76, 220
Southern La Cosa Nostra, 158, 165
Speck, Richard, 20, 45
Spree killers, 46
St. Valentine's Day Massacre, 65
Stationary killers, 75
Status and affiliation, 102
Stoker, Bram, 5, 54
Stonegate Christian Community, 85
Stranger abductions, 124
Strangers on a Train, 63
Strieber, Whitley, 6
Stubbe, Peter, 82
Suicide, 216-217
Surete, 18
Suspected felony murder, 44
Sutcliffe, Peter, 27, 73

Tape recordings, 73
Tarasoff case, 213-214
Temple of Set, 83
Territorial killers, 75
Terrorism, 180-193
    defined, 181-183
    group mentality, 188-190
    profile of terrorist, 186-188
Theatre of Blood, 64

Throwaways, 124
Tieck, Joann, 60
Toole, Ottis, 84
Torture, 74
Tranxene, 175
Traumatic crisis, 133-140
Triolism, 73
Tupamaros, 185

Urophilia, 110

Vacher, Joseph, 21-22
Valium, 175
Vampires, 3
Vicars, Henry Edward, 144
Victims, 127-140
    categories, 129-131
    Grief Process, 133, 136-137
    Post-Traumatic Stress Syndrome
        (PTSS), 133, 137-140
    profile, 131-133
    psychology, 133
    Rape Trauma Syndrome, 133,
        135-136
    Situation Crisis Response, 133,
        136-137
    traumatic crisis, 133-140
    Zodiac Killer, 132
Vidocq, Eugene-Francois, 18
Viett, Inge, 202, 204
Violence, defined, 32-34
Violent Criminal Apprehension
    Program, 41
Vision killers, 76
Vlad Dracula, 14, 69
Vogt, A.E. van, 13
Voyeurism, 74

Waco Massacre, 1, 90, 190
Weakness, 25
Welch, Robert, 148
White, Jimmy, 148
White Supremacist Murders, 90
Whitman, Charles, 20, 45
Wiccans, 87
Wilder, Christopher, 46, 75, 98
Wille, W., 71
Williams, Wayne, 102, 123, 125
Wilson, Charlie, 148
Wilson, Frank, 145
Wisbey, Thomas, 148
Witchcraft, 85-88
Witch Hunts, 14-15
Women who kill, 194-205
    assassins, 202-205
Women who rape, 104
World Terrorist Network (WTN), 191
World Trade Center, 1
World Trade Center bombing, 182,
    185, 191
Wuornos, Aileen, 75

Xanax, 175

Yorkshire Ripper, 73
Younger Brothers, 150
Young Germany movement, 181
Young Poland movement, 181

Zimmerman vs. Burch, 213
Zodiac Killer, 132
Zoophilia, 110

Other Books in the HOWDUNIT Series!